The English Travelers

Three Narratives

Sharon Hope

Sharon M. Hope

Sharon M. Hope Inc.
Sidney, B.C.

The English Travelers (2nd ed.)

ISBN: 978-0-9877459-1-0 (Book)

Published by Sharon M. Hope Inc.
301-2050 White Birch Road
Sidney, BC V8L 2R1 Canada

www.sharonhope.ca

Photographs in this book are used with permission. Many are from the Estlin family memorabilia collection in the possession of Sharon Hope. All sketches within John Prior Estlin's "London Visit" represented in Part II come from the original diary supplied by Sharon Hope. The photo of the Garden of Versailles on the Part I title page is courtesy of M. and S. Kirkpatrick.

Book Design and Layout: Paula Gaube, Editworks Online Design
www.editworksonline.com

v6-12-2012

Acknowledgements

Lynda Villeneuve kindly gave permission to use her compilation of Alfred Bagehot Estlin's memoir "The Old Commission Trail."

Fran Aitkens provided assistance in proofreading the London diary as well as with some family connections and information; she also offered the streetsweeper photographs.

Many persons encouraged me to prepare the book, including historians in Manitoba, family members, friends, and the members of the Sidney Write Group.

Paula Gaube of Editworks Online Design formatted the work for publication and made editorial suggestions.

Table of Contents

Part III: Prairie Winds 1880-1911

Preface

Three narratives are presented here: *Packet to France*, the diary of Susannah Estlin's journey to Paris in 1789, *London Visit*, the 1847-1848 diary of her grandson John Prior Estlin, bank clerk, and *Prairie Winds* 1880-1911, an Estlin biography, about immigrating to the Canadian prairies. The first two diaries are reproduced as direct transcriptions with notes inserted to explain obscure events or connections; in the *Packet to France* the original f's (the long s) have been replaced with s's. The last narrative is composed of letters by the Estlin brothers and sisters, particularly by Alfred Estlin, interspersed with his memoir, and other pertinent family documents. The diaries have been supplemented with images not in the original text. John P. Estlin's diary contained his own pen and ink sketches and some of these images have been reproduced.

In 1789, Susannah Estlin, a Unitarian minister's wife from Bristol, was eyewitness to the turmoil in France and the seizure of Paris. A woman of high spirits and opinion, she described travel by chaise, the scenery, the French customs, and the country's tourist attractions. In addition to her description of a city in political upheaval, she brings gentle humor and a critical eye to a range of topics. These include everything from impassable roads and Catholic services, to postillions and the height of French beds. Several years after her trip, Susannah saw the publication of journals from the men she associated with in Paris. She prepared her own diary for distribution at least within her family but the care she took over it suggests she thought of a larger audience.

In 1847, John Prior Estlin, Susannah's grandson, obtained an interim position with an affiliate of Stuckey's bank in London. He stayed almost a year, describing such well-known events as the Chartist movement, and giving readers an idea of the streets, entertainments, and nearby towns. He visited the London theatres, churches, and the docks. In particular, he recorded the social life of extended middle class families where soirees dominated. We share with him lazy weekend days rowing on the Thames and taking trips to Greenwich. John has an explorative nature, trying the public baths and strolling about Billingsgate.

In 1881, Alfred B. Estlin, John Prior's son, became the spokesperson for the settlement of the family branch in Canada. With the sudden death of his father, John Prior, Alfred evolved as the family decision maker in a new country. He had no experience with Canadian prairie farming, a path his father chose. The family endured the Red River flood, the Boundary Commission Trail and a plague of frosts, gophers and fires. This is a story of adaptation, ingenuity and survival in a harsh environment.

Writing was familiar to Susannah, John and Alfred Estlin. Susannah was well educated, and was acquainted with many of Bristol's literary and scientific elite from Priestley to Coleridge. She was a personal friend of Laetitia Barbauld whose work was well known in her time. Both John Prior and Alfred had letters and articles produced in their respective local papers.

The insights of these individuals would have been lost without the hoarding instincts of the Estlin family, which in turn led to an extensive collection of letters and memorabilia held by many generations. That tenacity and determination to preserve the past provided an opportunity to bring these documents and the authors to life.

Part I
Packet to France
1789

Susannah Estlin

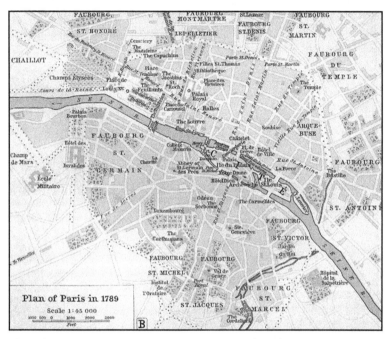

Plan of Paris in 1789. *Source:* en.wikipedia.org/wiki/History_of_Paris

Introduction

The Georgian period in England was one of cultural and literary development, as well as industrial and agricultural revolution. It was the golden age of architecture. In 1783, the Thirteen Colonies that formed the United States received formal recognition from Britain through the Treaty of Versailles. Botany Bay was established as a prison colony in 1788 and in the next year, Britain sentenced the last woman to be burnt. The crime was counterfeit. Prison reform was just being considered partially based on John Howard's assessment of prisons completed in 1777.

Women's fashions for the period involved a large mobcap and a simple dress with a high neckline. Men wore cut away coats, silk vests, knee length breeches, and silk or woolen stockings. Tea was not only served as a custom at home, but in various shops to potential customers. Foreign visitors to London noted that there were no sewage systems in the major cities and that educated middle and upper class persons were great letter and diary writers.

Society distinguished various "classes"—those that one believed equal in status compared to those above or below one's own standing. This hierarchy depended on good breeding, occupation and ancestry. Although upper middle class individuals earned a living, they owned property. They could be financiers, industrialists, merchants, lawyers, engineers, university dons and higher clergy. The "middle" middle class might include lesser clergy, artists, clerks, shopkeepers and innkeepers. Lower classes were usually those who had employers such as master craftsmen, labourers and servants.

Bristol had gradually become a literary, scientific and intellectual centre. The Philosophical Institution, which had two fine reading rooms on Park Street, held formal lectures and had a museum. The city had a theatre built in 1766 and a handsome bridge spanned the Avon built in the same period.

Bristol also had a flourishing slave trade that Protestant Dissenters strongly opposed. On December 18, 1789 (88 days after leaving Bristol), for example, the Sarah began purchasing slaves at Bimbia in West Africa, followed by additional purchases at the Cameroons River and at Calabar (one of the largest and most infamous West African slave ports). In total, 256 slaves were purchased. At this time, Bristol's principle raw imports were rum, tobacco, timber, sugar, tea and coffee.

In 1789, Paris was enduring difficult economic times. Farmers near Paris consumed over 80 percent of what they grew, so if a harvest fell by around 10 percent, which was common, people went hungry. At the same time, people suffered due to a decline in the textile industry. In addition to the economic impact on textile workers and farmers, people who worked at odd jobs such as carrying water were also vulnerable. Paris had many who stayed alive only by petty thievery or prostitution; individuals were being buried every day in paupers' graves.

On June 24th 1789, about the time Susannah left Bristol, Arthur Young of Britain, an agricultural advisor touring France, stated that 10,000 people had been at the Palais Royale and the king's propositions had been rejected. A few days later, he reported an attack on the clergy. As a lively 29-year-old Englishwoman, Susannah stepped into this environment.

Chapter 1
Finding Passage

June 23rd 1789

Preface: This little journal written on the spot, at intervals, early and late, is in consequence full of imperfections, but correct with respect to facts. When I have leisure, I will transcribe it.

Tuesday June 23rd 1789

Left home; breakfasted at Warminster, din'd with Mr. Buller at Wilton; took a peek at Wilton House, the seat of Lord Pembroke. Rumsey, (where we chang'd chaises), is a near pretty Town, pleasantly situated. Slept at Southampton.

Left: Rev. John Prior Estlin, Unitarian minister, and Susannah Estlin's home on St. Michael's Hill, Bristol. *Right:* Susannah Estlin at 67; she wrote the diary at aged 29. *Source:* Estlin family collection, Sharon Hope

Wednesday

Walked about the Town, saw the Baths, which are extremely commodious, and the Public rooms, which are finely proportioned and elegantly finished. The streets are spacious, the houses (in general) well built, of brick. From the Quay you have a delightful view of the river, which is properly speaking an arm of the Sea. Beyond it, the New Forest, and the Isle of Wight. The Country around Southampton is really charming, it abounds with roads, & a great number of gentlemen's seats are in the environs. The roads are delightful, of fine gravel, like the walks in a garden, a rais'd causeway makes it extremely convenient to foot passengers. There is a mineral water much esteem'd. The spring rises close to the Sea. The situation of Southhampton is remarkably healthy. The town is uncommonly clean, the general appearance of it cheerful, & the inhabitants look contented & happy. Not a Beggar to be seen, not indeed any appearance of poverty. It has a Mayor & Corporation, & sends two members to Parliament.

After dinner, the rain being very heavy, we were prevented from going far from our Inn; the tinkling of a neighbouring bell inviting us to church, we attended prayers. The congregation consisted of two old men, one old woman, my friend, & myself.

The Curate gazing at us (being strangers) unfortunately, lost his place, & was totally unable to proceed, till the benevolent Clerk set him right. I cannot say that his manner of reading the prayers inspir'd any great fervor of devotion. It is a sad mocking of religious duties to hurry them over in this slovenly manner, better not to pray at all, than pray thus. At the Star Inn we were well entertained.

Thursday

We left Southampton & arrived at Portsmouth; it is the most charming site imaginable. In the morning we walk'd about the Town & cross'd over to Gosport. In the afternoon went on board the Admiral's ship, the Barfleur, where we drank tea, and saw the accommodations, cabins etc. etc.

Samuel Hood. *Source:* en.wikipedia.org/wiki/Samuel_Hood,_1st_Viscount_Hood

The admiral might have been Admiral Samuel Hood appointed until 1789 on the Barfleur. Gosport was a major naval and military town associated with the defence and supply infrastructure of his majesty's Naval Base.

The officers of the Barfleur treated us with distinguished politeness and good breeding. In the evening we walk'd about the Ramparts & Garrison. The midshipmen's cabins are under water, not a ray of sun ever enters the dreary abode. What can induce young men of birth & fortune to submit to such hardships?

The B. is an extremely fine ship; most elegantly fitted up, carries 90 guns & 750 men. The middle deck exhibits an extraordinary scene—men, women, infants, eating, drinking, laughing, working, cooking. Never did I see such a motley group. The peace establishment consists of about 400 men. These were all on board. Some of the women sold fruit, gingerbread etc.

Friday

We breakfasted with Mr. Scott; visited the Dock, Store-rooms, rope walk, mast-houses, and Blacksmith's shop, all upon an immensely large Scale. At 12 o'clock the men leave work, the scene is really diverting, they all rush out as fast as possible, some on their way scramble for chips, others have permission to take home as much offal wood as they can carry under one arm. This indulgence they improve much to their advantage by taking each man as much as he can lift on his shoulder. This burden is with the greatest difficulty put under one arm when they pass the officer (who stands ready to examine them) but the instant they have pass'd the gates, the[y] sell their loads to persons waiting for that purpose.

Government has offer'd the workmen fourpence a day in lieu of these chips, but they are wiser than to accept the bounty, as they dispose of it for a shilling or eighteen pence. This indulgence must, I should think, have a bad effect on the morals of the people, as it unavoidable[y] leads to pilfering habits & contrivances to avoid the eye of Justice. The room where they make their cables is 1170 feet in length; the cables for first-rate ships are 24 inches round.

At one o'clock we took a Boat, & sail'd for the Isle of Wight; [which] is more productive than any other island of its extent in the known world. The sea was rough; I felt no disposition to be sick, but must confess I was a little frightened at the waves that appear'd to me tremendous. On our return the sea was charmingly pleasant.

The Island is an enchanting spot, Dr. Walker's house & lawn etc., is a Paradise. Every beauty of prospect is there; a rich wood, cultivated fields, a fine Sea, and beyond it a distant view of Portsmouth. We sailed thro' Spithead and saw the masts of the unfortunate Royal George, a considerable way above the water.

Mr. Russell Scott was minister of the High Street Chapel in Portsmouth and formed a Unitarian Society for South England in 1801 with two other ministers.

*On 29 August 1782 whilst undergoing minor repair work at
Spithead, the Royal George began to take on water. She sank very
quickly with the loss of about 900 lives. The dead included Rear
Admiral Richard Kempenfelt and as many as 300 women and 60
children who were visiting the ship at the time. Some parts of the ship
were salvaged at a later date.*

Saturday

Before breakfast we bath'd in the Sea, afterwards visited the Naval Stores,
saw the method of making & baking the Ship biscuits, salted provisions &
some curious brown birds brought from Guinea by Capt'n Inglefield on
board the Adventure.

*In 1788, Inglefield was posted to HMS Adventure (44 guns) which,
joined later by HMS Medusa (44 guns), also under his command,
patrolled the West Coast of Africa. In 1792 he served as one of the
judges at the court-martial of the mutineers from HMS Bounty.*

At two o'clock, the Duke of Clarence arrived in a post chaise and four,
alone. He pass'd close by us and afterwards we met him in the Street and
saw him go into his Boat, which waited to convey him to his own ship
the Andromeda, lying at Spithead. The soldiers were drawn up to receive
him on his entrance, the guns were fired and the colours hoisted. Very
few people took the trouble to look at him. The Bargemen were dress'd
in a handsome uniform and made a pretty appearance, but not a single
huzza was heard nor any demonstration of joy visible. I suspect he is not a
very popular character; they say here, he is arbitrary and tyrannical to the
ship's crew. He is handsome, but there is a great degree of hauteur in his
countenance.

*In 1788, William, the third son of King George III, assumed
command of the frigate HMS Andromeda. He became the Duke of
Clarence in 1789 and advanced to the rank of admiral in 1799. He
was known as the "Sailor King."*

In the eve^g walk'd upon the Gun wharf, saw the stores of Cannon Balls,
Guns and Shells. Drank tea with Mr. Scott, s[l]ep'd at our Inn. No Packet
ready to sail yet.

Sunday June 28[th] 1789

No Packet yet arriv'd: we propose going to Brighton and sailing from thence Tuesday next. I am glad of this opportunity of seeing so fashionable a place and travelling a little further on this delightful Coast. Went to Mr. Scott's Chapel both parts of the day; spent it rationally and comfortably. Breakfasted and drank tea at Mr. Scott's lodgings.

Monday

We set off from Portsmouth at 5 'clock in the morning. It is not unlike Plymouth but [I] think handsomer and cleaner; tis a pleasant town. Breakfasted at Chichester. Walk'd about the Town & saw the Cathedral, tis miserably shabby and extremely dirty inside; the Steeple is well proportioned, and there are three neat Marble Monuments, but nothing else deserving notice. Chichester is a clean pleasant town, and has several good houses and wide, airy streets. The ride from this place to Arundel is romantic; you have a view of the beautiful woods, and the seat of the Earl of Newburgh. At Arundel whilst the chaise was getting ready, (for we never lose a moment's time in traveling), we walk'd up the principal street and took a view of Arundel Castle, which stands at the very top of the Town, the seat of the Duke of Norfolk.

None of the family resides there; indeed it appears a habitation fit only for Bats and Owls. It is an immensely large castle, in ruins with an indifferent modern house built close the adjoining walls. Never did I behold a more dreary mansion. This Castle gives the possessor the title of Earl of Arundel. From this town we went to Shoreham, the next stage.

We pass'd over a prodigiously long bridge which is built across the Sea, that is, an arm of the Sea. The toll that we paid was two shillings. Shoreham is a little Town almost in the sea; from hence to Brighton you ride all the way on the beach, tis really delightful, as the sea is unusually bold and fine. Shoreham is seven miles from Brighton. The road from Chichester to Brighton is not turnpike; we saved, however, nothing by this, as they made us pay 15d a mile. Arrived in Brighthelmstone to dinner (4 o'clock). We had great difficulty in getting intelligence of a Packet, or even to find the Captain. We have, however, at length prov'd successful and are to sail to-morrow evening, wind and weather permitting. The Sea is uncommonly rough for this time of year; the Captain says he never knew such a stormy season. I wish we were on the other side of the water. This is the most beautiful bathing town I ever saw. A fine view of the Sea from almost every part of it, and a Square call'd the Heyne with elegant houses on all sides; the Prince of Wales' beautiful mansion, lately built, call'd the Pavilion, adorns it highly.

The wooden bridge over the River Adur at Old Shoreham was built in 1781, replacing a ferry. *Source:* en.wikipedia.org/wiki/Shoreham_Tollbridge

Tuesday

Bath'd in the Sea; the beach here is extremely smooth & fine, the bathing machines neat & convenient, & the guides admirably skilled in their profession. If you come to Brighton for the purpose of bathing, I recommend you to the care of Martha Gun [sic]; with her you will be perfectly safe. We have no prospect of sailing tonight. The Packets are on the other side & probably cannot get out of the French harbour, as the wind is set against it. How unfortunate! For if there were a Vessel on this side, the very wind which detained us here, would waft us on to Dieppe in eight hours. We have walk'd all round the Town and I believe through almost every street.

Martha Gunn, the most famous of Brighton's bathing women (also known as "dippers"), was born in the seaside village of Brighthelmstone (Brighton) in 1726. Martha came from an old fishing family, but when sea-bathing became popular in the 1740s, she found employment as a "dipper" on Brighton's seafront. The "bathing machine" was a small, wooden hut on wheels. The wheeled huts or "bathing machines" were then rolled or pulled into the sea by strong bathing attendants. (At some resorts, horses were used to pull the bathing machines out into deeper waters and to haul them back on to the shore when the bather had finished swimming). www.photohistory-sussex.co.uk/BTNCHAR_MarthaGunn.html

The Downs adjacent, are open and extensive, they surround the town except where the Sea comes. The Sea here is unusually bold, and bounds the prospect most beautifully. This afternoon we sat in one of the bathing machines to behold at our ease the noble sight before us. The Sea was calm, the weather clear and the Sun shone gloriously upon the swelling waves. I saw distinctly 70 vessels in full sail; some almost lost in the Horizon, but others near enough to perceive their motions; some fishing vessels, extremely small, some large with two masts and others with three. I must confess I am never tired of a Sea prospect, especially when it presents such a delightful moving scene to my view.

At ten at night we walk'd again upon the beach; the scene now was somewhat changed. The cheerfulness which the Sun occasion'd was gone. The moon's "wan lustre" gleamed faintly upon the waves which at this silent hour sound awfully, render'd the whole truly sublime. How can any Human Being who contemplates the boundless Ocean with all its wonders be an Atheist? "There are thy glorious works, Parent of Good."

Wednesday July 1ˢᵗ 1789

Again bathed in the Sea, it was extremely rough. We hear no tiding of a Packet. Two are expected in this day, but neither is yet in sight. The Captn assures us it shall return with us an hour after it arrives. I hope we shall sail tonight, as we have seen this place and its environs thoroughly. There are no public amusements yet open, & but little company. However I am delighted to see Brighton, tho' it was not part of our Plan. Tis really a charming place—the bathing is so commodious—the air so pure—the houses so pleasant—& the accommodations so good.

The Castle is a noble Inn & upon a very large scale; the coffee-room, card rooms, & Assembly room, are all here. The latter is a most elegant room, decorated and furnish'd in the first style. All the rooms are good, & the accommodations of every kind excellent, but—you pay for them handsomely. As I sit, I can see the Sea, with vessels gliding to & fro, the Square with the company walking, & the Prince's Apartments on the left, together with a peep of the Downs.

Castle Square became the commercial hub of the town in the late eighteenth century when the Castle Inn (q.v.), after which the square is named, became established. When the inn was demolished in October 1823 the square was opened up into a broad thoroughfare which became the main coaching centre of the town and later the terminus of the many horse-bus routes.

The Church is situated at a distance from the Town, upon a hill as you come from Shoreham; from the churchyard, which is very pleasant, you have at once a view of the whole town, adjacent country & Sea.

The Packet is just arrived. At nine o'clock set sail. Adieu sweet Brighton! My terrors were great on going aboard; they however soon abated, though I cannot say I was a moment entirely free from alarm, till we saw the French Coast. This was a truly welcome sight. We sat on Deck till the rain oblig'd us to retire to the Cabin. Here was a scene to me perfectly new. All the Passengers (a genteel party of a dozen persons) sick as death. I was soon infected by the contagion, which no human being could withstand; had I not witnessed this sight, I am confident I should not have been indisposed. At eleven we all went to our beds and there remained till the French Coast was in view. At ten in the morning we landed at Dieppe to our unspeakable joy.

Chapter 2
Travel by Chaise

Thursday

We went to Monr La Rue's Hotel, La Ville de Lourdes, refresh'd ourselves, & then walk'd to see the town. Dieppe is a large town, pleasantly situated and the streets wide, but the houses miserable in the extreme, built in the clumsiest manner & intolerably filthy. The women's dress (to English eyes) appears a complete Masquerade. They wear wooden shoes with very high heels, a petticoat that reaches just below the knees, made of striped woolen cloth, and a short jacket of a different colour and texture. They wear a small round ear'd cap which hides all the hair with broad lappets pin'd up. This dress is universal; I saw hundreds of women thus habited. They never wear hats, so that their faces, though naturally fair, are burn't like our English gypsies. Their caps are remarkably white, neat and high, some of fine lace or cambric. The dress is altogether tight and decent. It is not peculiar to Dieppe, but the same with very little variation all over Normandy. The people here are cleaner in their persons than their houses. I believe they never wash their floors or stairs, seldom sweep them and when they do they leave the dirt in one corner. Our dinner, etc., was but indifferent. From the Garrison we had a fine view of the town & its environs.

Monr La Rue furnished us with an old fashioned English Chaise, which is to take us all the way to Paris. We laughed incessantly for half the way to Rouen, at the droll appearance of our Equipage all together. The horses are fastened to the carriage with ropes, you are oblig'd to pay for four horses if you have a four wheeled chaise, though but three are usually made use of. These three horses run abreast, the middle one was a great hard trotting carthorse, with his mane flowing in a state of nature, just as the wind directed. The other two were little creatures, that cou'd scarcely keep pace with the great Elephant in the centre. One horse was grey, one black and the other sorrel. The Postilion had his hair tied, and a fierce cocked hat, his legs were plac'd in immense jackboots, which cannot be lifted but with the greatest difficulty. Boots, harness and horses are never cleaned, unless when a friendly shower of rain performs the office.

*The chaise was a closed carriage popular for traveling. It was usually
small, with seats for two people, occasionally one, but a side seat
could pull out to hold three, and with two seats, both facing forward,
it could hold four. The horses of a chaise were controlled, not by a
driver seated on a box on the vehicle, but by a post-boy, or postilion,
who rode the near, or left, horse. www.jasnanorcal.org/ink9.htm*

The road from Dieppe to Rouen is charming; of fine gravel, like walks
in a garden, very wide and corn [wheat] fields on either side, without a
fence. The last stage is beyond description romantic, you descend gradually
into a fine valley, enrich'd with trees and cornfields and adorned by the
beautiful windings of the river Seine, with here and there on the right hand
a venerable abby and on the left pleasant country seats. You enter the Town
through a double row of lofty trees that extends several miles. At the Gate,
a person waits to demand who you are. We lodg'd at Monr Valvis's Hotel
Maison Royale. Immediately upon arrival we were shown into the grand
Apartment, with two beds in it. Here our supper was served up, and whilst
we were refreshing ourselves, a smart man enter'd with sheets under his
arm and made our beds very dexterously; he placed all the proper furniture
in due order and then retir'd. He left us at liberty to indulge our laughter,
which it was impossible to suppress. The height of the bed was so prodigious
that I cou'd not mount it without a chair, and when I lay down and look'd
around me, I trembled at the frightful precipice, & feared lest in my sleep I
shou'd tumble down & be dashed to pieces against the stone floor beneath.

Friday July 3rd

We had with us on board (amongst other passengers) a French Abbe
who was extremely agreeable, & very intelligent. He overtook us at Rouen
& kindly offer'd to call upon us upon our arrival in Paris. I think he will
prove a valuable acquaintance. He speaks English perfectly for he was born
in Ireland but was educated & is now settled in Paris. He has purchas'd at
the great sale of Penelli's library in London, a curious Ximenes Bible for
which he gave £475.

*In 1788, London booksellers James Edwards and James Robson
bought the Pinelli library; an inventory catalogue had been compiled
by the custodian of the Bibliotheca Marciana, Iacopo Morelli, the
previous year. Although it was not a great success financially, the sale,*

which brought in £8,637, was the first auction of foreign books on a large scale to be held in London.

The streets of Rouen are narrow, dark, & dirty, the houses lofty and shabby, & the shops very mean. The women dress as at Dieppe; even the better sort never wear hats. Their dress is tawdry and vulgar, the smartest and genteeliest women, exactly resemble in their dress the lowest order of Ladies of a certain Description in London.

The Cathedral has a grand altar, & is also famous for the beautiful open ironwork around the Choir. It is a most magnificent edifice. In the tower is the famous great Bell. We did not take the trouble to mount the many hundred steps to see it. One may conceive the appearance of a Bell, if it be as large as a town. In the library we saw the most beautiful book, containing certain services peculiar to that place. It is printed on the finest vellum, adorn'd with paintings of exquisite beauty and bound in brass with two locks and keys. The staircase leading to the Monks apartments is very fine; the garden at a distance, (for women are not permitted within), look'd pleasant. The

A Rouen street. *Source:* Sharon Hope

church of St Ouen has the finest altar imaginable; it is all of Marble & surrounded with brass work remarkably curious. In the Choir is buried the heart of Richard Coeur de Lion, on the other side his son, & in the middle the tomb of Henricus. Six immense wax lights are plac'd around his tomb and a grand silver lamp suspended over it. Here are a number of fine paintings; Madonna and Crucifixes, as in all the churches in this country. With all this grandeur you see cobwebs hanging over the beautiful painted windows, and the pavement of the Churches much dirtier than our streets. The church is reckon'd one of the finest pieces of Gothic architecture in France, several kings and nobles are buried there.

From the walks adjoining the old Castle we had a fine view of Rouen, the beautiful avenue of trees leading to the gates of the city, the Quay, the river Seine, the Exchange, and Walk where merchants meet to do business. The greatest curiosity here is the bridge of Boats, which rises and sinks with the tide. I cannot say that the appearance of this bridge answer'd my expectation; it is not handsome, nor could I admire anything but the singularity of the contrivance. It is attended with considerable expense to keep it in repair. It is pav'd with stone and has a raised causeway on either side.

Saw the Square where Joan of Arc was burnt. Here is her statue. Monsr Valois gave us an excellent dinner & dessert, in our chambers where the Abbe and a young Oxonian join'd us. We set off from Rouen after dinner and arriv'd at Porteau de Mer, a market town at night. Here we met with great civility & good accommodations, though my terrors were renewed at the sight of the bed, I was destin'd to climb.

Rouen Cathedral. *Source:* Sharon Hope

The road from Rouen to this place is enchanting; the prospects are beyond conception beautiful. I shall never forget the impression. As we look'd back on the city we beheld the Seine embellished by many small islands with trees, sometimes a building on them, winding through rich fields, and then lost sight of for a few moments, a grove of trees intervening. Again it appeared in view, forming a serpentine, with here and there a vessel sailing gently along. Woods, cornfields, valleys, and the sight of this river, render'd the prospect compleat.

Saturday

Let me here describe our breakfast; the tea was brought in, ready made, but no cups or saucers; pint basons & plates with large spoons supplied this defect. The milk was in a large dish, & scalding hot. We had also coffee & sugar, cherries, cheese, sweet cakes, & good rolls. I never breakfasted better in my life. Ponteau de Mer is a pleasant little town. I was surprised at the grandeur of the altar; the church itself was mean, but the paintings good & the candlesticks & crucifixes costly. The apartments are cleaner here than any I have yet seen.

The children in Normandy (for I have taken particular notice of them) are very handsome & uncommonly fair, but their dress is strange indeed. Whilst they are very young they are swath'd up that they cannot move, their dress is of thick flannel with three caps on their heads. At ten months they wear stiff, long stays, & something resembling a hoop. The parents seem proud of them & are extremely pleas'd at any attention given the little creatures.

With a great thumping carthorse, & two poneys, we left Ponteau de Mer & reached Harfleur to dinner. On the road we overtook a Lady of some importance, riding on an Ass, veiled, and holding an umbrella. She had a maidservant on each side, and two men after, all on foot. This was travelling in State. We had fine prospects, & good road all the way.

At Harfleur, we saw Harve de Grace, Harfleur, and the Seine which here joins itself to the sea. The hotel where we dined is delightfully situated on the Pier, from whence the prospect is charming. The town is dirty and mean, but the country round is very fine. We had an excellent dinner; the poultry uncommonly large and well flavour'd. I never saw such fowls in England. Our dinner was served up in the apartment that the present Emperor of Germany occupied lately on his visit to this place.

We set off from Harfleur in high spirits, hoping to arrive at Caen the same night. Till now, all had gone smoothly—we had met with no accident —we thought of none. We have no right to expect uninterrupted comfort in a journey through Normandy, or a journey through Life. In each the scene is chequer'd. The hind wheel of our Chaise flew off after we had travell'd a few miles; fortunately the carriage was hung low, which prevented it from oversetting. This accident being soon repaired we reach'd Pont Eveque, where we had four horses as we were informed the road to Dive was not excellent. Had the stupid souls assur'd us that it was absolutely impassable, we cou'd not even then have form'd an idea of half its horrors.

The horses flew like lightening through the miserable streets of Pont Eveque, & down we came in the midst of the town, the wheel coming off a second time. Here we waited a considerable time to have it thoroughly repaired & once more mounted the vehicle, which owing to its old fashion'd make, had been the means of preserving our bones. After ascending a steep hill we enter'd a narrow lane full of deep holes, with a high bank on both sides, so that we had no prospect to enliven the dreary scene. The horses could hardly drag us along, & every two or three feet down sunk the carriage in a deep hole full of water. A violent effort was necessary to raise it from thence each time. This dreadful Lane was twelve miles long; two miles an hour was the quickest pace we could possibly go. Not a human being (save one wretched old man), or single habitation did we behold. Night came on apace, the rain grew heavy and the jolts we were perpetually receiving bruised us so that we resolv'd to quit the carriage which we expected at any moment wou'd be dashed to pieces. We proceded on foot many wearisome steps, filled with the most gloomy apprehensions, unable to Discern many paces before us, when the Postillion inform'd us we were near Dive.

This sound cheer'd our hearts; we car'd not in what poor hovel we pass'd the night, cou'd we but get to the end of our misery. "The cobwebbed cottage with its ragged wall of mouldring mud" would have been welcome to us. At length we reached a wretch'd Post house, where we gladly rested our wearied limbs in a room over the Stable, the stench of which together with the continu'd trampling effectually prevented our sleeping. We had a dish of fried eggs, & some bread for supper, with a bottle of tolerable wine. The people were civil & attentive.

The line in quotation marks is from a poem written in 1745 by Edward Young who became an English minister late in life. It was an extremely popular poem in its day.

Chapter 3
French Towns

Sunday July 5th

At four o'clock in the morning we left this wretch'd Dive, which I hope never more to behold. All the road to Caen was miserable, through deep heavy sands, & continued rain. At ten we reached Caen & arrived safely at the house of our friend Madame de la Motte Paisant, where we met with affectionate reception, & were rejoic'd that our sufferings were ended. After breakfasting and dressing, we sallied forth to visit the churches & streets. Nothing but my almanac reminded me that it was Sunday; tho numbers of persons were assembled in the different churches and repeating their prayers, not the least appearance of devotion was visible. The streets presented a spectacle still worse. Fruit selling at the stalls, shops open, men fiddling, in short every noise that can be imagined at a fair. The crowds of people in the streets were prodigious; it seemed one perpetual procession.

In the evening, a vast concourse of people assembled to see the grand procession of the Host, with all the Priests, crucifixes, banners, etc., etc., attended by the Military, and a band of musick. This is a grand festival kept once every seven years, when prayers are offer'd up to heaven for us poor heretics. (Kind souls!) The weather unfortunately proving very bad this great spectacle was defer'd to our no small disappointment.

Monday

Visited the church of St Peter, which is esteemed the handsomest in the city. It is a fine building, & highly adorn'd with paintings & grand Altars. Here we saw several persons at confession; Priests look'd wonderfully sapient, & consequential while the poor deluded creatures confess'd their various inequities. I should like to know whether they actually tell the truth.

Caen is a large town & very populous, I think it is a handsomer town than Rouen, tho the streets in the midst of the town are dirty & narrow, and the shops mean. There seems to be but little business carried on, indeed the inhabitants wholly employ'd in sauntering thro the streets, & telling their beads at different Churches. I went into a shop to buy some lace, the woman who kept it, did not take the trouble to rise but pointed at a seat for me, & then ordered some lace to be brought. After I had chosen what I lik'd, I paid the money, which was rec''d without a compliment. I left the shop disgusted with French laziness, and impoliteness. But, this was not Paris.

The chief trade of this place is lace making; the lower order of people seem industrious and work very late of an evening. Their fare is very hard; they have no cheese, little butter, & indifferent bread; no malt liquour of any kind but slight cyder. Their chief & standing dish is Soup which they make of all kinds of herbs & roots, with little or no meat. The butchers' meat is good, & the Poultry excellent; soup & boulie is always a part of the dinner. They are a long time at their meals, especially at dinner. As soon as it is over, Coffee is introduc'd; the cloth is never removed until the Desert [sic] and wine are finish'd. With respect to their dress, the lower kind of women dress as at Dieppe, the middling class universally wear Jackets & long flounced color'd linen cloaks, neat caps, but never any hats. The Ladies walk everywhere without hats, & appear generally much dressed, even early in the morning.

Tuesday

We went a Party of five upon Asses to La Folie, Madame De la Motte's country house. When I mounted, and beheld the calvacade, I was ready to burst with laughter. Five asses all in a row; no sidesaddles, but seats like pillions cover'd with old fashion'd tapestry, and ropes for bridles. After the first emotions of laughter were over, & we had proceeded a few paces, I began to like my Ass prodigiously, he went at an even, pleasant, easy pace, and I cannot help thinking that asses are more adapted for Women, than great headstrong horses, & more delicate & feminine, besides much safer. La Folie is finely situated, and is a very handsome house. In this Town there is a remarkably fine Square, with good houses on all sides; in the midst stands a statue of Louis the fourteenth. This Square is called Place Royale.

Wednesday

Went to visit the Monastery of the Benedictines, founded by our William the Conqueror; also the beautiful Church of St Stephen, which he built & where he lies interred. The Abbey is a most noble edifice, the situation enchanting, & the Gardens very large & pleasant. The prospects from the different Galleries are superior to most I ever beheld. In short, within these walls every comfort and luxury of life are to be met with; nor can I guess what they mean by mortification & self-denial. There can be but one ingredient wanting to make their cup of felicity full to the brim. Need I say it is the company and conversation of us politely denominated by a polite Nation—the best part of the human species. The Monks received us with great politeness; they are men of sense & good breeding. They permitted us to see their Treasury that consists of gold Crucifixes, Cups, etc. etc., and immensely rich robes of gold and embroidery. The Church is beautiful. The Choir pav'd with fine marble, the Altars rich, & the building light & grand. It was also clean. In the evening, we looked into the church of the Trinity, belonging to the Nunnery close adjoining. Built & founded by Matilda, the wife of William the Conqueror; her tomb is in the Choir. This church is very grand and the Altar immensely rich. The endowments here are vast. Shocking reflection, that the Riches of the Nation shou'd be heaped upon Altars, & thrown away upon enthusiasts, whilst the poor, actually want bread. From the Castle we had a fine view of the Town and Country round. There is also a charming walk near the town, between a double-row of trees, with the river on one side.

William the Conqueror had attempted to capture the French town of Mantes, where the king was injured when he was thrown against the pommel of his saddle and his internal organs ruptured. William returned to his capital at Rouen. His condition continued to worsen and William confessed his sins and sought pardon. His treasure was distributed to the churches and the poor, "so that what I amassed through evil deeds may be assigned to the holy uses of good men." penelope.uchicago.edu/~grout/.../anglo.../williamdeath.html

Abby of Men founded by William the Conqueror. *Source:* Sharon Hope

Thursday

We left Caen, & journey'd on with some of the best horses in the world. How can people rail at French horses; all that we have had have been excellent, full of life & spirits, and remarkably strong, nay handsome, if the slightest attention were paid to their appearance. But I believe they are never clean'd or cropp'd. As we were ascending a steep hill we met a waggon heavy laden, coming down with three horses, four were taken from the team & fastened on behind to keep it back. It was a droll sight to see them tugging and pulling the wagon back with all their strength lest it go too fast. This is a French idea & <u>wonderfully ingenious</u>.

We breakfasted at Lisieux, a city in Normandy, & proceeded on, as there was nothing worthy of attention, towards Evreux.

The town Lisieux is in the heart of the Pays d' Auge, of which it is the capital. Lisieux is therefore surrounded by Normandy's typical hedged farmland, where there is a mix of livestock farming (mostly milk cows) and cider apple cultivation.

I must not omit, however, mentioning our breakfast, which consisted of coffee, radishes, rolls, cherries, & butter. We din'd at a poor little cottage, called an Inn; we had, however, the best they could offer us, & consequently were content. The miserable accommodations, and the awkwardness of our attendents serv'd only to make us laugh. I will always remember Marche – neuf with a smile. We passed through a small town call'd La Riviere, the situation of which was uncommonly fine. Here stands the House of the Farmer-General, surrounded with Woods, a beautiful vale below, with a clear river gliding at the bottom; it is altogether one of the sweetest places I ever saw. I understand there are twelve of these men called farmer generals in France, who raise themselves immense fortunes by taxing the poor Peasants, in what mode, and as heavily as they think proper. I envy them not their splendid institutions, thus dearly bought.

At the end of the 18th century, the Ferme générale had become the symbol of France's inegalitarian society. The men involved became extremely rich.

We arrived late in the evening at Evreux, where we supp'd very well and slept. Late as it was we walk'd out to see the town, which I have a clear idea of, as the moon shone brightly. In the public walks were numbers of persons enjoying the fine evening, and at ten o'clock at night, the whole town seem'd alive. The Cathedral is a beautiful Gothic structure. Here is also the Palace of the Duke of Boullion and that of the Bishops. Evreux is a pleasant place, & the entrance to it, charming, thro double rows of trees as at Rouen.

Friday

At three o'clock we set off from Evreux, and reached Mante where we breakfasted. This town is in the Isle of France, & has a fine stone bridge of twenty to thirty arches over the Seine. It is also famous for excellent wine. From thence we proceeded to St Germains (after eating eggs and drinking coffee for breakfast). The prospects here were again enchanting, all the way along, everywhere enlivn'd by this beautiful river. Gentlemen's Houses were profusely scatter'd on all sides, and our road lay thro charming vineyards, & rows of walnut & cherry-trees. I never saw so luxuriant a scene. I cannot attempt to describe it. We arrived at St. Germains to dinner, fatigued & half dead with heat. This town is pleasantly situated on a hill with the Seine at the bottom, twelve miles from Paris. The Palace is immensely large & grand, built in the form of a castle. Here James [II of England and VI of Scotland] resided during his exile [driven out of England by William of Orange]. Here he died. The terrace is more beautiful than can be conceived and the view from it astonishing. We saw Marli, the Waterworks, the Windmills adjoining Paris; a fine valley below, with the Seine winding along, & to the left the grand forest that contains five or six thousand acres.

> Marly-le-Roi, a village lying between Versailles and St. Germain, supported the palace at Marly. It was near a forest of that name, and was close to the site of a large water-raising machine. Both the smaller palaces of Marly and Versailles were fed by this machine. Water transported to Versailles via aqueduct supplied its many fountains and gardens. The chateau at Marly was destroyed in the early 1800s.

The terrace is broad & seems to have no end. There are several fine walks & shady retreats. It is altogether a Paradise. After we had sufficiently view'd this scene of enchantment, we set off from St Germains & soon reached the grand road, or Avenue, leading to the Gates of Paris. Here, the entrance is truly striking. The road perfectly straight, continues thro a double row of trees a considerable way, till you are brought to the beautiful Gates, with two fine portals on either side just finished. Here our carriage was stop'd but not searched as we assur'd them we were not Merchants and

In foreground: formerly the Hotel d'York at 56 Rue St. Jacques, Paris, in 2007, now an office building. *Source:* Sharon Hope

had nothing with us except our cloaths. A small fee we paid, as was customary, & then were permitted to proceed.

The coup d'oiel as you enter Paris, is noble, the grandeur & walks of the Thuilleries, and the number of gay equipages you meet, is, to a stranger, a most striking scene. We arrived at the Hotel de Yorch in Rue de St Jacob, got rid of our chaise, & were soon settled in apartments splendid enough for a crown'd head. We have a grand suite of rooms; the sitting rooms are adorned in the highest style of elegance hung with silk, border'd with gold; beautiful Chandeliers suspended from the ceilings, and looking glasses from the top of the room to the bottom, besides in the panels and doors. We could get none less splendid, so the Maitre handsomely lowered the price. I already feel quite at home as the fatigues of travel are over for the present.

> *There is a plaque on the former Hotel d'York which reads that in this place Benjamin Franklin and David Hartley signed the Treaty of Independence in 1783.*

Saturday Paris 11ᵗʰ July

We have agreed with a Traiteur [caterer] and Valet de Place. In the morning we went to the English Convent, in Rue de St Antoine, to deliver our letters to Mrs Stock. At our entrance we rang a bell, an inferior Nun appear'd at the grate to whom we gave our letters; we were then directed into a parlour, Mrs Stock appear'd & convers'd with us thro' a double grate. She receiv'd us with vast politeness, and will send our names to the Arch Bishop for permission to shew us the Nunnery. We shall also see a procession next week.

*The student learning was fairly superficial consisting of a little
drawing, music and Italian. The convent became extinct as a result of
the French Revolution.*

On our way to & from the Nunnery, we had a compleat view of the
Bastile. This horrid abode of misery occupies considerable space of ground
& is surrounded beyond the moat with houses, so that little more than
battlements appear in the front. Behind you have a better view of it. Its
appearance is not unlike the Tower of London. The Guards will not permit
any person to stand still in the street to view this infernal Mansion, but
immediately orders them to proceed, (which is the safest thing to do)
about their business.

We then visited the church of Notre Dame; here I was struck with
astonishment! The building is noble; but the beauty of the paintings, the
grandeur of the Altar & Choir, with the extreme elegance of the private
Chapels & their monuments, is wonderful indeed. The front of the Altar is
gold; the marble figures on it are finer than can be imagin'd; they represent
the Virgin Mary with the dead body of Jesus Christ lying across her knees,
with Angels on each side. Death is strongly express'd in the countenance of
our Saviour & in the attitude of the falling limbs. Expression of woe in the
Virgin's face can only be felt. The tears streaming down her cheeks appear
liquid tho' in marble, & the drapery is wonderfully fine.

On each side the Altarpiece is a fine statue of a king presenting his
Crown to the Virgin. The whole of the Choir is beautiful marble, on
each side are figures in brass holding instruments used at our Saviour's
crucifixion. The private chapels here are very grand, adorn'd with rich
paintings and Altars. In that of the Harcourt family, is a most beautiful
marble monument, representing the Countess kneeling before her dead
husband, an Angel lifting up the lid of the Coffin and Death standing by in
a menacing posture, shewing his hourglass. The expression of grief in the
lovely features of the Countess is life itself. I cannot enter into a detail of
the beauties of this magnificent Church nor can you form an idea of half its
grandeur unless you were to see it. The Paintings are innumerable & all by
the best Masters. I never saw any to equal them.

Here we saw the Vespers performed in great perfection. Such a scene
of Mummery surely was never exhibited. It was a Pantomimical farce
consisting of singing, bowing, curt'sing, parading up and down in costly
garments, and tossing from one to the other silver lamps of incense. Not
the least appearance of seriousness or devotion could I discover. The Priests

have it all to themselves, as the People are kneeling outside the Choir, which is the stage for these <u>religious Actors</u>.

In the afternoon we amus'd ourselves in visiting the shops, & making some trifling purchases. Their mode of transacting business is clumsy & extremely fatiguing; they have very little civility to customers, are wonderfully slow in their movements, & have very little choice of goods. I think their prices are extravagant, at least the English find them so. You must be sharp to deal with them, bid them little more then half their demand, and you may get things tolerably cheap. The best shops make a contemptible appearance, in comparison with those in London & the Principal Towns in England. The streets in the middle of the city are narrow, dirty, & without drains, so that the smells are very disagreeable; & after a shower of rain, boats are more necessary than any other conveyance. Tis hardly possible for Women to walk the streets; especially if they be well dressed. Here is no foot pavement, so that you are in danger every moment of being run over by carriages, which are passing continually, not to mention the extreme vulgarity and rudeness of the lower kind of people. People in the higher walks of life are uncommonly polite & attentive to all strangers, but to English in particular.

The Publick Buildings are much grander than we have in England. From the different Bridges across the Seine, you have a fine view of the Palace of the Louvre which is large enough for a Town. On the Pont-Neuf is a fine Equestrian Statue of Henry the Fourth. The building called the Thulleries is extremely grand.

Left: Henry 4th Paris. *Right:* Portion of the Louvre. *Source:* Sharon Hope

Paris: Palais de Justice, south range. *Source:* Sharon Hope

Chapter 4
Revolution

Sunday July 13th

After breakfasting early & dressing ourselves (fit to appear in Court) we went off to Versailles; proceeded immediately to the Palace & travers'd the magnificent apartments until the King appear'd. He pass'd close by us to Chapel, where we immediately follow'd him and had a full view of his Majesty & the ceremonies below. We were in the gallery on the King's right hand; the Priests in the body of the Church under us. The King has good-humour strongly imprinted on his countenance; he is handsome, & not unlike our own King. After he had said his prayers he left the Chapel, & the Queen soon appeared with some Ladies attending her. She sat in the King's place, & the same ceremonial farce at the Altar was repeated. The Queen has a fine person, and a beautiful face, but I do not admire the expression of her features, tho tis said she was remarkably handsome a few years ago. She has a deal of hauteur in her looks, & a strong expression of something like contempt. They both appear'd anxious and discontented. Probably the awkward situation of Public Affairs made them uneasy. The band of Musick at the Chapel was charming, & the voices very fine. As soon as Mass was ended, we went into the diningroom to see the King <u>eat</u>.

In the main palace, the king usually dined alone at a table in view of hundreds of onlookers. On other occasions, diners were seated in his presence in strict protocol by rank; cooking for the palace's banquets required a kitchen staff of 2,000.
adventure.howstuffworks.com

The dishes are all of gold. This ceremony he goes thro every Sunday in Publick. The Queen sits at table but does not eat. The King tastes several dishes & then they retire to dine en famille! I was charm'd with the politeness of the gentlemen who everywhere made room for us, & placed us in the best situations they cou'd procure. Why cannot the King & Queen pray together? After dinner we walk'd in the Royal gardens & in full view of this grand Palace. But here I must leave all description—No words of mine can convey an idea of the surprising magnificence of this wonderful Place.

Chapel at Versailles. Note the upper gallery.
Source: M. and S. Kirkpatrick

Statues in the gardens at Versailles.
Source: Sharon Hope

In England there is nothing like it. Louis the fourteenth made this surprising place, it was his Hobbyhorse, & because it was difficult, he delighted in it the more. He caused water to be brought from Marli to supply the beautiful fountains here. The wealth of the Nation was drain'd to compleat the plan.

The outside of the Building is astonishing; the inside immensely rich. The gardens are vastly extensive, & everywhere enrich'd with marble statues of exquisite workmanship, & immense value.

The fountains are wonderful & almost numberless; the water is thrown up by marble figures and returns into immense basons of marble. From this scene of inconceivable grandeur we went to visit the beautiful little Palace of Trianon; where their Majesties retire from the fatigues of a Court, to taste the luxury of repose, in the most elegant retreat imagination can paint.

Here tis all enchantment! The house is comparatively small; the furniture of the rooms is rich in the extreme & filled with expensive ornaments. I cannot help mentioning one room, the furniture of which is a rich blue silk bordered with fine point lace. From this specimen you may judge of the rest. The gardens are delightful not unlike Mr. Hoare's at Sturton, but on a larger scale.

After winding through the gardens a considerable way, you arrive at a cluster of Cottages in a rural situation, cover'd with thatch like ours in England. I declin'd at first entering the rooms, imagining that the inside corresponded to the outward appearance, but the attendants seeming desirous of it, we went in. Never was I so mistaken in my conjecture; the rooms were finish'd in a superior style, & furnished with great elegance. What refinement of taste! The outside a cottage—the inside a Palace. In the garden is a most beautiful Theatre where sometimes Plays are acted to select Parties of the Queen's appointment. Trianon is an earthly Paradise. At some little distance is another Trianon with a most beautiful double Collanade of the finest marble.

Evening now drew on apace, and we thought of returning to our Hotel, we had witness'd the grandest spectacle of Art, & were fatigu'd with attending to them. We entered our carriage & drove on to Paris; when after a few miles, before we reached the Gates, the Military stopp'd us, order'd us to turn back, and informed us that there had been a revolt at Paris & no one cou'd be admitted within the Gates. We saw the Barriers [toll houses] on fire.

Our consternation was great, but hundreds were in the same predicament, this supported our sinking spirits. We all turn'd back, but where to go we knew not. Versailles was worse than Paris. We agreed to drive to a small village at some distance, & if no better accommodation offer'd, to spend the night in our coach.

We were however, overtaken by some other carriages, & all stopped to call a counsel of war. It was at length agreed to proceed to Paris by some other road, & to try to gain admittance. This we easily accomplished, & arriv'd at our Hotel in safety though we found the city in utmost confusion, a report that Mr. Necher and the Duc d'Orleans were exil'd from Court & probably confin'd, occasion'd the revolt.

Necher was former French Minister of Finance who resigned his
position in 1781 but remained in political life.

The Citizens broke open the shops where guns & pistols were likely to be found, arm'd themselves, disarmed the Guards, & burn'd the barriers near the Gates. A party of the Queen's horse fir'd upon them, but were oblig'd to retreat instantly; some were killed. The Solders in great numbers revolted and join'd the people. They have secur'd the Gates leading to Versailles, & cut off all communication with the Court. Our Hotel is some distance from the scene of action, so I hope we are secure.

The state of Politicks upon our arrival in Paris was this: a considerable army had for some time surrounded the Metropolis which gave just cause for alarm to the Citizens. The Stats [sic] General had requested the King to remove his troops; he refused and order'd them to retire from the Assembly. Their answer to the King's Message was truly noble; they inform'd his Majesty that they never wou'd quit the Assembly till they were carried out Dead!

Monday July 14th 1789

What a scene presented itself to our eyes this morning! The shops shut throughout the City—all business at a stand—every individual furnishing himself with some kind of weapon; those who cannot get swords or pistols, have hatchets, reaping hooks, pitch forks, and iron spikes. Tis terrible to see them. We have ventur'd through the streets in a coach to see the beautiful Church of St. Sulpice; here again I was struck with wonder at the grandeur of the building, but above all the dome or calvery behind the high Altar. It is crowded with rich paintings, & the light artfully thrown in you know not how. In a vast niche in the centre, is the Assumption of the Virgin in purest marble. It is wonderfully fine. The pulpit here is very remarkable, so is the Organ. All the Churches are shut today on account of the trouble, except those where citizens hold their Assemblies. We look'd in on the English Benedictines, and saw the coffin of James the 2nd, also his bust in wax. The Monk was polite.

We visited at the same time the chapel belonging to the Carmelite Nuns. This is the most elegant little place imaginable. The Altar is rich, and the paintings admirable, but the beautiful picture of Madame Valiere in the act of tearing off her ornaments, and renouncing the world, is the most enchanting portrait I ever beheld. She was some years Mistress to Louis the 14th before she took refuge in this convent. Louis threaten'd to burn the convent, in order to regain her, but she vow'd she wou'd perish in the flames. Here she died, and is buried.

The confusion seems hourly to increase; where will it end? They threaten to set fire to the houses of those who are obnoxious. O that we were safe in

England! They say we cannot quit the city, as every carriage is stopp'd & the baggage seized.

We have ventur'd another ride to see the foundling hospital. This is a noble institution; infants are rec'd at any age & no questions asked. They have now seventeen thousand children! We saw but few, as the major part are at nurse in the Country. The beds etc. are remarkably neat and clean.

In 1784, Jacques Necker prophesied that this institution would
seriously embarrass the state. From 1452 to 1789 the law had
imposed on the seigneurs de haute justice the duty of succouring
children found deserted in their territories.
www.answers.com › ... › History 1450–1789

Our carriage has been stopp'd several times by persons arm'd with drawn swords who demanded whether we were for the Tiers/Etat. We replied we were English, & friends to liberty; they then gave us loud huzzas and suffer'd us to pass on. We go to bed—but with the strong persuasion that we shall be suddenly rous'd by some calamity. Tis unfortunate that we are here in this crisis, as the end of our coming is defeated. Every public amusement & spectacle of any sort is shut. But the spirit of the people I revere. They are making a glorious struggle against arbitrary power, and are unanimous in the cause of liberty.

Chapter 5
Military Rule

Tuesday 15ᵗʰ

No excesses were committed last night. Some of the shops are open'd and the people seem under regular discipline. Every individual is under arms. They have hung five men this morning for robberies; this I hope will prevent outrages. Several Convents were broken open early this morning and the corn secreted there, brought out and sold in the public market. The price of it has lately been doubled. We have ventur'd out again in the coach, but it shall be the last time. We were stopp'd eight times by large bodies of the Bourgeoisie, who opened our coach & sometimes search'd to see if we had any arms secreted. Though the idea of having our coach surrounded by fifty men with drawn swords & bayonets fixed was not very agreeable, yet they always treated us with politeness & respect.

We went to see the King's botanical garden, and from the Belvedere, which is considerably elevated, we saw a sight which made my heart rejoice, in the midst of terror. The Bastile, stormed – & taken. Glorious moment! Down goes that horrid monument of Arbitrary Power, which has so long stood the disgrace of this Country. Some circumstances of horror attended the Siege, but the vile dungeon will be demolished. The Bourgeois demanded arms of the Governor of the Bastile, he promised a supply, permitted a party of enter, & then drew up the Bridge, and basely fell upon, & destroy'd them. Vast numbers, upon seeing the bridge drawn up, suspected the fate of those who enter'd & immediately storm'd the Bastile & got possession of it. They seized the Governor, cut off his head, and hew'd his body into ten thousand pieces. (Tis said they eat his flesh). The Governor's head, with two more it was reported, were carried about in triumph, & stuck up in the Palais Royale.

We have introduc'd ourselves to Mr. Wilkinson, who accompanied us today, & will not leave us. He is extremely kind and attentive, & we will put ourselves wholly under his care for the remainder of our stay here. He has already animated & raised our drooping spirits. He tells us we have nothing to fear.

Dr Rigby and his party, with whom Susannah later connected, viewed two heads stuck up at the Palais Royale. John Wilkinson, the industrialist, employed a son of Joseph Priestley, an individual who was also in Paris at the time. Wilkinson began to spend time with Susannah's party. He had dissenting connections, and connections to Priestley by marriage. The Estlin family was acquainted with Priestley since he was an instructor at Warrington Academy where Rev. John P. Estlin attended.

We have seen the beautiful statues & paintings in the Louvre. This is a charming place! The collection is prodigious, & by all the most approv'd Masters. One room is appropriated for the reception of Portraits of the most eminent Masters. The other rooms & the long Gallery are full of fine Statues, Busts, and paintings.

At twelve o'clock at night we were dreadfully alarm'd. A rumour was spread that an immense number of troops were marching to attack the city. The people were all in commotion, and immediately put themselves in a posture of defense. At the end of each street, barriers were plac'd to prevent the enemy from entering; the stones of the pavement were torn up, and carried to the tops of houses, with an intent, and a request to us all, to shower them down upon the army. With these expectations and fears we went to bed, nay slept –& slept soundly. I think no number of troops can enter Paris such amazing precautions are taken to guard & defend it. I believe it was this assurance that compos'd our spirits & enabl'd us to sleep, though in such critical circumstances; not to mention our great fatigue.

Wednesday 18th

Orders are given that no strangers may quit the city. Not a horse to be hired for any sum. Well! Hundreds are in the same situation, and that is some consolation, although we are to all intents and purposes, prisoners. Mr. Challen has join'd our party, this is very agreeable, as he is courageous, polite, & good-temper'd and in these times of distress such a companion is an acquisition. We din'd with Mr. Wilkinson at the Palais Royale. This is a noble building, & for grandeur & extensiveness, exceeds anything one can form an idea of in England. In one wing the Duc d'Orleans resides, the rest is let to different persons for shops, coffee houses, eating houses, etc. etc., at a vast rent. In the middle, is the Garden or public walks, where people continually resort; today it exhibited an interesting scene indeed, crowded with persons full of anxiety, all waiting for the King's answer to their message. At length it arrived—and was propitious. A Grand procession now took place. The Deputies, the Archbishop of Paris—the revolted troops—and an infinity of the Bourgeois march'd in triumph to Notre Dame to thank God for their Liberty. It was a noble procession.

In 1788, with the Revolution looming, the young Louis Philippe showed his liberal sympathies when he helped break down the door of a prison cell in Mont Saint Michel, during a visit there with the Countess of Genlis. From October 1788 to October 1789, the Palais-Royal was a meeting-place for the revolutionaries.

Entrance to courtyard area at the Palais Royale Paris. *Source:* Sharon Hope

Immediately after the cannons fir'd, the bells rung, and every token of joy was visible throughout the town. Just before the Procession arriv'd, we went to the top of Notre Dame where we had a fine view of the city and environs. The unusually white appearance that the houses make, adds (in my opinion) greatly to the beauty of the prospect. The country round is charming. Whilst we were in the Palais Royale, Henry Dubois, a private soldier, who first enter'd the Bastile was carried round in triumph, adorned with flowers, and preceded by a band of music and officers of distinction.

This man also join'd the procession to Notre Dame, deck'd with the dead Governor's ribbon. After him was dragged the Bastile canon in triumph. The whole procession form'd a grand spectacle. A good old lady receiv'd us into her house, where from the windows we had a view of the whole group. We return'd to our Hotel on foot, in perfect safety, notwithstanding the immense crowds in every street.

Thursday 17th

Unfortunate indeed! We arriv'd at the Convent of Blue Nuns two hours too late to see the Procession. The Abbess (our friend Mrs. Stock) expected us, and had given orders for our reception, and even waited some time for us. I shall repent this as long as I live. I may never more have such an opportunity. Writing letters to England (which by the way were not permitted to go) and an idea that the present troubles might prevent the ceremony, or at least retard it, detained us at home the greatest part of the morning. Marin thinks us safe only at home. He is a prudent and judicious Valet but has no spirit. Perhaps, so best. Mr. Wilkinson took us to the Luxembourgh where we din'd, and afterwards walk'd in the Gardens, which are extremely pleasant, though not to be compar'd with the Thuilleries. We drank coffee at a coffee-house, our friend told us it was customary for ladies to frequent those places. I had no sort of objection; the novelty pleas'd me.

We contrive to see a great deal, notwithstanding the public places are all shut. I rejoice that I am in Paris at this time, and shall ever look back upon this fortunate event with pride and pleasure. I shall (probably) tell my grandchildren with exultation and triumph that I was an eye-witness to the glorious revolution in France—that I saw a nation that deserv'd liberty throw away their chains of slavery and become free!

I honor the spirit that I see in the people here; they are wise, brave, and unanimous. The order and regularity with which everything is conducted is really surprising. All orders come from the Hotel de Ville and are punctually obey'd. They have established there a permanent committee, the wisest and ablest men in Europe are at the head. There are this day in Paris two hundred and eighty thousand men in arms, (besides the military) whose names are enroll'd. On the Bridges, and at the entrance to the city, cannon are plac'd and the tinderbox and matches stand close by. At night the streets are barricaded, and day and night innumerable Patroles are marching to and fro. The troops have deserted their King and joined the citizens; none prov'd faithful and loyal but the foreign troops. They have this morning retreated from the Champs de Mars, leaving their baggage and stores behind them. We are now free from alarm on account of a Siege.

The King has not a man to send against Paris; and if he had thousands they would find it a difficult matter to effect an entrance.

The Parisians have sent to Versailles requesting the King would come to Paris, and assure them of his determination to accede to their proposals. He has return'd an answer, that he will consider of it. This will not do; they have sent again telling him, that he has eight and forty hours to consider of it, and if at the expiration of that time he does not make an appearance—they will fetch him. I believe that this is the first time that a Monarch of France ever endur'd such language. What will be the result we know not. If he does not come, the consequences must be dreadful. Arbitrary Power seems now to have receiv'd its fatal wound! It is at its last gasp in this country.

The people have found vast stores of corn secreted in various places. This is reviving news, as famine star'd them in the face. The cool determination of the noblesse and clergy was to starve them into submission. The Authors of this infernal plot will meet with no mercy from the populace.

The Luxembourgh is a handsome Palace; the Gardens are extensive, but not very beautiful; laid out in the taste of the last century, with formal cut yew hedges etc., etc. The Balustrade that encloses part of the garden is entirely of marble.

Chapter 6
Keys to Paris

Friday July the 18th

Early in the morning the King sent word to Paris, that he wou'd entrust himself to his citizens, and visit them on that day. Preparation was immediately made for his reception. The Bourgeoisie form'd two lines which extended five miles, for the King to pass through, all bearing arms. Our friend Mr. Wilkinson procur'd us an excellent situation on a balcony, from which we had a near view of this grand sight. After standing six hours, the guns announc'd the King's arrival. The procession soon pass'd before us. But, how shall I describe the grand spectacle! The King's guards attended him to the gates of the City, and then withdrew leaving him to be escorted by the people, to the Hotel de Ville. First came parties of light horse—next the revolted troops—close to them an innumerable multitude of the Bourgeoisie on horseback. Then on foot, dressed in the habits of their different orders, the Three Estates compleat. The clergy (with the Archbishop of Paris), the Noblesse, and the Tiers Etat. This group form'd a most noble spectacle; and the Tier's Etat were welcom'd with rapture. Then follow'd the King in a gilt coach drawn by eight horses, and proceeded by the Marquise de la Foyatte [sic] and Monsieur Bailey, the new provost des Marchands. In the coach with the King were Compte d'Estang and four other persons of distinction. Another coach with eight horses follow'd the King's. Then came the Bourgeoisie on foot, their number seem'd almost infinite.

Dr Rigby, George Cadogan Morgan and his party viewed the event from the balcony of a Mr. Sykes at the Palais Royale. Susannah dined with them later at the Palais Royale, likely introduced through Mr. John Wilkinson.

The king alighted at the Hotel de Ville, & there assur'd the people (by proxy, for he was unable to speak for himself) that he would comply with their wishes and do everything to promote the prosperity and peace of his kingdom. He then returned, and was escorted in the same manner to the gates of the City; there the Bourgeoisie left him to make the best of his way to Versailles, which he did with all possible speed, and no doubt congratulated himself that he was got off in safety. He certainly had rather not have paid the visit, but it was indispensible. Tis said that the queen and her party urg'd him to refuse the request of the people, be the consequences what they might; but more prudent advisors persuaded him to the conduct which he wisely adopted.

I forgot to mention some of the most distinguished personages in the Kings procession to the Hotel de Ville. These are the Poissonienes or Fisherwomen, or countrywomen who sell vegetables, who constantly make a part of every procession, and are permitted on certain days to approach the Grand Monarque, when, and at no other time, he stands a chance of hearing the truth.

15 July 1789: Voters in the town hall welcomed Messers. Lafayette and Bailly, heads of the delegation of the National Assembly, with shouts of: Long live the Nation and its deputies! M. LaFayette became the general commander of the militia, called the bourgeois National Guard. Bailly was named provost for all merchants. larocheusa.org/ bastil.htm

Hotel de Ville. *Source:* Sharon Hope

The Duc d'Orleans the idol of Paris, remain'd at Versailles a hostage for the king. Cockades of blue, pink and white were worn by every individual, by express orders from the Hotel de Ville. They presented one to the King & adorn'd the hats of all his attendants in the same manner.

When the King arriv'd at the City gates on his entering Paris, the new Provost des Marchands presented him with the keys saying "I bring your Majesty the keys of the good city Paris; they are the same that were presented to Henry the fourth. He had regained his people, here the People have regain'd their King". It was proclaimed death to say "Vivre le Roi", when the king made his appearance, till he had been to the Hotel de Ville & assur'd them of his approbation; then they were loud in their acclamations and "Vivre le Roi, Vivre le Nation", "Vivre le peuple", resounded on all sides. At night a general illumination took place, the Hotel de Ville was beautifully illuminated and in the center a transparency with this inscription "Louis Seize Pere des Francois et Roi d'un Peuple Libre" –Juillet–17–1789–.

We din'd at the Palais Royale with Mr. W.; Mr. Morgan & his party join'd us, & a most pleasant day we passe'd together. It was a glorious, animating sight, to see a People thus made free, and without (comparatively speaking), any bloodshed. For my part, I am such a citizen of the World, that I rejoic'd most heartily in their liberty, & felt an ardour in the cause which could scarcely have been greater had I been personally interested.

George Cadogan Morgan was a Welsh dissenting minister and scientist interested in electricity. While traveling with Dr. Rigby, he also wrote letters from Paris concerning what he experienced. Morgan died in 1798 from inhaling poison during an experiment.

We went in the evening, late, to see the illuminations; all was peace, order & sobriety. We were astonish'd at the tranquility that reign'd throughout the city. No drunkenness—no tumults—no discord. The conduct of the lower class of people in Paris, upon this great occasion & indeed through the whole of this business, must be remember'd to their immortal honor. In a window very near us, stood the unfortunate Count d' Auch to see the king's entre. He had been confin'd in the Bastile 42 years. His offense was writing against the Jesuits, which made him obnoxious to the People then in power. The unhappy man had the appearance of an Idiot.

Dr. Rigby described the Count as being dressed in a greasy reddish coloured uniform when released from the Bastille. There is some question as to whether the Count was an Idiot because Dr Rigby

*believed the man at the window close by was not Count d'Auch but
another prisoner released at the same time.*

Saturday

Today the city appears tranquil; people are return'd to their respective
employments, except those who are on Patroles, which are very numerous.
All the barriers & entrances to the Town are strongly defended even the
matches and tinderboxes, are plac'd close to the Cannon's mouth. They do
not relax their vigilance in any respect. The solders are separated from each
other, & intermix'd with the Bourgeoisie so that you will see in a Patrole
two solders to six or eight citizens. This is undoubtedly a wise precaution.
Indeed Wisdom & Prudence seem to regulate all their proceedings. From
the Hotel de Ville all orders come; and there sits a permanent Committee,
day and night, in order to frame a free Constitution. In the gardens of the
Palais Royale it is no unusual thing to see persons mounted on stools and
harangueing on the rights of mankind. We have heard several orations of
this kind which were receiv'd with rapture by the gaping audience.

Chapter 7
Paris Sights

Mr. Wilkinson took us this morning to see the Charity school for Blind children. Here they are cloath'd & taught free of expence both boys and girls. The girls learn to knit and read; the boys learn writing, arithmetic, reading, printing, & other arts, as their different tastes direct. They are all musical, and learn to play on various instruments. We saw them at their respective employments, & were astonished at their dexterity. Afterwards, they perform'd a little Concert, two of the girls play'd, the rest sang, and the boys accompanied them on violins, flutes, etc, etc. This is a noble Charity; but the sight of the poor creatures is extremely affecting. After the concert there was a collection for their benefit. The publick day is on a Saturday, when all persons are admitted.

John Wilkinson supplied the Paris Waterworks with forty miles of piping. books.google.ca/books?isbn=0811716430...

Valentin Hauy, who was blind himself, started the school. It was almost self-sufficient; the pupils made almost everything. All the instructors were blind. Children, if received gratuitously, were between 9 and 14. There was no age limit for boarders. The school later produced books using a series of raised letters invented by Hauy to allow the students to read. M. Louis Braille a later professor at the School, who died in 1852, forwarded the idea.

We din'd in the garden of the Thuilleries, and afterwards walk'd to see the famous works that supply Paris with water. They were made under the inspection of our friend Mr. Wilkinson. In the evening we crossed the Seine and visited that amazing structure the Hospital or Hotel of Invalids. This magnificent building forms a square on the outside, but when you get within you find five compleat Squares, the largest in the center. The church is extremely grand, & has a most beautiful dome richly ornated with paintings. The pillars near the altar are also most beautiful. In this Hospital or rather Palace, (and a superb one too) are 7000 Invalids. There is nothing in Paris more worth the attention of strangers than this vast structure. Besides the grand dome, there are smaller ones, each richly embellis'd with paintings. The pillars represent palm trees. From hence we went to the Ecole Militare but didn't gain admission. The Hotel of Invalids surrendered to the citizens the third day of this revolution & furnish'd them with arms, and cannon, ammunition etc., etc.

Passage at the Hotel des Invalides. *Source:* Sharon Hope

Sunday 20th

Went to Notre Dame. We were too late for the Farce of High Mass—but we were gratified by a sight of the Treasury. The costly robes and habits, for the different priests and occasions, are cover'd in gold and fine embroidery. Here we saw the collarbone of St Dennis, the leg of St somebody, a drop of the Virgin's milk, & a part of the real cross. These precious relicts were preserv'd in glass cases, and richly ornamented with gold & precious stones. Here we saw crosses of gold enriched with diamonds of immense value, Cups, Saints, Virgin Marys etc., etc.

We visited also St Roch, which is a fine church, & had, behind the altar, a large Sepulchre, to represent our Saviour. Here stands a coffin cover'd with black; the light is artfully thrown in, and just enough of it, to make darkness visible, and to discover a crucifix which appears to be at a great distance, surrounded with clouds. This gloomy spot is called the chapel of the Sepulchre. From this we went to the church of St. Eustachius; the roof is extremely light and beautiful, & very high.

The churches this day in Paris, exhibit an extraordinary appearance; they are turn'd into Barracks for the Military; who have their beds, arms, etc., here, and are eating, drinking, sleeping, dressing, whilst service is performing in another part of the same church. I never beheld such a motley scene, nor is it easily conceiv'd. I looked towards the high Altar, & saw the priests celebrating mass, & the multitude kneeling by. In the body of the church were the solders marching with their hats on; & sleeping in the beautiful chapels; others eating & drinking.

We next visited the House of Justice, where the courts of justice are held (similar to our Westminster Hall) and where the Parliament us'd to meet. The front of this building is very beautiful; a court stands before it, and is divided from the street by vast iron palisades & gates, gilt at the top. In the Chapel—conceal'd behind the high altar are said to be deposited the instruments that were used at our Saviour's Crucifixion. The greatest curiosity here was a resemblance of some Saint or great personage cut in Agate. Over the door were painted figures exactly resembling fine sculpture.

Left: Notre Dame.
Below: Stained glass window at Notre Dame.
Source: M.and S. Kirkpatrick

At four o'clock, by appointment, we went to the English Convent. The gentlemen were left at the Hotel, they were not permitted to tread this hallow'd ground. The gate was opened by the Abbess herself; she saluted me on both cheeks with her veil over her face, then introduc'd us to the Nuns who were assembl'd to see us. The Abbess after making affectionate inquiries for her relations (with whom we were intimately acquainted) conducted us to the Chapel, Refectory, and apartments belonging, particularly, to herself. All was neat—but very plain. We then ascended the stairs which led to the different Cells; they were on each side of a long gallery; and at the entrance was written in large letters STRICT SILENCE. I cou'd not help asking the Abbess if this law extended to me, assuring her that if it did—I cou'd proceed no farther. She smil'd at the question & we pass'd on.

The Cells were small but pleasant rooms, in each there was a white bed, chair, table, Altar, Crucifix, death's head & bones, holy water, and a crown of thorns hanging at the head of each bed, also a Virgin Mary and a very few devotional books. Till this moment I always imagined, that Nuns, though excluded from the world, had in their own Convents an agreeable society, which might make their time pass away pleasantly enough. Alas! Poor creatures, they are debarred this comfort. When they retire to their Cells, (which is at an early hour) each one is shut in alone—no sound is heard, and, that this awful silence may not be broken whatever, each Nun puts on a pair of woolen slippers to tread softly across her room.

One nun is never permitted to enter the cell of another, or even to speak outside the door, unless sudden illness obliges them to break through this law, but even then, the conversation must be short & on their knees. They have what is call'd an hour's recreation after dinner, when they are suffer'd to converse freely with each other. Seven times a day they have Masses, which, with a little necessary needle work, and cleaning their apartments (a task they are oblig'd to perform themselves) fills up their time.

Close to the House is their burying place. They have a spacious & very pleasant Garden, abounding with all sorts of vegetables and fruits; here they are indulg'd with walking during the hour of recreation. They also have a pretty wood adjoining, where they enjoy the same liberty; in the midst of the wood stands a mount called Calvary on which is erected a vast Crucifix stuck full of thorns. Here they come to meditate. The Abbess appear'd very affectionate to the nuns whom she call'd her dear daughters, they at the same time giving her the title of dearest mother. I cou'd not help being surprised at the look of cheerfulness each countenance wore, till I recollected, that the sight of a stranger was undoubtedly the occasion of this momentary joy.

Whilst we were walking, one of the nuns came running to the abbess exclaiming " Oh my dearest mother! Sister Catherine has a return of her fits. What shall we do for her?" It made my heart ache. Oh, I thought, this is some miserable creature just awaken'd to a sense of the horrors of her situation, and repenting too late of the rash vow she has made. The dress of the nuns is frightful in the extreme. A white cloth cap covers the head, forehead & ears, & is fastened to a large white bib, which is tight under the chin, over this is worn a long back veil, which is usually thrown back from the face. [There is] A robe of coarse white stuff, with immense sleeves, tied around the waist with a cord, [where a] crucifix and a string of beads [is] suspended. A medal of the Virgin is fasten'd on the bosom of the robe. Over this dress they wear on great festivals, a large blue mantle—from this they are called "Blue Nuns". In my opinion, the finest feature in the world wou'd appear disgusting in this abominable disguise.

In this convent there are a number of young Ladies, pensioners, who are plac'd here for education. They are enter'd here for two, three, or five years, & at the expiration of that time, return to their Parents or Guardians. During their stay, though they are not subject to the cruel laws the nuns obey, they are, like them, denied the privilege of going outside the gates, or of seeing their dearest friends upon earth except through the iron grates. The Abbess saluted us again at our departure, & after a profusion of compliments, open'd the horrid Gate, and clos'd it after us. Devoutly did I thank Heaven that I was not doom'd to pass my life within those dreary walls!

I piti[ed] most sincerely, the miserable victims I left behind me, for miserable they must be, notwithstanding they professed the reverse. When the French Government is settled, there will, I doubt not, be a reformation in matters of religion, and then, I heartily wish [that] the Convents [might] share the same fate with the Bastile—not one stone left upon another.

Abbess Elizabeth Stock was replaced in 1794. She died in Jan. 30th 1799.

We return'd to the Hotel, join'd our party, and to dispel the gloom our visit had occasion'd, took a ride to see the beautiful bridge call'd Pon Neuli. It is remarkable for the uncommon size of the stones with which it is built, and the wonderful lightness of its appearance, notwithstanding the immense size of the Arches. The prospect from the bridge is rural and very beautiful. This little excursion finish'd our day's work.

Chapter 8
City Icons

Monday July 21ˢᵗ

At seven o'clock we went to Notre Dame, to see the farce of High Mass. It was well performed, & the costly dresses of the Actors (or Priests) added much to the splendor of the puppet show. Who shou'd breakfast with us, but our sensible mess mate on board the Princess Royal, Abbe Kernay [sic].

> *A regular packet service began in 1790, the year after the French Revolution began, when the packet Princess Royal left Shoreham every Tuesday evening, and returned from Dieppe on Saturday evening. A contemporary leaflet announced that the vessel had two elegant cabins, each containing eight beds, and that "horses and carriages must be sent on the day before sailing".*
> *www.dieppe.fr/mini-sites/a-taste-of-dieppe/pages/ferry-tales*

> *In 1793 Abbe Charles Kearney, who had been superior of the Irish College watched the execution of Louis as a "simple spectator".*
> *www.irishmeninparis.org/framesets/abbedefirmont.htm*

We had never seen him since our arrival in Paris, the truth was he knew himself to be obnoxious to the popular party, and dar'd not venture abroad till now. Abbe K. lives in Tell [sp?] street near Toll Gate. After breakfast he attended us to the King's Library. This is well worth attention. Here is a noble set of apartments fill'd on all sides with books, written in all tongues and languages. In the middle of the rooms, rang'd on tables, there are beautiful models of various manufactories & a surgeon's dissecting room. The tools & apparatus are in miniature and finish'd with the nicest art. Here are also two vast globes 12 feet in diameter and a curious Mount Parnasus in bronze.

Abbe Kearnay says there are several other public libraries belonging to the King in Paris, to all which persons without distinction have free access. This is really a noble Privilege, and shows a liberality which under such a Government one should hardly expect to find. From the library we went to the Sorbonne, a college of great reputation, from whence the students receive their different degrees. Here they study law, Physic, & Theology. The church belonging to this university is a very fine one; in the middle of the Choir stands the famous monument of Cardinal Richlieu.

Sorbonne. *Source:* M. and S. Kirkpatrick

Nothing can exceed the beauty of the figures. The whole is of white marble, though now somewhat discolor'd by time, & is said to be the finest monument in Europe. Religion supports the Cardinal who is in a reclining posture, whilst Science kneels weeping at his feet. His arms are supported by two Angels in tears, one holding the Cardinal's hat.

After paying a due tribute of admiration to the Sorbonne, we visited Gobelins, where the tapestry is made, We saw several men working at the looms, & some pieces of tapestry that were finish'd. Never surely was any work so beautiful as this. The figures in the historic pieces are as large as life, and really look alive. The colours are exquisite, I never saw any to compare with them, and blended together with inimitable skill. The house is named after a famous dyer called Gobelin. There is a little dirty river called Bievre, where they dye their wool; to the quality of this water is ascrib'd the uncommon beauty of their colours, particularly scarlets and purples. The Paintings from which they work, are all done by the best masters; we saw several which in my opinion exceeded all I had ever seen. I am no Connoisseur, far from it, but if I might judge from the effect the beautiful picture of Andromachs and

Gobelins manufacturing and the Bievre River. *Source:* en.wikipedia. org/wiki/Gobelins_Manufactory

Hecuba lamenting over the dead body of Hector had on me, I shou'd not hesitate to pronounce it one of the most perfect pieces of painting in the world.

In returning to our Hotel, we stopp'd in to see St. Genevieve; this church, if ever it shou'd be finished, will be more magnificent than all the rest. The Domes are surprising, & the Porch, which is compleated, is extremely grand, supported by vast Corinthian pillars of beautiful workmanship. The sculpture over the great door is very fine; £30,000 per ann. is allow'd for the building of this church. The bare scaffolding cost £10,000, & is so curious, that all the great architects in Europe have been here to see it. After dinner we went to see the Duc d'Orleans Palace. This forms a part of the Palais Royale. The staircase is grand and the rooms most elegantly and superbly furnished. The paintings are very numerous but in general are so indelicate that I confess I formed no very favourable opinions of the morals of the Possessor, however high as a great political character he may rank. This Duc d'Orleans is the idol of Parisians, & has acted nobly in the defense of liberty.

In the apartment belonging to the Duke's son, I remarked that the bed was laid upon the floor; our conductor told us the children were not permitted to sleep on bedsteads. The Lustres in the grand suite of rooms call'd the Duchess's apartments, were made in England and are singularly elegant. In the midst of the Palais Royale gardens the Duc d'Orleans has built an immense oblong room underground. The decorations, boxes, orchestra, and gallery somewhat resemble Ranelagh. The ceiling is level with the gardens; there is a vast sky-light & on the top of the building a garden is rais'd; the whole surrounded with water to keep it cool. What this whimsical (though beautiful) place is design'd for, or by what name to call it, no one knows. Abbe Kernay [sic] is extremely imprudent, even in the apartments of the Duke he expressed his indignation at seeing citizens at arms, seem'd hurt at their victory, & wish'd success to the Court party. Priests are always firm friends to arbitrary power. I think it is hardly safe to be seen with him on account of his political sentiments, which are doubtless known.

In 1741, the Ranelegh [sic] house and grounds were purchased by a syndicate led by the proprietor of the Theatre Royal, Drury Lane and Sir Thomas Robinson MP. The Gardens opened to the public the following year. Ranelegh was considered more fashionable than its older rival the Vauxhall Gardens; the house was torn down in 1805.

The Palais Bourbon belonging to the Prince of Conde next engag'd our attention. This is esteem'd one of the most elegant buildings in France. The furniture is extremely superb, indeed everything in this place is in the highest style of magnificence. The beauty and variability of the clocks pleas'd me extremely, they are made as elegant ornaments for chimneypieces & are supported by small pillars of white marble in glass cases, through which you see the movements. The garden is laid out in the taste of the last century, not very charming to English eyes, but the prospect of the Thuilleries etc., etc., is delightful. A new palace close adjoining is just finish'd and is a most magnificent edifice. It is destin'd to command the prospect of a new bridge, which is now building. We cross'd the Seine to the Thuilleries, walk'd thro those enchanting walks, & late in the evening, arriv'd at our Hotel.

Tuesday 21ˢᵗ

Employed the whole morning in rambling amongst print shops & calling on Mr. Griegson, the watchmaker, from whom we have received many marks of attention and politeness. We collected a few prints, portraits of the King etc., which are admirable likenesses, & then proceeded to the Bastile, where we saw with satisfaction five hundred masons at work pulling down this horrid mansion. They intend to level it with the ground, & erect upon the spot a Temple sacred to Liberty.

Pierre Gregson, an Englishman in Paris from 1788–1790, became clock maker to the King of France. In 1790, he moved to Switzerland and then back to London.

They have found (as yet) but five prisoners within the dreadful abode; one of whom we saw—Count D'Auch, his offence writing something against the Jesuits, which made him obnoxious to the persons then in power. He made a shocking appearance, pale emaciated and almost idiotic. We cou'd not gain admittance, indeed it was extremely dangerous to attempt it, as the stones were constantly falling but we procur'd a piece of the stone, which we brought off as an invaluable relick. It will be a long time before this building is compleately down, the walls are fifteen feet thick & the whole covers a considerable quantity of ground.

All the amusements in Paris have been shut since the beginning of the Revolution; this night for the first time, they were order'd to be open'd; a sign that peace and safety are again restor'd. We went in the afternoon to the Opera, & were highly entertain'd. The dancing was exquisite. Vestris was there & many others that equall'd him.

Auguste Vestris followed his father in dance starting at the age of
12, and had become a premier dancer by 21. He left for London
for four years because of the Revolution, but returned to France.
encyclopedia.stateuniversity.com/.../Auguste-Vestris.html

The last scene representing a wedding entertainment was beautiful. The scenery, illumination, dresses & numbers of personages, had altogether a fine effect. The lively animated airs [with] which the Opera abounded, pleas'd me much better than the intolerably tiresome recitation at the Italian Opera in London. But the London Theatres are far superior in elegance and convenience.

Abbe Kearnay breakfasted with us, he said he had a little business at the Convent in the next street, and wou'd return to us in half an hour. He went—but we have seen nothing of him since, I strongly suspect he judges it prudent to secrete himself as he is a person obnoxious to the friends of liberty. We have obtain'd leave for horses, & a Passport, not from the King, but from the Hotel de Ville now the only seat of power.

Chapter 9
Leaving Paris

Wednesday July 22ⁿᵈ

We rose early, pack'd up our cloaths, paid our bills, and left Paris without the least difficulty; our good friend Mr. Wilkinson accompanied us to the barriers, lest we shou'd meet with any impediment, then took his leave.

We then proceeded on to St. Dennis where we stopp'd to visit the Abby which is remarkable for being the burial place of all the French kings. Here are some noble monuments, & finely painted windows. They have a singular custom here, of keeping the last deceas'd above ground till another dies of the Royal family, and then the body is interr'd. The coffin stands cover'd with a rich pall, under a canopy of black velvet adorn'd with the crown & scepter. The architecture of this church is extremely famous. The treasury here is immensely rich; I believe it is reckon'd the most valuable in France; but we did not stay to examine it. We had seen that of Notre Dame & therefore cou'd guess at its contents. Gold crosses, diamond crowns & dead bones. We did not allow ourselves time to stop for dinner, but ate a cold chicken and a luncheon of bread as we travell'd on.

We had been requested in Paris not to travel thro' Chantily [sic], upon any account, as the village was in a state of the utmost confusion, & the woods so infested with robbers that it was highly dangerous to travel that way. We had been told, that a gentleman the last evening had been robb'd, & almost murder'd there. We ventur'd to Chantily, however, & found the information totally without foundation. The villagers were peaceful & happy, & the woods fill'd with nightingales, instead of robbers. We were charm'd with this beautiful place; the Palace belongs to the Prince of Conde & is only inferior to Versailles. The gardens are delightful & very extensive, the canals and fountains numerous. The carp in one of the canals are so tame, that they eat bread out of your hands & follow you up and down the water. This singular sight pleas'd me extremely. I longed for more time to spend with these rational & friendly fish. In the midst of the gardens there is an enchanting little Island call'd L'Isle d'Amour. Here you walk under the thick shade of evergreens, roses & jassamine, till you arrive at a beautiful Pavilion built chiefly of marble.

Here are eight little fountains, cover'd with glass in the form of Pyramids, so that you distinctly see the spouting of the water, without suffering any inconvenience from wet. This pavilion, by moving certain springs or screws separates from the walk, & floats down the canal. We did not see the inside of this beautiful Palace, but were greatly struck with the magnificence of the buildings. The furniture, paintings etc. are said to be very sumptuous. The stables are perhaps the greatest curiosity at Chantily. The building is extremely fine, & very spacious; it looks much more like the residence of a Prince, than a place for horses. It was now time to make the best of our way to Clermont where we propos'd sleeping.

In Chantilly, the Hamlet dates from 1775, and influenced that of Marie Antoinette at Versailles. Composed of 5 Norman cottages, the Hamlet was fashionable for nobles seeking a change of scenery in villages in miniature. They would travel there from elsewhere in "dugouts", spraying themselves heartily amid laughter. Servants would dress up as peasants and shepherdesses, and sing while welcoming visitors.

We bid the Postilion hasten forwards but a violent shower of rain happening to overtake us as we were driving through the beautiful woods belonging to the Prince, the Postilion with great composure and deliberation, got himself snug under a tree, & there waited until the storm was past. We sat very patiently, for what avail'd hurrying ourselves, or him, stir he would not till he cou'd proceed with a dry skin. We arriv'd late at Clermont, & there took up our abode for the night; it appeared to be a small town, & contained nothing worthy of notice.

Thursday

Left Clermont at two o'clock in the morning; breakfasted at Breteuil a shabby little town or village. The Maitre d'Hotel, a remarkably handsome man, stood leaning against the fireplace in his night-cap, gown, & slippers, totally inattentive to us, and everything around him, leaving the whole business to his wife, who appear'd to have more than she cou'd easily perform. I have observ'd this frequently in France, at shops as well as Inns, the management of all the affairs devolves entirely on the wife whilst the lazy or ignorant husband stands by an idle spectator; nor does he even by conversation attempt to amuse his customers. The French politesse certainly does not extend to the middling, & lower ranks of people; or else the Women of France having more patience & better understanding than the men, are fitter to conduct business. The husband therefore, seeing this, wisely resigns the reigns of government to the hands of his Wife. At Amiens (which is about six posts & half or near forty English miles from Clermont), we stopp'd to see the Cathedral, which is a most beautiful church & the inside remarkably light & airy. Here are a number of fine marble monuments, & the whole is highly adorn'd & decorated with gilding and sculpture, but what struck me as rather extraordinary, the church was entirely destitute of paintings. This is very unusual, as the churches in France, but especially at Paris, are crowded with pictures.

Amiens is the capital of Picardy, & I believe reckon'd a handsome and a pleasant city. To us, I cannot say it appear'd a very inviting place to remain in, the people look'd sour & suspicious; they regarded us, I verily believe, as disaffected persons, perhaps Noblesse flying from the capital. They look'd at our passport, & suffer'd us to proceed, without any further examination. We felt some unpleasant sensations during our short stay & were heartily rejoic'd when we turn'd our backs on Amiens.

Besides, added to the looks of the people, the beggars beseig'd us so closely, by twenty at a time, that it was with the utmost difficulty we cou'd get off, though we had given them all the small money we had. I think one of the most unpleasant circumstances in travelling through France, is the number of beggars which constantly surround your carriage, wherever you stop. They have permission to beg, & they follow it as a trade. When you have reliev'd a dozen or a score, of these poor creatures, as many more advance, & so on, till your Postilion cracks his whip as a signal for your departure. It is not merely the torment & the expence, (which is by no means inconsiderable) but really it shocks humanity to see so many miserable & destitute objects. We staid nowhere on the road to dine, but far'd as yesterday; a chicken & a roll, with a little brandy & water, was our repast, as we travell'd onward.

Pass'd through Abbeville, & had a fine view of it just before we entr'd. This is a large city, pleasantly situated & strongly fortified. This Town was never taken by an enemy & from that circumstance is call'd the Maiden Town. We had some hopes of sleeping this night at Montreuil, but finding ourselves much fatigued, & night drawing on apace we determin'd to stop two posts short of Montreuil, & accordingly slept at Bernay; a shabby house, the resort of waggoners, in a small village consisting of four or half a dozen small houses. The people however, were honest and innocent, deep politicians, & extremely anxious to hear some particulars of the revolution. We told them all we knew; but when we related the circumstances of the Bastile being nearly demolish'd their joy was excessive. Postilions, waggoners, servants, all crowded about us to hear the interesting narration. We assisted them in preparing our supper, for really their rage for news prevented them from attending to the wants of us poor hungry travelers. Eighty miles on a hot summer day is enough to make one weary; we had travell'd more.

The accommodations at the Inns in Picardie, are so very inferior to those of Normandy (the country not half so beautiful—the roads much worse) that I'm astonish'd people go by any other route to Paris than from Brighton to Dieppe. The road from Dieppe to Paris, passing through Rouen is delightful, and the prospects truly charming. Besides, it is not so long a journey as from Calais to Paris. The only disadvantage is, that you are a little longer at Sea; but this, when you have made up your mind about venturing on board (if you have any fears), is scarcely an object worth attention. I think Picardie is not to be compar'd to Normandie in any respect. There seems to be more wretchedness & poverty here than in the other Provinces. I believe it is esteem'd the poorest.

Chapter 10
French Coast

Friday

We set off from Bernay early in the morning as we'd hop'd to sail from Bologne or Calais (if possible) at night. We pass'd through Montreuil which is a pretty fortified town situated on a hill. At Samers (a little market town) we had a dish of coffee & were inform'd that a vessel was ready to sail from Bologne & only waited for passengers. We hasten'd on with great speed & arriv'd at Bologne by twelve o'clock. We found, however, that there was no probability of sailing till midnight; we therefore sat down to a comfortable <u>English</u> dinner, & were much pleas'd with the attentions of our landlady Mrs. Knowles whose house accommodations & <u>manners</u> were perfectly <u>English</u>. After our refreshment, we sallied out to view the town which is a pleasant seaport and well fortified. There were a number of charming little places, half conceal'd in the adjoining woods, which were the retirements of some of our own countrymen who had taken refuge at Bologne. Here the arm of Justice cannot reach them and they enjoy as much happiness as a troubled conscience will let them. We saw old England (that is, the white cliffs of Dover) distinctly from the Citadel; indeed we cou'd discern them before we reach'd Bologne. The sight delighted us. We return'd to our Inn & lay down desiring to be call'd when the vessel was ready. We sent our Passport to the Custom House, but were extremely loath to part with it, as it was a curiosity; being one of the first that had been signed at the Hotel de Ville by a FREE PEOPLE. We could not, however, get it back again.

Mrs Knowles was a well-known person who ran an Inn in Boulogne, and in 1790, identified Mrs. Swinborne as she left France for England to escape the Revolution. It was rumoured she had died, but references to her running an Inn in Boulogne after marriage to a Mr. Parker persisted into the 1830s and 1840s.

Lady Massarene & her suite arriv'd at Mrs Knowles' whilst we were there. Her husband was just landed at Dover. He had been confin'd in a prison in Paris for debt above twenty years, & was now liberated. When he arriv'd on English ground he knelt down, and kissed the earth with rapture. It was reported that he was confin'd in the Bastile but this was a mistake.

Lady Massereene was Marie Borcier the daughter of the M. Bousier in charge of debtors in the Chatelet, a jail where the Irish Lord Massereene was incarcerated. They were privately married by the prison chaplain in 1786. Urged on by Lady Massereene in 1789, the mob blew the Chatelet gates open at the same time as taking the Bastille. The pair was married again in London. The Lord was again incarcerated there but she did not wait for him after he was released for the second time.

The Duc Fitz James was at Bologne with part of his Regiment; these were attach'd or suppos'd to be so, to the Court Party. Their frightful whiskers, & grim visages struck me with horror; I had the assurance to wear my National cockade under their noses. A few miles from Bologne we met some of the Irish Brigade and baggage; we thought it prudent to hide our cockades, not caring to expose ourselves to the sour looks, perhaps insults, of half a Regiment of soldiers. By accident part of my colours were visible; one of the men perceived it with pleasure and putting his head in at the window cried: "Vivre le tiers etat". These men were to fight against freedom. Such is the dependence which the Court of France has upon the Military!

At twelve o'clock at night the signal arriv'd for sailing. We immediately went on board & bade adieu to France. The cracking whip that made the forests echo to the sound no longer vibrates in my ear! The dapper Postilion with his fierce cock'd hat, vieing in size with an umbrella, the huge jack boots—the harness of rope—the horses flying off free of each other, and trotting, galloping or walking as their fancies directed, all with the laugh-provoking equipage, adieu.

It was a wet, uncomfortable, dreary night; and as it was impossible to remain on deck, we got into our little cabin beds, and remain'd there until Dover. We had three other persons aboard, one of whom was a Courier to England conveying dispatches from Paris.

Saturday July 25ᵗʰ 1789

At seven in the morning we landed safely at Dover, & we pleas'd to set our feet again on English soil, though we did not, like Lord Massarene kiss the earth with extacy [sic]. In a moment, I was sensible of the difference in climate, or rather of the disagreeable smoke, which is a thing never perceiv'd in France, and which single circumstance makes the air so much purer and pleasanter on the continent than here.

Chapter 11
British Soil – Epilogue

We made the best of our way to London being anxious to arrive before dark. We got in about nine o'clock, and now a thought occur'd that we were in a land where attention to our baggage was absolutely necessary. In France we never had any occasion for this sort of caution. I verily believe in the streets of Paris every article wou'd have been secure, had it been left there half the night. At the little Towns in Normandy the people at the Inns were hurt when we propos'd removing our boxes into our rooms at night & assur'd us all was perfectly safe with them. This we found to be true. Must not their Police be better than ours or why is it that travelling is safer in France than in England, and that there are fewer robberies and thefts of every sort committed than with us? The fact is, I believe, undeniable.

Sunday we spent most pleasantly with Dr. Price at Hackney, Monday with my brother, and in the evening at the Haymarket to laugh at Edwin.

Dr Price moved to the village of Hackney in 1783 and became principal of the newly founded Hackney College in 1786. He was a dissenter, friend to Priestley, wrote letters of introduction for George Cadogan Morgan, and corresponded with Benjamin Franklin. Nicholas Bishop, a solicitor in London, was Susannah's only surviving sibling.

"Jack" Edwin first appeared as an actor in 1778 as a boy of 10. He continued appearing in theatres from then on and married in 1791.

Tuesday evening we left London, & Wednesday spent at Hartham with our friends [that] we hop'd to have met in London but were disappointed. Thursday we arriv'd to our inexpressible joy & comfort after all our perils and adventures, safely at our journey's end, and enter'd our own habitation with heartfelt satisfaction.

I shall ever look back on this very interesting little tour with pleasure, as it will afford me a fund of amusement during my whole life. I shall tell my children, and I hope my grandchildren, with pride and exultation, that I was present at the glorious Revolution in France & that I saw the Bastile seiz'd and demolish'd. I admire the character of the French; they are at this period enlightened, liberal, and brave. They have overturn'd an infamous Constitution, and upon its ruins are erecting a free & happy one. They deserve a good Government, & I ardently hope they will obtain it. We saw none of that frivolity which I was taught to expect in Frenchmen. Quite the reverse; indeed, the situation of their grave affaires gave them a wonderfully thoughtful and anxious appearance. I never saw finer countenances than those of the French Officers at Versailles. Countenances full of intelligence & animation; manly and handsome. Excepting at some moments when the horrors of War seem'd to surround us, which Providentially were soon dispers'd, we had altogether a most delightful ramble.

We set off with a determination to laugh at trifling difficulties, to be pleas'd with everything barely tolerable, and to give pleasure to every creature around us, as often as possible. I think we shou'd be wiser, and certainly happier, if we were to adopt this maxim more than we do, in the journey of life. The people lik'd us (for this reason) wherever we went, & we had the satisfaction of seeing merry countenances everywhere. Tis true we never sour'd them by complaints of heavy charges, tho' sometimes there might be ground enough for them, but it was not worthwhile to plague ourselves and them for the value of a few more sous or livres. Besides, we went to laugh, not to quarrel. I would earnestly recommend this plan to all that travel for amusement, and if upon the whole it shou'd cost them a guinea or two more they will find they have had Value Received.

It has been more than thirteen years since the important events hastily recorded in this little journal took place. Alas! How is the friend of humanity—of temperate reform—of rational liberty—griev'd at the sad disappointment of all his hopes and expectations. In 1789, all the friends of liberty throughout Europe wish'd success to the overthrow of Despotism in France, and the establishment of a better Government. Little then did we forsee the sad consequences that followed.

Appendix 1

On Monday the 13th not knowing the exact situation of Public Affairs, we went out with the intention of visiting some Churches. Upon arrival at the "Val de Grace", we were much surpris'd to see the body of the church fill'd with some of the principal Citizens who seem'd assembl'd to transact some important business. We were not mistaken; the President of the Assembly advanc'd towards us, and with an honest emotion expressive of the keenest sensibility, hinted his surprise at our indulging our curiosity at a moment when they with breaking hearts were assembl'd to defend all they held dear. He, however, added that we might see the Church if we pleas'd;

this we declin'd and retreated with many apologies for the interruption we had undesignedly caus'd.

Appendix 2

The following is a translation of a Paris newspaper [that] made its appearance on July 15th. The style is so singular that we look'd upon it as a curiosity.

"The horrid conspiracy which was to reduce Paris to ashes, & bathe France in blood is at an end. Fifty thousand men, one hundred cannon, six thousand 'banditti', [&] six Princes of the blood, had on Monday resolv'd the destruction of this Empire. The States General were to be murdered, the horses of the Patriots destroyed, the public libraries in flames, the Palais Royale pillaged, sacked, laid waste. Everything was ready torches, poignards, gibbets and the fatal which devoted all our heads. Sunday night whilst the assassins were descending from the eminence of Mont-martre to assail us, whilst the embodied murderers spread themselves like lava from a raging volcano in the Champs Elysees; in these bloody hours the banditti of Versailles were singing in a brutal orgee, the departure of Mr Necher and the proscription of his party. The wretches danc'd to the sound of the German band. Such was the preface of this St. Bartholemew.

A sudden energy takes possession of every mind. The Tocsin sounds the alarm 'Liberty in Cabon', utters a groan & gives existence to Patriotism in every heart. The Churches are fill'd, not with women in tears, but with armed men determined to sell dearly their lives. The whole of this horrid night those vile Clans who come out of Germany only to assist Tyrants in the overthrow of liberty, run about the streets firing on the people & their retreats.

The Gardes Francoises join the people, they do not desert their colors, they walk under the standard of their Country, they combat, they disperse on these ferocious strangers. At the Place Louis Quinze, at the Boulevards, at the Barriers, these contemptible panders trampled the people under their horses' feet. Their Chief (Worthy) descended from a family always inimitable to the Bourbons and the French, their Chief ever exorable & vile, fell sword in hand upon the women and children, and profaning the garden of his King basely assassinated a feeble old man who extended his arm to him for protection.

Monday it was reported at Versailles that 100,000 arm'd men were going to fall upon the Castle, not to attack the best and most deceived of Kings, but to seize the Chiefs of the formidable conspiracy. This fortunate report saves Paris and France. Terror takes possession of these Catalines & their friends. The defection of the troops compleats their dismay. A few hours after, they learn a crowd of events, such as the history of fortunate rashness never presented before. The Camp of the Germans dispers'd, the Invalids surrender'd, the cannon in our power, the Bastile taken by assault, the bloody heads of the traitors carried about the City on Poles—a guard of 280,000 men suddenly raised, order'd, posted; a permanent committee sitting at the Hotel de Ville day and night. The conquer'd cannon plac'd at all the barriers & bridges of the Capital. The National Assembly constantly sitting for sixty hours. This is the great, the glorious spectacle, offer'd by the impetuous Nation. All their deliberations, all their resolutions, were sudden, were wise. The activity of the Counsel, the harmony of the Chiefs of the Districts, the indefatible docility of the new Militia, was constantly kept up night & day.

And what days! What nights! Grand Dieu! You must have witness'd that gloomy illumination, that stern silence, that hollow & dismal noise which awaken'd the most gloomy apprehensions, you must have felt during three days those convulsive & rapid sensations. Let the eloquent pen of Mirabeau, of Lally Tolendal, of Clermont Tonnerre consign these facts to posterity. Let them hasten to devote to the execution of every age those base & sanguinary ministers, accomplices in this infernal project, this grand assassination of a whole people. A crime which Caligula had only wish'd. A few moments more, it wou'd have been executed. The Bastile wou'd have protected with its fire, the fire of the troops.

The road trac'd at Montmartre under pretense of occupying the unfortunate, finish'd Saturday, offer'd them on Sunday an easy way, & a thundering situation for fifty cannon [that] were to be brought from St. Dennis to the fatal eminence which has threaten'd us so often. Immortal Thanksgiving be offer'd to the protecting God of the French Enpire! Honor and Glory to that brave Defender of his Country the Duc D'Orleans for having first inspir'd us with the thought of arming, & made us repulse with incredible vigor these assassions, who fill'd with wine at Versailles, had sworn to exterminate us that fatal night. Infamy, Disgrace, eternal execration to that aristocratic band, to that hundred headed monster who is just expir'd roaring under the victorious arm of Liberty."

This newspaper translation marks the end of Susannah's diary

Part II
London Visit
1847–1848

John Prior Estlin

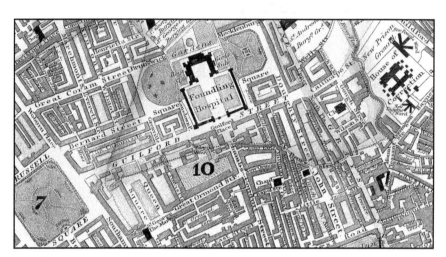

This 19th century map of London includes Woburn Place and Russell Square (left), Foundling Hospital and Upper Calthorpe Street (center), and the House of Corrections (right).
Source: Gen Maps. Free access–Internet source.

Introduction

Susannah's family grew and prospered. Two sons, John Bishop and Edward Rochemont, became doctors, and another son Alfred Estlin, became a solicitor. Her stepson Joseph became a successful wine merchant. Edward died of consumption at 24, and Joseph also died young, leaving a wife and three children. John Bishop Estlin became a famous eye surgeon, and a supporter of the anti-slavery movement like his father. His daughter Mary Ann, who sustained the Estlin family later from time to time, continued to support the anti-slavery movement.

One of Susannah's daughters, Ellen Fox, lived in India with her soldier husband, William Milbourne Fox, whom she married against family wishes. When he died young, she returned to England, childless. She is mentioned in John P. Estlin's London diary featured next.

John Prior Estlin and his brother Alfred were raised in Somerton when their father, Alfred a solicitor, moved there from Bristol. In coming to London, John Prior joined Robarts, Curtis and Company, an affiliate of Stuckey's Bank. In 1847, Alfred Estlin was articling with John Lawford attourney, his sponsor for the bar at the Draper's Hall in Throgmorton Street, where Edward Lawford was also part of the firm. Although it appears that John was replacing Fred Stuckey, who had gone to the country, we have no further information on how this arrangement was made. John Prior may have been with the same bank in Ilminster before coming to London and the arrangement could have stemmed from there.

London was a foggy, dirty, noisy city. There were a myriad of street vendors calling their wares, trades wagons clattering, street urchins begging, and labrours at work on buildings and roads. A traffic count in Cheapside and London Bridge in 1850 showed a thousand vehicles an hour passing through these areas during the day. The vehicles produced a vast amount of manure that had to be removed from the streets. The smells from the garbage, sewage and industries would have overwhelmed our sensitive noses today, but John Prior rarely remarks upon these conditions. It was just part of his day-to-day life. In 1841, London life expectancy was 37. In 1839, half of the burials in London were for children under the age of 10. There were more deaths than the graveyards could sustain.

London air was foul and sooty; even the soil was decayed. Where there were no sewers, excrement and urine were thrown into the street. Drains, sewers and gutters emptied into the only source of drinking water, the

Thames. Bathrooms were still rare in 1849 but there were public baths and washhouses introduced only a few years before. In 1849, there were about 300 baths taken a day, at the George Street Baths. There were slightly over 14,000 robberies reported in 1847; London had about 5000 police and a population of over 2 million.

Within this setting, John Prior describes his contact with a web of acquaintances, distant family connections and closer relations with whom he spends most of his time. Since the number of children in families was large, it took very little effort to put together dances or soirees.

Persons mentioned in the diary

Individual	Event / Comment	Source
Alfred	Alfred Estlin, John Prior's brother, 21 on Jan. 21st 1848	Diary
Alder	Participant in Prichard soirees	Diary
Aggie	Agnes Letitia, John Prior's sister	Diary
Aunt Prichard	Woburn Place, Anna Marie Estlin, Prior's aunt married to Dr. James Cowles Prichard	Estlin family tree (Fran Aitkens)
Albert Prichard	Youngest Prichard offspring born in 1831	Prichard family tree (Fran Aitkens)
Dr. Augustin Prichard	Born about 1818; was at the Estlin Eye Dispensary in Bristol	As above
Con Prichard	Rev. Constantine Prichard, 7th offspring, officiates at the 1848 Moline wedding	As above
Miss Parkes	Bessie Raynor Parkes, feminist, likely to be one of the Parkes that J. P. met in Bristol	Internet
Dr. Prichard	James Cowles Prichard, Lunatic Commissioner, resides with his family at Woburn Place	Prichard family tree
Edy	Born about 1829, Edith Prichard is the 10th offspring, and married Nicolas Pocock in 1852	As above

Individual	Event / Comment	Source
Aunt Fox, Aunt Ellen	Elen [sic] (Eleanor) nee Estlin, Susannah's daughter and Prior's aunt, married William Milbourne Fox; he died in India and she returned to England	Estlin family tree
Bacchus	George Woolgrove, childhood friend of Prior's, merchant midshipman with the East India Company on the Alfred in 1847 but becomes master of a vessel by 1860	Diary and data from Val Wright
Bagehot Edward and Walter	Edward Bagehot, merchant of Langport, brother of Margaret who married John Bishop Estlin, John Prior's uncle. Edward is also the uncle of Walter Bagehot, the economist	Bagehot family tree (Fran Aitkens)
Bateman	Eliza Senior married Henry Bateman in 1845. She is the daughter of Bernard Martin Senior of Jamaica, brother of Letitia Senior Estlin	Fran Aitkens
Miss Bacon	Amelia Bacon was living with her father William, an artist, in the 1841 census for England	Diary and vital statistics through ancestry.uk
Hardwick	May be Phillip Hardwick, architect, who lived at Russell Sq.	Internet
B. H. Hunt	Cousin Bernard Senior took the name of Husy Hunt in order to inherit property from his wife's family that required a male heir carrying the name	Fran Aitkens
E. Lawford	Alfred's supervisor, along with John Lawford who sponsored him for the bar	Internet
Uncle Innis	Likely a Pocock since Innes is a family name within the Pococks	Personal knowledge

Individual	Event / Comment	Source
Mathews family Captain, and Mrs., Ellen and Graham	Captain Richard Hunt Mathews, Buxar, West Indies married the eldest daughter of Nicholas Donithorne Bishop, solicitor. Nicholas was Susannah Estlin's only living brother. James Bogle Denton Graham Mathews a cousin to J. P. Estlin became a soliciter and died in 1870 aged 52. Born at Deep Close Lodge	The Law Times 1849
Moline Family	Cousins of the Prichard's—parents are: Mary Prichard d. 1868 married Robert Moline. They had 12 children; the following are mentioned from the diary Emily Moline born 18th March 1827, married cousin Iltudus Thomas Prichard in India in June 1848, Anna Moline born June 30th 1818 married Robert Haines August 1848, Charles Moline born Aug 30th 1819, Married Margaret Wylie, Ellen Moline born 23rd Feb. 1821 married Johann von Lendendorf in Nov. 1851, Mary Jane (Jeanette) born April 27th 1827, married William Moline 16th Nov. 1847, Agnes Moline, born 24th May, 1824, married Thomas Gee 12th Aug 1849, Francis (Frank) Moline, born 19th Sept. 1825, married Emma Kranz 20th Oct. 1852, Richard Moline born March 8th 1829, married Mary Haines, 8th Feb. 1855, Susan Moline born 18th Jan. 1831 married Arthur Cayley 6th Sept. 1863, Louis (Lewis) Prichard Moline born 18th April 1832 married Jane Tripp 9th April 1863	see IGI for more details
Mrs Nash	Ian Harwood's prior landlady—the place to which he retires while his wife is away	Diary

Individual	Event / Comment	Source
Old Paul and son Edward	Likely the manager of Stuckey's Bank in Langport, Thomas Paul	Internet
Pocock Family	2 male Pococks and a sister: One may be Nicholas Pocock (born abt. 1814) who marries Edith Prichard in 1852, John Carne Pocock (born abt. 1815) and the sister Charlotte Pocock (born abt. 1812)	http://web. ukonline. co.uk/bean95/ ft/frippuk/ pafg05. htm#149
Mr George Rozia	Weds Miss Amelia Bacon in 1848, the couple had several children only a few years later	Vital records for the United Kingdom
George Henry Sawtell	In 1847–1848, clerk in London with Robart's bank. Was apparently a distant cousin of the Langport Stuckeys and was in the Bagehot household from time to time. He wrote (in 1882) about his recollections of Walter Bagehot's childhood around 1835	Internet
Senior Family, Cousin Bern	Agnes Letitia (Prior's sister) said in a note: Lewis Senior took the name Husey Hunt and was succeeded on his death in 1843 by his eldest son Bernard, who also took the name Husey Hunt. Bernard died in 1894 and was followed by his brother James (d. 1897), rector of Blackford and Compton Pauncefoot. Bernard's brothers Jem and John Senior referred to in the diary. Lewis is brother to Prior's mother, Letitia Maria Senior Estlin	www.british-history.ac.uk/ report.asp? compid= 18759
Sherwood family	Alfred and John Prior boarded with the Sherwood family in London	Diary

Individual	Event / Comment	Source
John Simon	John Simon became the City of London's first medical officer of health in 1848 and in that capacity issued annual reports that led directly to the Sanitary Act of 1866	Internet
Mr. Frederick Stuckey	It appears John Prior was exchanged for Fred Stuckey	Diary
Tegetmeir	Likely Henry Walter Tegetmieir listed as a banker's clerk and married in 1849. His brother corresponded with Charles Darwin on scientific matters	Internet
Uncle James Richmond	Probably James Gale Senior brother of Letitia Maria Senior Estlin	Fran Aitkens
Uncle John & Miss Ann	John Bishop Estlin and his daughter Mary Ann Estlin born in 1820	Estlin Family tree
Uncle William	Likely William Moline whose marriage is described	Diary
Walter, or Walter B.	Walter Bagehot, born 1826, who was attending London University at the time of the diary. His father was Thomas Bagehot	Internet
Ward family	Attorney from Bristol	Internet
Weak boy	Assumed to be Emily Moline's brother	Diary
White and J. Noon	White begins a school in Cheswick and J. P. Estlin later sends his two boys Euty and Charles Prior to the school	Alfred Estlin memoire and Estlin family letters before 1881

Chapter 1
Settling In

Common Place Book
Epochs in the life of J. Prior Estlin

Left School for Wells (arrived there) 10 December 1844
Left Wells for Ilminster 29 February 1845
Left Ilminster for London 9 November 1847

9th Nov 1848

Quitted the paternal domicile at 6.30. I was driven, with Papa, to Bridgewater by Mr. O. who manifested great concern for our welfare, & was about consigning all my luggage to the tender mercies of a coal down train to Exeter, & was very anxious we sh'd take our places in the same; took the 9-20 train to Bristol & arrived there at 10-25. Saw Uncle John [Bishop Estlin], Miss Ann [his daughter], Augustin [Prichard] & his wife. Two Miss Parkes at Uncle John's, shook hands with one of them in mistake for Miss Ann (I beg Miss P's pardon) was weighed and not found wanting, weight 141 lb. Left Bristol by the 12-45 train, Alfred's ill conditioned & sneaking one, & reached London at 5-15. Got out on the road at Swindon, to admire the rooms, pay 6d, & eat 3 sandwiches. Found Alfred waiting at the station & looked unavailingly for my luggage, but found none.

John Prior Estlin taken about 1855.
Source: Estlin family collection,
Sharon Hope

Dr. Augustin Prichard, son of James Cowles Prichard, held an appointment with the Bristol Infirmary; he was concerned about the use of chloroform during operations. Bessie Rayner Parkes, noted feminist, the daughter of the solicitor, Joseph Parkes, was born in 1829. Her grandfather was Joseph Priestly, the scientist and political reformer, who was forced to leave the country in 1774. Bessie's father was also a Unitarian with radical political views, and was a close friend of several reformers.

Took a "keb" to 17 Upper Calthorpe Street, & made a low mock bow to the Sherwood family, but could not keep my countenance. Thought Alfred's account of the concentrated ugliness was fallacious on seeing a pretty girl among them, but afterwards discovered she was a Miss [Amelia] Bacon on a visit there. Slept that night like a top.

November 10th Wednesday

Walked with Alfred to Lombard Street & saw Mr. Sawtell, my future Govenor, whom I'm inclined to like. Did 3 hours work and, the Lawfords having given Alfred a half-holiday, went with him for a walk. Took a 2c Steamer and saw the Houses of Parliament a magnificent pile of building. Walked back via the Penitentiary, Horse Guards, Strand etc etc. Paid an evening visit to Woburn Pl found Aunt Prichard, Mrs. Fox, & Albert existing.

Very kind of them here to give me an iron bedstead, bugs don't patronize them, and they possess this advantage, that one can swing oneself to sleep as in a hammock.

The Houses of Parliament London. *Source:* M.and S. Kirkpatrick

Woburn Place is the home of James Cowles Prichard, the husband of Agnes Estlin, J. P. Estlin's aunt. When Prichard was made a commissioner in lunacy, he went to London to take up his post. He died three years later on the 23ʳᵈ of Dec 1848 of rheumatic fever: at the time of his death he was President of the Ethnological Society and a Fellow of the Royal Society.

11ᵗʰ Nov – Thursday

After the usual routine of business went with Alfred to the Terminus to enquire for my luggage; but heard no tidings. Left the address. (Mem. When travelling by rail, to write Mr. J. P. Estlin, 17 Upper Calthorpe St. London, Passenger to Paddington, or wherever it may be). Returned through Oxford Street & Holborn & was astonished, bewildered and utterly confounded at the number, size and brilliancy of the shops there and elsewhere. Danced in the evening.

12ᵗʰ Novʳ Friday

Luggage arrived this evening. Went to the office by myself and lost my way of course, but soon got right. Got a jaw for being late. Saw Harwood the paterfamilias in the evening.

13ᵗʰ Novʳ Saturday

Funds up again today and firm. Glyn & Co refused to honor Messrs P &W.E. Gundry's notes and drafts. About £1,000 due to us. This will cause some excitement in the country and will injure us for a time, but I think we shall ultimately gain by it. Bought some gloves in Holborn and an Illustrated London News to send to Bacchus at Calcutta.

A private bank in 1841, Glyn's took many of the customer accounts of Ladbroke & Co (est. c.1770), bankers of Cornhill, City of London, upon that bank's closure and from 1851 was known as Glyn, Mills & Co. In 1845, Trueman & Cook was described as, "...the leading colonial broking house in Mincing Lane: such is the extent of their operations, that it is said, they dispose of produce of the worth of several millions of money in the course of the year. They are general brokers, ...they sell largely... sugar, coffee, spices, indigo, etc, upon which they take a commission, which is their remuneration." home.clara.net/mawer/city.html

St Andrews church is in Holborn. Part of the churchyard became the
Holborn viaduct opened later by Queen Victoria.

14ᵗʰ Novʳ Sunday

Patronised Woburn Pˡ Aunt Ellen & Emily Moline the only visitors and
her brother, the weak boy came in the evening. Went to Woburn Church
in the morning, lunched & took a walk with Alfred and Albert to see
Buckingham Palace, the Duke's Statue, Hyde Park & parts adjacent. Went
to Sᵗ Andrews Church in the evening where they chant the service.

15ᵗʰ Novʳ Monday

Another large failure in the city today: Trueman and Cooke produce
brokers went for £2,000,000.

Scene: London Department Office, time dusk, Clerks busy writing,
enter lady dressed in black.

"Is Prior here? That's you, Prior, is it not?"

"Yes Ma'am"

"That's Mr Prior Estlin, is it not?"

"Most certainly it is, I should be very sorry if it was not"

"Oh then Prior, your Uncle John has sent me £100"

Conscience flashes on the bewildered clerk that it is his Aunt Ellen Fox,
come to obtain the long contended £100 for the purpose of protecting the
remnants of her departed husband's remains from the desecrating unshod
feet of the niggers.

16ᵗʰ Novʳ 1847 Tuesday

A most miserable day, tho' free from fog. There has been just sufficient
rain to make the streets one mass of thick, black, greasy, sloppy, sooty,
sticky, nasty, slush. Very dark all day; Alfred's fellow article Allen went up
for his examination the second time today, but the result is not decided yet.
News of a wreck on the coast of Ireland attended with great loss of life, and
several more murders there.

Cork Examiner Nov. 5ᵗʰ 1847: Major Mahon, whose murder is the
latest stain upon Ireland, was returning home about twenty minutes
past six o'clock in the evening of Monday, from a meeting of the
Board of Guardians of the Roscommon Union, when he was shot
dead by an assassin, about four miles from Strokestown. There were

two persons engaged in the murder, according to our informants.
vassun.vassar.edu/~sttaylor/FAMINE/Examiner/Archives/Nov1847.
html

18th Novr Thursday

Allen's passing has been a source of rejoicing to Alfred all day, he thinks there is some chance for him now. I do not believe he really fears it the least, but tries to make himself and others believe that he does. I called at Woburn Place in the evening & met Walter [Bagehot]; Alfred having an appointment at Counsel's chambers was prevented. A slow evening, nothing but talking; people seemed resting on their oars after the excitement of the wedding of Jeanette Moline on which occasion Uncle William [likely her husband] was in great force, taking on himself the duties of a waiter and helping everybody to wine at dinner. He had the service shortened, & it was over in 5 minutes with no crying: a picnic dinner was prepared in the country, & the torrents of rain must have been very enlivening. Alfred exclaims, "Happy is the Bride whom the Sun shines on", goggles his eyes, & goes on about his work.

19th November Friday

A small taste of London fog, though only what Londoners call "rather a misty day". Lights in the Banks all day. The fog was not a genuine London one, but still more than we have in the country. I was sent about a good deal today, and am getting more into the business. How stupid it is of Jones' people not to burn gas, they have more than 100 candles burning in one room exclusive of the interior offices. Most of the old banks have arms suspended "in terrorem" over the fire-place, but they are generally old & useless, being chiefly blunderbusses, flint and steel pistols, or carbines with bayonets, much out of order, never cleaned & never loaded. If I were one of the nobs I would see it altered. I'm sure the Bank of England sets them a good example: it would stand a siege for a considerable time (provided the garrison had something better than Bank notes to live upon). Julien gives his last concert for the season tomorrow and the Bal Masque the next evening. We accepted an invitation from B. H. Hunt Esq. [see listing] Sunday. I suppose we shall hear him play the cello.

Julien: In 1847–48, he was the director of the Drury Lane Theatre, London and engaged Berlioz to conduct concerts and the orchestra of the Grand English Opera at the theatre.

20th Novr 1847 Saturday

20th Novr 1847 Saturday

Of all fogs I ever saw, the one today has been the densest, yellowest, darkest, smotheringest and palpablest. Candles & gas were used in all places of business most of the day. Yesterday we could see the sun looking like a red-hot penny piece through the mist, but today it was quite excluded. Getting more into business now, was sent about more, & some of the Bankers required a letter from Mr. Sawtell authorizing me to receive the bills, accounts, letters etc as being more regular and to show that I was not one of the swell mob "up to a thing or two" and personating a clerk to get possession of bills and tin, I suppose. A great quantity of gold arrived today from the Emp. of Russia. The S. family retrograde awfully on acquaintance. If they were high enough in the brute creation I should detest them but, as utterly unworthy of, and below any one's hate, one merely regards them with the same kind of feeling that you feel for an exceedingly ugly piece of dirt or coal that is in your way, or a badly made scarecrow that offends the eye.

21th November 1847 Sunday

Another fog today. We went to Woburn Place, & met the people just starting for church. Just before service the fog became so thick that no one could see & the service was delayed to get candles. We took a walk afterwards in the Regent's Park came home wet, dressed and took a cab to Cousin Bern's. Met John Senior [Bernard's brother] there, and came home early.

23rd November Tuesday

Nothing particularly exciting occurred today except I was frightened by the apparition of a large, black bonnet on my bed at night left there, I presume, by Miss Bacon.

24th November Wednesday

One of the greasy days. Dance in the evening. Mr. Alder & Miss Bacon the only strangers present. Alfred's library night. First polka lesson.

1840: Among the new dances: the polka.

25th November Thursday

4 failures in the City today. Called at Woburn Place in the evening. Had

some music there, Edith and Emily Moline songstresses. The Doctor not returned from his expedition with the "lunatic commissioners". No Mrs. Fox, she having taken lodgings.

26ᵗʰ November Friday

Four failures today, the whole amount to something considerable. A most beastly day, wet squashy & soaking. Alfred has gone off to lecture under Harwood's care.

28ᵗʰ November Sunday

In very inauspicious weather, we set out for Woburn Place. Went to Church in the morning, & afternoon, it being too wet to walk in the evening, we set out for St Andrews Church Wells St but Service having begun there we went on to Margarete's Chapel where we heard the full cathedral service conducted on tractarian principles. A very handsome cross something in this style, adorned the altar with two silver candlesticks with large wax tapers burning in them on either side, while the altar cloth was embroidered with various symbols. The Chancel was railed off for the officiating clergymen (of whom there were 4) and the choristers.

Samuel Daukes architect built St Andrews: WELLS STREET, 1844-47, Gothic, taken down and rebuilt at Kingsbury (Middx) by W.A. Forsyth, 1934.

Monday 29ᵗʰ Novʳ Monday

As Alfred had to go very early to business, I went down with him, walked on to London Bridge; was nearly overwhelmed by the number of Clerks hurrying to business.

There was little doing on the river.

Sketches on this page from J. P. Estlin's diary.

Wednesday 1ˢᵗ Decʳ Wednesday

The Acct Genl paid us a visit today bringing with him a large quantity of Silver and notes. A large fire occurred at Hoxton, burning a timber yard & 7 houses. I did not know it till over. I called on Mrs Bateman in the evening and saw all the family including the slow bookseller. Mrs B. wonders the Prichards don't call on her. I don't.

Eliza Senior married Henry Bateman in 1845. She is the daughter of Bernard Martin Senior of Jamaica, brother of Letitia Senior Estlin.

Thursday 2st Dec^r

Alfred and I called at Woburn Place in the evening; conversation & music as usual.

Self sketch from J. P. Estlin's diary.

Saturday 4th December

This has been the heaviest day since I have been here in consequence of bills drawn on 1st falling due today. I was sent to Temple bar, & Charing Cross, & had a delightful walk.

Sunday 5th December

After a tremendous night's rain, the morning turned out so fine that I was tempted to go to Twickenham, so parting from Alfred who went to Woburn Place, I found my way to Temple Pier, & took a boat to Nine Elms Station. Arrived there, I found the train did not start till 1-10 so I wandered about the country for an hour & a half, & at last started by the narrow gauge oscillating Southampton Line. I then walked from Richmond to Cross Deep (my malediction be on the place and people). After wandering up and down at least 6 times & enquiring of every body & at every house (during one of which enquiries Ellen and Graham Mathews [see list] passing behind me, wondering who I was) I at last found the Lodge, & got in there at 20 past 3 having been 5 hours 45 m. going a journey of 12 miles. I found Mrs M., Graham and Ellen at home, & a Mrs. Hogg there, & afterwards our party was increased by the arrival of Capt Mathews. He talked about Egypt and India, & was very pleasant only rather prosy. Graham is like a sheep. I returned by the Bus with Capt M. not over pleased with my visit being tired, & out of temper when I arrived. However, I was very kindly received. They have a jolly rocking Horse in the Hall.

Captain Richard Hunt Mathews married the eldest daughter of Nicholas Donnithorne Bishop, solicitor, who lived in London. Nicholas was Susannah Estlin's only brother. In 1839, Nicholas Donnithorne Bishop made an unsuccessful petition to the House of Lords on behalf of his wife and grandson Graham to claim a right to the Earl of Monteith. The Law Times Volume 49 1870. books.google.ca/books?id=Mp4DAAAAQAAJ.

Monday 6th December

My Birthday, & Aggie's too. I wrote her a long letter, & received a packet from home. I also hear there is to be a "swarry" at Woburn Place in honor tomorrow. I bought a canister of snuff for Papa today "which I hope he will like". There was a dance in the evening rather better than usual. I can manage the Polka now. Punch in the evening.

Chapter 2
Pastimes

Tuesday 7th December

A beastly wet day in the morning then dry and frosty in the evening. I went to Woburn Place at 8-30, & Alfred came an hour or two after being detained on business. We met Walter, Anna, Susan & Emily Moline there. After tea and some music we acted charades (handkerchief) in one of which Nep was introduced as a cur, & was so elated at being taken into the drawing room, that he behaved anything but decorously. I had hoped that people there would have had sense enough to omit all health drinking, but I had to submit to it.

Friday 10th December

Nothing today out of the usual routine, except that Alfred had a fall down some dark stairs.

Saturday 11th December

While I was at dinner Mr. Tegetmeir (one of my fellow clerks) heard someone enter the door & come up stairs, after straining his eyes in the direction of the sound & seeing nothing, he concluded it was Mrs. Clarke going out, when lo in a few minutes Mrs. C. appeared making tender enquiries for the large doormat which proved to have been taken away by some person or persons unknown, under our very noses & with a glass door only between. While Tegetmeir was sitting with some friends in the inner room of an Inn, smoking etc one day, a tradesmanlike looking man entered with a blue bag & having looked at the clock, nodded & placed a chair on the table, proceeded to unscrew it, deposited carefully in the bag, got down, replaced the chair & walked away with "Good evening Gentlemen". The landlord soon entered.

Log. Teg. "What's the matter with your clock that you've sent it to be mended?" Landlord looking up: "Why it's gone who took it? It's been stolen." Rather a bold trick.

The clerk is likely Henry Walter Tegetmieir listed as a banker's clerk on census records, and who married a Jane Hope. They had numerous children. His brother, a surgeon, corresponded with Charles Darwin.

Sunday 12th December

Alfred having procured orders from the Soli Genl David Dundas & Sir T. Thesrigen to carry six, Edith, Emily Moline, Albert, & ourselves went to the morning service at the Temple Church. Oh that gorgeous building taking a volume to describe. I must content myself with a short and lame description. On entering a magnificent gothic archway you come into the circular part in which lie the figures of 8 knights Templar in black marble beyond which is the barrier at which the orders are taken. The altar is at the east end and close to it the pulpit. The organ is in the north. The columns supporting the roof are of black, polished marble, & the arches meeting in the centre form the ceiling which is beautifully painted, the cognizance of the winged horse & the lamb & flag & beau saint appearing everywhere as well as on the floor, which unfortunately is modern* tho' in keeping with the rest of the noble pile. The chanting is magnificent. In consequence of the halls, windows, floor ceiling and every part being painted it has a very gorgeous appearance though at the same time to unaccustomed eyes rather gay. *By far the greatest is ancient—this I have learned since.

David Dundas was appointed Solicitor General. In February 1846 he was knighted, a traditional prequisite of the office, but he resigned the position in March 1848 due to ill-health and returned to the backbenches.

The church built by the Knights Templar, consists of the Round and the Chancel. The Round has a wonderful acoustic for singing, and contains life-size stone effigies of nine knights. Most famous of these knights was William the Marshal, Earl of Pembroke, an important mediator between King John and the Barons in 1215.

Monday 13th Dec^r

No circumstances worth recording save a visit from Mr. Edwd Bagehot who is looking better than usual.

Thursday 16th Dec^r

There was a "swarry" at Woburn Place tonight, & we acted a charade that we had been preparing for some time.

1st Scene: A lawyer's office, with clerk writing. (JPE). Enter a lady & friend (EM & EP) to consult the lawyer (ALE) about bringing an action of breach of promise of marriage. The lady much overcome.

2nd Scene: A moustached Gent^{an} (Louis M) reclining in a chair. Enter a tailor (JPE) who measures him for a suit of wedding clothes, during which time he talks about his approaching marriage with the lady. Final Scene. A court of justice. The judge (Albert P) arrayed in scarlet & ermine & wig, before him two counsel (ALE & Walter B) in wigs and gowns. After a long preliminary speech & reading of letters, Amelia Gordon (EP), friend of the pltf, is examined, then Mr. Gray grandfather to pltf (JPE) dressed in an old waistcoat reaching to his knees & covered with bugles, d° coat. Powdered hair and stick, very deaf, then Miss Gray's waiting maid (Agnes M.) who was behind the curtains. This was a very good witness & answered the council very pertly. Then the tailor (JPE) who had heard the Gent say he was going to be married, then summing up etc. Damages for pltf £500,000.

We acted another after. Mr. Paul & his wife came up, & stayed till today.

Thomas Paul was the manager of Stuckey's bank in Langport according to an 1850 directory.

Sunday 19th Dec^r

Woburn Place as usual. We went to Woburn Church in the morning & St Andrews in the evening, & took a walk between, intending to go to Westminster but found ourselves in Edgeware Road, & afterward under the Duke's Statue. We received 3 invitations today, one to go to Aunt Ellen, one to spend Xmas at Woburn Place and one to go to Greenwich on Monday.

Note: Early maps show Christ Church (Church of England) in the middle of the eastern side of Woburn Square only a street west of Upper Woburn Place. Unfortunately the church was demolished sometime after 1972. This church was, no doubt, the Woburn church referred to by John Prior Estlin.

Monday 20th Dec^r

As arranged we went to Greenwich. Taking some clothes to Lombard St we dressed there, took the train at London Bridge. We found Mrs., Anna, Emily, Susan, Agnes, Frank and Louis Moline. Edith and Albert there & two Misses Pontifex. After acting some charades, dancing was introduced, & having settled that Edith & Emily should stay, we left them at ¼ past 11. It was a most magnificent party, people were so much at ease & free & enjoyed themselves immensely. We took an omnibus to Charing X & walked home. I hope they will ask us again. We received an invitation from Mrs. Nash to spend Xmas day with them but being under orders for Woburn Pl we could not go.

John Pontifex, solicitor, who lived at Croom's Blackheath, had one daughter Jessie born 1843; his son Charles also became a solicitor. There were two other Pontifex brothers and all three married Marshall daughters. Edmund Ponifex lived in Kent and the other brother lived in London. The Misses Pontifex mentioned in the diary could be related to this family.

Chapter 3
Attractions

Tuesday 21ˢᵗ Decʳ

Alfred has an infernal toothache. I expect he will have to have it out tomorrow. The weather is rather frosty today. I hope we shall have a fine Xmas.

December 19ᵗʰ 1846 marks the first use of anaesthesia in Britain by James Robinson, a dentist in London. Cavities in teeth have been filled since earliest times with a variety of materials: stone chips, turpentine resin, gum, and metals. Arculanus (Giovanni d' Arcoli) recommended gold-leaf fillings in 1848.
www.carabelli.com/pages/patient_library/history.htm

Wednesday 22ⁿᵈ Decr

When we came home in the evening at ½ past 6, we found a note from Albert stating that they had arranged to go to Aunt Ellen's that evening at 7. So we trudged off & got to Woburn Pl just at 7, where we found Con [Rev. Constantine Estlin Prichard] & Walter [Bagehot]. Leaving them and the ancient ones to chat, Edy, Emily, Albert, Alf' & I travelled off, walked to Fleet Street, took a bus, and after a great many enquiries & wrong turnings found our selves under Aunt Ellen's window with herself looking down upon us. People were very merry & laughed a great deal. We (the male part) acted a charade & broke up. Walked to the Elephant and Castle, bus to Holborn Hill, & walked home.

The Elephant and Castle has been a traffic junction since the 17ᵗʰ century and got its name from a tavern, converted from a smithy around 1760. It became a terminus for coaches and later trams.

Friday 24ᵗʰ Decʳ

We had a dance at home this evening. I can do the Polka now, & am getting into waltzing.

Saturday 25th Dec', Christmas Day

We went to Woburn Place. Church twice; some music and chess in the evening. Con, Augustin and wife there, & Dr. and Mrs. Tweedy. Unpacked a box of sculls from Stockholm. Found them dancing here, with Misses Sherridan & Alder. Joined them till 2 o'clock.

May be Joshua Alder, the naturalist, who was in close contact with Darwin.

Sunday 26th December 1847

Went to Woburn Place again today after having first been to church. We first assayed to go to St. Paul's but on arriving there at 11 & finding the service commenced at ¼ to 10 & being refused admittance, we went on to Bow church, a very ugly place with bad pews & no people to sit in them. We visited the Duke's Statue as usual & went to St Andrew's in the evening.

The Duke's Statue.
Source: M and S. Kirkpatrick

Duke of Wellington's statue built in 1844. J. P. viewed this several times "…under the Duke's statue…"

Tuesday 28th Dec'

Received a note from Uncle George today, & went to see him at his Hotel in Covent Garden, waited for him some time & went away leaving a message.

The Piazza was designed by Jones with arcaded houses to the north and east. To the west was the church of St Paul, flanked by two houses, and to the south there was at first no development because the Piazza backed on to the mansion of the Bedford family, which faced the Strand, the main artery of London connecting City and Court at Westminster. The market building that we know today appeared in 1830, and other buildings in the square went up later that century.

Wednesday 29th Dec[r]

From my message, Uncle George was able to find us out, & called chatting some time. We danced in the evening. Mr. Alder, Miss Choice & Mr. Rosia, Miss Amelia Bacon's [see list] intended, present. Polka, Waltzing, Spanish Dance, Quadrilles, Connor, & Calidonian the order of the day.

The quadrille, according to most reports, was brought to England in 1815 by Lady Jersey who introduced it at London's leading assembly, Almack's, where "she was perhaps the most formidable of the Lady Patrons" (Richardson 1961, 58). At Almack's, and consequently elsewhere in Great Britain, sixteen different "sets" of the quadrille were performed. http://www.standingstones.com/cotill.html
The Calidonian was apparently invented in 1816.

Friday 31st Dec[r]

We went to a splendid soiree at Greenwich this evening, but unfortunately I had a tremendous headache. We were invited at 6 but did not get there till 7 & found they had been dancing some time. We acted 2 charades. Witchcraft.

1st Scene: A lady and prince (Edith: Louis M.) call on a sorceress (Agnes) to look into future. She summons spectres and satisfies them.

2nd Scene: The witch as a washerwoman with her associates (F. M) ironing. Enter Mathew Hopkins (JPE) in costume & who secures them, and searches the house.

3rd Scene: Trial of the witch Judge (Albert) counsel (Alf) in black skullcap, ruff, gown and beard. We danced (Cardinal) afterwards & came back by the omnibus.

Queen Catherine the Great, in 18th Century Russia, used to make up her own dramatic proverbs to be acted out and solved by her court. The noted poet Alfred de Musset wrote his own proverbs for the game in 1831, and by the mid 19th century, charades were the rage in England.

From a 1834 article by Dickens on omnibus travel:
As we arrive in the vicinity of Lincoln's-inn-fields, Bedford-row,
and other legal haunts, we drop a great many of our original
passengers, and take up fresh ones, who meet with a very sulky
reception. It is rather remarkable, that the people already in an
omnibus always look at newcomers, as if they entertained some
undefined idea that they have no business to come in at all.
Conversation is now entirely dropped; each person gazes vacantly
through the window in front of him, and everybody thinks that his
opposite neighbour is staring at him.
charlesdickenspage.com/omnibus.html

Saturday 1ˢᵗ Jan. 1848

Hard at work all day, so much so that I had to go without dinner. Hurried back in the evening to go to a party at Woburn Pl but found it was put off on account of Mrs. Gelt's death. Went to bed with another headache.

Sunday 2ⁿᵈ Janʸ 1848

Not wishing to be at Woburn Pl we took a trip to Richmond and Twickenham. Got to Nine Elms at 11-30 waited about at Battersea etc till 2 minutes too late & went at last at 1-45. Dined at Richmond, & walked all about the Park. Called at Mrs Mathews, went to Richmond (a horrid) church, & came home.

Wednesday 5ᵗʰ Janʸ 1848

A most beastly day, all squash & mud. Went with Sherwood to a tailor's & got measured for some clothes, & having used up so much time found I had none to spare for dinner, so as on Saturday, I went without.

Thursday 6ᵗʰ

Albert came down and asked us to go up this evening, but Alfred having an attack of cholera was prevented. I went at ½ past 8, had a game of blind man's bluff with the Greenwich mamselles who left at 9. Acted a charade for Aunt Prichard's amusement (Serenade) Sir wry naid & came home early. Misses Ellen, Susan, & Emily Moline & Charles and Frank were there.

The second major epidemic of cholera began in Scotland in October 1848 but did not establish itself in London until February 1849.

In relation to the number of fatalities, this was the most serious of all 19th century epidemics and around 53 000 deaths were registered for England and Wales compared to around 20 000 for the 1831–1832 epidemic. Between 1845 and 1856 over 700 individual works were published in London on the subject of cholera.

Dr. Snow's preventive measures concentrated on scrupulous personal hygiene—he drew attention to the fact that doctors rarely caught cholera from their patients—and…suggested improving the conditions of working groups like miners in order to limit the potential for fecal-oral transmission.
www.inthesetimes.com/article/2942/cholera_and_the_city/

Friday 7th Jany

As I was going into Jones' Bank today, I stumbled on a person standing on the steps who turned out to be Frank Moline. After talking a bit, we parted on our different ways. Mr. E. Bagehot & Gen Luce came up today to buy a ship.

Sunday 9th Jany 1848

This was a most beautiful morning & as we were going to Richmond to dine with Uncle James we took Westminster Abby in our way. Afraid of being late we walked very fast & got in heated, but the worst draft (save a black draught), I ever felt soon cooled us & kept me like a piece of ice. The sudden change from muzzy to frosty weather made it feel colder than it really was. The singing & chanting was beautiful, but the appearance of the choir was spoilt by some being obliged to wear great coats instead of white gowns to keep themselves warm. The Abbey is a splendid place but spoilt inside by the monuments & 2 screens. Some of the carving outside is fit to lay on a drawing room table (saving the roof) it is so fine & well preserved. After service we went to Richmond via train, walked over Richmond Hill, crossed the ferry & into Uncle Jim's. I found Alfred's account of our fair cousins not exaggerated at all. They are more like wax dolls than Girls.

Sir Joshua Reynolds painted Richmond Hill in about 1780. William Wordsworth heard choirs of nightingales here, recording them in a sonnet of 1820, and a century later, the Austrian Expressionist painter Oskar Kokoschka produced one of the more striking contemporary depictions of the view.

<u>*Monday 10th Jany 1848*</u>

White called at breakfast time & walked with me into the city. In the evening I called at J Noon's & went with him to Exeter Hall but not having procured a ticket he could not go in so I gave him mine & he went in by himself.

> *Exeter Hall opened on 29 March 1831. Although designed for meetings of religious and charitable institutions, the Sacred Harmonic Society gave concerts in 1834 in the smaller of its two halls. Following the establishment of singing classes in 1841 in the hall, the decade 1840–50 saw a series of popular Wednesday concerts, whose programmes included symphonies by Haydn and Mozart. In Queen Victoria's London, in 1848, Jenny Lind, a famous singer, could be heard each Wednesday at Exeter Hall.*
> *www.hberlioz.com/London/BLExeterHall.html*

<u>*Tuesday 11th Jan^y*</u>

Went as usual to work had not been there more than half an hour before White and Noon came in, so I got a holiday and went with them to the Tower. There we saw the armoury & regalia, but they hurry one through it so fast that there is no time to examine things. The jewels are said to be worth £3,000,000 and the crown itself £1,000,000. Then we took a boat and went to the National Gallery & examined all the paintings, after that and dinner, we patronized the Valhalla, which is well worth seeing once, being beautifully arranged & having the effect of a very good wax-work. Having parted with Noon, we went to the Strand, to the Divan, had coffee and a game of chess (in which I beat) and then crossed over to the Lyceum. The press going in was awful but we got through at last.

The decorations of this theatre is said to be the best & most chaste, (one would hardly expect that from Maid "Vestris"), in London. They certainly are most beautiful. We saw the "Tragedy Queen". "The Golden Branch", & a farce "Box & Cox". The last scene in the Golden Branch was magnificent. The back scene (of gold) was this shape. I can't draw it. A kind of beautiful star formed of fairies and beautifully executed foliage intermingled with gilt, on the stage were groups of Arcadian peasantry with garlands of flowers beautifully arranged. Suddenly red lights were lit which threw a most beautiful warm luminous glow on every thing during which the curtain fell.

The Tower. *Source:* M. and S. Kirkpatrick

On 14 July 1834 a new Lyceum designed by Samuel Beazley opened with its main entrance now on Wellington Street. Edward Stirling's adaptation of Martin Chuzzlewit ran for at least 105 performances from July 1844 through April 1845 there. On 13 December 1845,

Photo of the Lyceum. *Source:* Matthew Lloyd

Mary Ann Keeley, the comic star and the co-lessee of the theatre, applied to The Examiner of Plays for the licensing of Albert Smith's "official" adaptation of Dickens's The Cricket on The Hearth: A Fairy Tale of Home. J.P. lists the plays he saw.

Chapter 4
Family Gatherings

Wednesday 12th January

It was arranged to have a dance this evening here but we found a note from Albert summoning us to Woburn Place, which of course [we] obliged & on arriving there we found Misses Anna, Agnes & Emily Moline, 2 Pococks, & their sister a lamentably heavy person & some "friends of Con's". We had a polka or 2 but the arrival of the ancient ones & especially of Miss Pocock, threw a weight on it & stopped it. There was some eternal acting, magical music, & special pleading. We broke up late it being after 12 & received & accepted (of course) an invitation for Greenwich on Tuesday next when I hope to have some enjoyment.

Saturday 15th Jan^y

I am happy to say that scamp of a tailor has sent my clothes at last. I fear I have a sty coming in my eye.

Sunday 16th Jan^y

Woburn Place as usual. W. Church in the morning & it being fine, Albert, Alfred & myself walked to Knightsbridge & went to St. Paul's, guided there by observing several ladies with Resezite [uncertain transcription Ed.] looking prayer books with crosses on them. This is a very splendid church inside, very spacious & lofty with Galleries constructed so lightly as to be almost an ornament. It is very bright with candles burning on the altar; the choir is likewise very good. We had a christening & the children were catechised in the place of a sermon. A visit from Aunt Ellen and Miss Wilkins (not together) at No. 1. Emily Moline tried hard for a moonlight walk to "the Duke" but we having been there before that day & on the opportune arrival of Frank Moline it was dropped.

St Paul's Knightsbridge is an Anglican Church in London's West End, one of the most beautiful Victorian Churches in London. Set in the heart of the Grosvenor Estate in Belgravia, St Paul's dates from 1843.

*It is of brick and stone, with a lofty tower, in two stories, each having
a window on its sides and front, and the whole terminating in a rich
embattled parapet of open work, with eight crocketted pinnacles.*

Monday 17th January

Sty rather worse. Went with White to the Coliseum saw the Swiss Cottage, Sculpture room, Stalagmite cave, conservatory & Panorama of London. This is splendid. The effect being such that though the picture is not far from you it makes you giddy to look down. I never saw anything so real in my life, every house being done,

Sketch from J. P. Estlin's diary.

the ripple of the water, the Aurora Borealis, change in weather, thunder, lightening, hail, & all was splendid. It was a beastly night, raining in torrents, & White (who was going to a party) was splashed from head to foot. I returned by myself, & got out of my way into Oxford Street, so that when I got home it was fine and promised fine for tomorrow.

Tuesday 18th January

It was as I wished, & hoped, but hardly expected, fine. We did, as usual, took our clothes to the office and dressed there, but while so doing our guilty consciences alarmed us when there was a ring at the hall, fearing it should be old Paul. Got to Greenwich at 7-20 & danced away splendidly, mingled with some acting and supper till 1-30 or 1-45. Company: Mr. & Mrs Anna, Emily, Agnes, Susan; Frank, Charles & Louis Moline, Edith and Albert, 3 Pococks, Mr. Thomson, (Susan M.'s admirer), Mr. Haines, a stranger & ourselves & Miss Wilkins. We had some splendid dancing, & one polka was kept up for nearly a half an hour. Knighthood and coffee were acted. After it was over we walked home. Mr. Thompson, Curator of the Anatomical Museum Som. ho., going partway with us. Got home at 3-20. Sty bad and looking red. Made me feel uncomfortable when dancing if my partner looked at me, told them I got it in a pothouse brawl with a drunken navvy. Emily played the guitar and sang to it very nicely. A little magical music.

Wednesday 19th January

Sty much worse, obliged to leave work, & instead of going to see the Museum with White as intended, had to stay in with a poultice on. Ditto Thursday.

Friday

Aff's Birthday /22/ Dance here. Got the back waltz.

Self-portrait of John Prior Estlin with bandage, sketched in his diary.

Saturday

An invitation from Bern for tomorrow which Alfred declined. Sty better but eye still "bunged up", & bandage on.

Sunday 23rd January

Woburn Place as usual. Alfred went to church in the morning & to St. Paul's Knightsbridge in the afternoon but they would not let me go out so I staid in & read. I heard read 6 whole sermons & some parts. Bandage off of course: but the air very cold & frosty, & snow falling a little. Talk of a party on Albert's birthday, a long time hence though. Saw a chimney on fire in Guilford St.

Monday 24th January

Returned to work as usual & found Mr. Sawtell gracious. A jolly hard frost.

Tuesday 25th Jany

Still frosty. Old Paul came up today and brought his kid Edward (£15 to petty exps). Mr Tegetmeir damaged his right fin by a fall: more work for me as a consequence.

Sketch from J. P. Estlin's diary for 25th Jan.

Wednesday 26th Jany

A splendid frost. No dancing here (C St) today. Paid Alfred a visit in Mr. Barlee's room. Was sent to St. Paul's Churchyard & went on to Earl Street & paid my tailor. Received some tin from home.

Sketch from J. P. Estlin's diary for 26th Jan.

Thursday 27th Jany

The weather still beautiful. Had a walk to Temple bar on business. Went to Woburn Place in the evening but found only the Dr. and aunt P. at home, the rest being gone to drink tea with C Moline & Robt Haynes at Finsbury. It began to snow in the evening.

Temple Bar was one of the City of London entrances or gates through which people and traffic had to pass. It originally stood where Fleet Street now meets the Strand, which was actually outside the London boundary wall. A bar is first mentioned in 1293, at which time it was probably no more than a chain (or bar) between wooden posts.

Its name derives from the fact that it was next to the Temple law courts. It is the only surviving gateway to the City of the original eight because, when it was removed to ease the flow of traffic, it was taken away and re-erected in Hertfordshire. The other gateways, Aldgate, Aldersgate, Bishopsgate, Cripplegate, Ludgate, Moorgate and Newgate, were all demolished before the end of the eighteenth century.

Saturday 29th

Had an awful Headache, & was obliged to go home. Invitation from cousin Bern.

Sunday 30th January 1848

Sketch from J. P. Estlin's diary for 30th Jan.

Went to Woburn Place as usual in the morning, and took them, Aunt P. & all, to the Temple. It rained furiously, and was very beastly. We then went to Cousin Bern's, & dined there with John Senior. Had some sacred music, & some not, Bern

accompanying with his weapon. We received invitations to Greenwich on Wednesday & WP on Thursday.

Monday 31st January

Man proposes and fate disposes. I was to have gone tonight to Woburn Place to make toffee but had a note from Edy to say they were obliged to go out. Also a note from Greenwich to say that Dick Moline was ill in a fever, & so the party was postponed: also a note from Albert saying that the Molines were not going there on Thursday. It was intended to go in costume, and keep it up the whole evening, which would have been jolly but that was knocked on the head. We shall go, but I'm afraid it will be slow.

Tuesday 1st February

We were honored with a visit from Albert, who asked us to Woburn Place to an "old swarry". Dr. & Mrs. Tweedy, Mr & Mrs & Miss Ward, Mr & Mrs Ridout & her brother a green eyed curate. Some talked, some played chess & the rest conglomeration. Mr.Ward is an immense man & represents Osborne and Ward of Bristol. Miss Ward played the Hermilie and Olga Waltz beautifully.

From Pigot's Directory for Bristol
OSBORNE & WARD Attorney 41 Broad Street, Bristol
Alexander Tweedie: (1794 – 1884) Physician and Author. FRS.
Expert on fevers. Physician to the London Fever Hospital 1829;
publications through the 1840s.
In 1854 Dr Tweedie was appointed as an examiner in surgery for the
University of London.
books.google.ca/books?id=jBVAAAAAcAAJ

Mr Ward. Sketched in John Prior Estlin's diary.

The Hermilie, or The Bridal Waltz, composed and dedicated to Madame H. Terre. ... The Olga, or, Princess waltz for the pianoforte. The Sir Roger de Coverley is the only one of the old English social dances that has survived to the present day, and it is frequently danced at the conclusion of the less formal sort of balls. ... men and women fac[e] each other in two long rows. The dancers are constantly changing places in such a way that if the dance is carried to its conclusion everyone will have danced with everyone else. http://encyclopedia.jrank.org/DAH_DEM/DANCE_Fr_danse_of_ obscure_origi.html

Thursday 3rd Feb^y

The swarry in honor of Albert's birthday came off today. We went, expecting it to be slow & nobody there but we found Agnes, Susan, Emily, Frank & Louis Moline, Aunt Ellen & Ellen Mathews, Miss Ward, Mrs & Miss Tweedie and Walter there. We did dance (but not in costume) & had a jolly evening. Aunt Prichard danced a contre dance & Sir Roger. We broke up at 11-30 much too early for such a splendid party. It was excessively hot & obliged one to have recourse to the handkerchief after polkaing.

John Prior Estlin's self-portrait after dancing.

Saturday 5th February 1848

When I returned from work, I found a note from Edy asking me to go & make toffee, so I manufactured a cap etc & went up Alfred coming afterward to read to us. We made the toffee, which turned out very good.

Making toffee sketch from J. P. Estlin's diary.

Sunday 6th Feby

Woburn Place as usual. We went earlier than usual, & took Albert to Westminster Abby. We saw the Horse Guards Red return Guard as we went. The cold in the Abby was so intense that on coming out the air & pavement felt quite hot. Great talk of celebrating the Doctor's birthday by a Bal Masque, but I am dubious of it's being so. If it is, I think I shall go as a sailor. Alfred is considering, & thinks he will go as a Knight Templar. It is difficult to choose.

Sketch of sailor from J. P. Estlin's diary.

Wednesday 9th February 1848

There was a procession of 20,000 sailors today to present a petition to the Queen. They went up the river in boats belonging to all the vessels in the Thames. All the ships had their flags flying & the boats had also. It was a very pretty sight indeed.

Thursday 10th February

We did not go to Woburn Place tonight as all the young people were out & Aunt Prichard wrote us a note to say so.

Sunday 13th Feby 1848

At Woburn Place. After church we took a walk to Highgate & Hampstead & passed close under Mr. Reynold's windows. We discovered a pretty church or chapel with Norman doorways & painted windows. Mem. To go there some day. We were very much tired. That horrid creature Miss Wilkins makes a point of dining at Woburn Place. Emily & Louis Moline came from Greenwich in the evening. They are expecting accounts from Dick Moline who is, or was ill in Montreal. No tidings. I hope the party won't be put off for him, or that he'll get better (the most charitable wish certainly).

Monday 14th February

No Valentines. I finished the cardboard part of Alfred's armour. The quipon etc is to come. The most difficult part is to get a white plume.

Wed. February 16th

Went to Woburn Place this evening, but found the whole family on the point of emigrating to Dr. Tweedie's to a grand soiree. It was very aggravating to one's feelings to see them all come down dressed in white etc when we were not going. They gave us an invitation for tomorrow night, & also put doubts to rest as regards Monday week. R. Moline is quite out of danger so the party will take place, but I fear Agnes Moline will not be there which will be incalculable loss. It is a great nuisance, as I expect she would have been the best of the party.

Sketch of Alfred as a Knight Templar in John Prior's diary.

Thursday 17th Feby 1848

Went as commanded to Woburn Place & found Mr & Mrs., Anna, Susan & Louis Moline there. They had been dancing but did not resume it unluckily. We had some music & 4 handed chess, but the board was upset before the game was finished. Afterwards we had conglomeration. Albert's, of course, was the best. It indeed was splendid, & beat everything of the kind I ever heard. Full as good as an Ingoldsby legend. Some words were difficult to bring in, such as Euphemism, others easy.

The Ingoldsby Legends are a collection of myths, legends, ghost stories and poetry supposedly by Thomas Ingoldsby of Tappington manor, actually a pen-name of Richard Harris Barham. The legends were first printed in 1837 as a regular series. They proved immensely popular and were compiled into books published in 1840 and 1843. They remained popular through the Victorian era but have since fallen out of fame.

Sketch from J. P. Estlin's diary.

Friday 18th Feb

When I returned from the city tonight, I was rather flabbergasted to see the room full of damsels in white dresses, & kid gloves. It turned out that we were to have a dance, which took place accordingly.

Sketch of glove in J. P. Estlin's diary.

Sunday 20th Feb 1848

It having been arranged that the younger portion of the Woburn Place establishment should go to Twickenham on Saturday we did not call for them, but went direct to church, when after the service had commenced, we were frightened to see them come in panting, & increased by the presence of Anna Moline & Robt Haines. I had a tremendous headache, & left after dinner. I lost 2 sermons (which being read by Miss Wilkins, was great gain), & some conversation about next Monday week. They told Alfred they wanted me a day at W Pl & 2 at Greenwich. I should like nothing better.

Monday 21st Feb

Hearing that there was a whale to be seen at Greenwich, I ran down there by train but found it had been taken away about ½ an hour before, so I comforted myself with a call at No 18 but found only Mrs. & Susan Moline at home. I went in the time usually occupied by dinner. After business, I walked down to the Minories & paid a visit to E. Moses & Son & there bought a sailor's jacket to appear in on Monday. It is a most enormous establishment, & splendidly lighted with beautiful chandeliers. I then dined and came home & sewed the buttons on my jacket. Expected a box from home but none arrived.

The Minories is the name of both an area and street in the city of London close to the Tower of London. It refers to the Abbey of St Claire or the Abbey of the Minoresses of St. Mary of the Order of St. Clare, which stood on this spot. www.eduqna.com/Words-Wordplay/2097-3-words-wordplay.html

A printed booklet produced by E Moses and Son, tailors, clothiers, hatters, furriers, hosiers and outfitters, contains light verses on the art of dressing, price lists, letters to public, exchange and refund policy, and closing days and times in the year 1848.—The booklet states

(on page 24) that E Moses and Son is closed "Every Friday Evening at Sunset until Saturday Evening Sunset when Business is resumed until 12 o'clock". This corresponds to the Jewish Sabbath ('Shabbat' in Hebrew) that begins from sundown on Friday and continues sundown on Saturday.
www.movinghere.org.uk/search/catalogue.asp?sequence=410&resour cetypeID=2&recordID=57934

Chapter 5
Billingsgate and Engagements

Monday 28th Feb'y 1848

Having been so busy the last week preparing for the party tonight that I haven't been keeping up with this as I ought. On Saturday I went to Paddington on business and asked about the box which ought to have arrived on Tuesday & found it there so having paid the carriage I found I had no money left & consequently I had to walk back in the pouring rain. That having come, we were able to finish our dresses. We left here in a cab at 8 in the evening & found all the company assembled. The principal characters were Bluebeard, Tatania & sister, Am. Rajah, New Zealand chief, Templar, sailor, Spanish slave holder, Spanish Don, 2 Tyrolese, Gypsy queen etc. We had a good deal of dancing, & a most jolly evening. Some talk of a party at Greenwich.

Thursday 2nd March

We went up to Woburn Place this evening with the strong presentiment that we should find them out, which was true for Aunt P & Mrs Moline, were the only ones at home. The former wished much for an Aolian [sic] harp. Mem: To see if I can make one. I also received instructions to make some sketches of the dresses on Monday which I will do tomorrow & Saturday.

The traditional aeolian harp is essentially a wooden box including a sounding board, with strings stretched lengthwise across two bridges. It is placed in a slightly opened window where the wind can blow across the strings to produce sounds. The strings can be made of different materials (or thicknesses) and all be tuned to the same note, or identical strings can be tuned to different notes. The sound is random, depending on the strength of the wind passing over the strings.

Saturday 4th March

A hard day's work. Finished the sketches for Aunt P., 13 figures.

8 dancing Pastorale & 5 looking on etc., & done up flash in blue red & black ink, & gold ink.

Sunday 5ᵗʰ March 1848

Woburn Place. Found Miss Swingly Moline there & all went to church. Miss S contrived to give a most secular turn to the conversation very unusual there. I went home for my sketches but people found fault with them so much I was constrained to make another. Swingly asked me for the old one, but I refused flatly.

Monday 6ᵗʰ March 1848

I received a visit from John Senior & went with him to his rooms.

Thursday 9ᵗʰ

Went to Woburn Place and presented my drawings which were more graciously accepted not without some criticisms. Music etc., found a note of invitation for a party on 21ˢᵗ. Miss Bacon's wedding day. Wrote to White. Funds 80 1/8.

Sunday 12ᵗʰ March 1848

Alfred having 2 orders for the Temple, we, of course, went there. Emily, Edy, Albert & ALE & self. Heard a most beautiful anthem. Walked about a little, & returned home. Emily Moline told me that she was going to keep her birthday twice. At Woburn Place on this day week by ordering the dinner, (an old custom there), and at Greenwich in a much better way viz a great swarry. It is the custom to tell us when there are going to be parties and not to ask us, so I made up my mind not to be asked. Not that I don't wish to go, but I may not be invited and then I might promise myself some pleasure & be disappointed in the end. The Dr just returned from York. We went to St Andrews in the evening.

Monday March 13ᵗʰ 1848

I took Alfred to Billingsgate to have a fish dinner. Boiled cod, & skait [sic], fried sole, conger, eel, skait, brill, cod, whiting, & place went pretty well.

In 1699 an Act of Parliament was passed making it "a free and open market for all sorts of fish whatsoever". The only exception to this was the sale of eels that was restricted to Dutch fishermen whose

The London Fishmonger scene at Billingsgate mid 1850s.
Permission from Ken Baldry.
www.art-science.com/Ken/Genealogy/PD/ch02_Fishmongers.html

boats were moored in the Thames. This was because they had helped feed the people of London during the Great Fire. Until the mid-nineteenth century, fish and seafood were sold from stalls and sheds around the 'hythe' or dock at Billingsgate.

Tuesday March 14th 1848

An old lady & her daughter turned up this evening. The old lady talked domestic arrangements to an awful extent, descriptions of 16 sons & 25 daughters, turkeys that lasted the whole family forever, burst water pipes etc. Immense preparation for Tuesday 20th.

Thursday 16th March

Went to Woburn Pl. Nothing particular doing. No invitation for Monday however, if they have a swarry, they won't dance during Lent.

Friday 17th March

Alfred's last lecture tonight.

Sunday 19th March

Woburn Church in the morning & St Andrews in the evening. Emily Moline's 21st birthday. Swarry of Aunt Ellen and the weak child. Alfred & I instituted a phillipena each with Edy, & Emily, how we shall get on I don't know. Headache as usual on Sunday.

Phillipena—a game of forfeit.

Tuesday 21st March

This was a very grand day here. Miss Bacon's wedding day to Mr. George Rozia, for which vast preparations have been going on for the last month. The ceremony breakfast, bride & bridegroom went off much as these things usually do. The party in the evening was also good. Company: Mrs., Misses Mary Ann, Harriet & Kate, Wm & George Law, Mr. Lombard, Mrs Hardwick, Alder & selves. Miss Choice, Miss Bradshaw, Miss & Master Hughes, & Lons. We began at 8 & finished at 3. Mr. [William] Bacon was very melancholy (with wine) & Mr. Sherwood very merry. After supper he discoursed in a style peculiarly his own & unintelligible to anyone else & danced in a similar manner. When the company had gone he paced the room, crying out that the picture of Hannah Moore was his mother & vehemently requesting everyone to tell him if he had killed his poor father & uncle, then seizing two of his sisters he fell weeping on them & hugging them (yetch!!!) & was borne up to his bed watering the stairs with his tears. However, it all went off well together.

> *In early Victorian times, weddings were required by law to be before noon. Because of the early hour for weddings, the reception was traditionally a breakfast. It was an English custom to have a noon ceremony with the breakfast thirty minutes later at the bride's home. There, the couple received the guests and accepted congratulations.*

Wednesday 22nd March

I was not at the office till ¼ to 11 this morning & then I fear not good for very much. Resumed flute practice—hope it'll last.

Thursday 23rd March

We lost our phillippena tonight, or rather Alfred lost his & I won mine, but the lady disputed, so I agreed to have it over again. My aunt was not well, & we had it all to ourselves. I got some eighths of farthings, & Aunt P was so pleased with them that she told me get some more.

Friday 24th March 1848

I dressed up as an old woman & went to W Place. Nobody could have known me but they suspected something from Billins' manner, & when Emily came to the top of the stairs, she called out Phillipena & floored me. I went into the parlour, & Albert did not suspect for a minute who I was till I embraced him when he started back horridly frightened. Aunt P. was better. I stayed till 11. Was weighed 135 lb 5 ft. 7¾.

Sunday 26th March

Woburn Place. W. Church in the morning, & St George's in the evening. Miss Wilkins turned up, [having] been absent in the country, wish t'was forever. St George's is a regular London church, square roof with X beams.

The sketch is likely of Woburn church. Taken from J. P.Estlin's diary for Sunday.

St George's church may have been the one near the British Museum as it would have been close to Woburn Place.

Monday 27th March

A visit from Aunt Ellen. Letter from White. Bought the Marcellaise. Spent the day cogitating what Phillipena to give Emily Moline & have rather felt inclined to bon bons.

Wednesday 29th March 1848

Dined at Billingsgate off fish. I went to Howard's, which is not half so good in anyway as Bowlin's, so I shall return to the old place.

Thursday 30th March 1848

I bought a flash battledore and shuttlecock for my Phillipena with catgut web instead of parchment & velvet handles & gold lace. We went up in the evening, & chatted on various subjects.

Battledore and shuttlecock is a "keeping up" game dating from at least the 14th century. Evidence for this is to be found in the British Museum Library in a [circa 1390] manuscript wood cut engraving depicting two medieval peasant boys playing the game. They are wielding two blunt ended, paddle shaped bats, curiously reminiscent of butter pats. [implements for patting butter into shape.] ourworld.compuserve.com/homepages/Rexhaggett/battledo.htm

Chapter 6
Chartists

Friday 31ˢᵗ March

A beautifully warm day. Took a walk on London Bridge. The air was very clean & I could see Greenwich & all the shipping. I dined with Premett [Primett] in the evening in Islington. Rather like his wife (a Miss Carson of Taunton).

Saturday 1ˢᵗ April

A reprieve for a month. Mr. Sawtell wrote to Stuckey to tell him to stay another month. This will carry me on to Alfred's Examn & perhaps to Bacchus' return from India which will be about 10ᵗʰ May. I heard from him this morning. They had a mutiny at Calcutta, & 7 midshipmen & the troops got a 1,400-ton vessel under weigh without the assistance of a single sailor. He has my hookah, whether I shall get it, or not, I know not.

J. P. Estlin's impression of his hookah sketched in his diary.

Bacchus is George Woolgrove, apparently a school friend, currently a mid shipman on the Alfred, who will eventually become a ship's captain.

Sunday 2ⁿᵈ April

Woburn Place. A most beautiful day, we took a walk to the Serpentine (so called I suppose from the fact of its being quite straight), & inspected people sailing numerous small boats. It was immensely hot. A Chartist meeting took place today at Kennington Common (the favourite place for such things now) which was very orderly. Had a long argument with Mr. Alder about the Chartists.

The boats were introduced to the Serpentine in Hyde Park in 1847, but that was not the first occasion on which a craft had scudded the waters of the Serpentine. From: 'Hyde Park', Old and New London: Volume 4 (1878), pp. 375-405.
www.british-history.ac.uk/report.asp?compid=45205
Date accessed: 19 November 2006

From the Illustrated London News Aug. 12th 1848:
Although complaints have been made, and justly, of the very dirty and stinking state of the Serpentine River, at the west end of the waters, in Kensington Gardens, yet nothing seems to be done, ... in order to remedy this glaring evil... it really seems a pity that this handsome piece of water should be left in such a shameful state, as not only to be most unpleasing to the eye, but actually, from its stagnant condition, rendered most obnoxious to the sense.—Times

Hyde Park. *Source:* M. and S. Kirkpatrick

Monday 3rd April 1848

Another Chartist meeting in Kennington Common but disclaimed by the real chartists, this being composed of blackguards "out of luck" prigs, rummy hunters, knucklers & such like.

The Chartist movement was established and controlled by workingmen in 1836 to achieve parliamentary democracy as a step towards social and economic reform. It was an emotional reaction against a changing economy and society, which was unjust and bewildering to the workingman.... It expressed the resentment of conditions and movements which had promised so much, but which

had failed the workingman. It was greatest, therefore, in the times of
depression such as 1847-1848.

Wednesday 5th April

A number of delegates have been fixed on & are paid, holding their
Parliament somewhere in the Edgeware Road. They summon meetings
in different places & speak at them, 3 or 4 times a day. Mr. Alder, who
has just come from one, is completely confirmed in his Chartism & talks
loudly thereon, not admitting one word in favour of the opposite side &
pertinaciously maintaining the impossibility of anyone's fighting, but the
mob, should it come to blows. The important arrival of Mr. Charles, of
whisker notoriety, & his kid today.

May be Charles Paul of Bristol known as a banker and affiliate of
Stuckey's who had 10 children. One born in 1848 was named Walter
Stuckey Paul. Charles Paul died in 1857. Mr. Charles E Ward was a
member of a Bristol merchants association in the directory for 1863
that included a Charles Paul likely a son. In 1848 a Charles Paul was
a new legal assignee in Bristol.

Thursday 6th April

Still great Chartists meetings at the usual resorts. There seems to be a
feeling abroad as if something oculi cit would happen on Monday, the day
on which they intend to meet to the number of hundreds of thousands &
carry their petition to the house. The Bank guard is to be doubled (170
men), all the clerks (900) are to be armed & detained (being treated with 6
hogsheads of beer & beef, bread and cheese, ad libitum), & an astounding
number of special constables sworn in. Report says that all the bridges
particularly Blackfrairs, over which they will pass, are to be occupied by the
Military & guns to be planted on them. Some Irish news of importance has
arrived this afternoon, but I have not been able to ascertain the particulars.
Woburn Place as usual. Albert indisposed attributed to overwork. The
Doctor told us he had just heard from Lord Ashley that the preparations
against the mob were to be very stringent & determined. The Lord
Mayor was to issue a proclamation forbidding a meeting in the city & the
Government was to issue one at the same time prohibiting it out of the
city: that the police and special constables were to occupy the Common &
disperse the mob as it assembled: that the military was to be ordered out &

stationed near, but not to charge or fire, but if the mob resisted, the artillery was to come up and fire grape without hesitation accompanied by charges of soldiers.

Saturday 8ᵗʰ April 1848

The Doctor's report is true. Today the Proclamations are placarded all over the city, 40 rounds of cartridges given to the soldiers, & orders to have the bridges guarded by cannon. The different Bankers have armed their clerks (I wish ours was not an agency office), & ordered most of them to remain all Monday night. It is the universal theme of conversation.

Sunday 9ᵗʰ April

We went to Twickenham today, it was wet going and coming back, but fine while there. We had to wait some time at the station of course. We took a walk by the riverside, & Graham & I took a boat apiece, two little nutshells built like sea boats, about 7 feet long, exceedingly light & very crank, the turning of the head will tip them. We rowed some way down, below the railway bridge, & came back against tide & current, it was tremendous hard work. We played about on the green & examined curiosities & polished pistols afterwards & returned via Kennington. The common was perfectly quiet & wet, it raining hard at the time. There were 30 or 40 people waiting for the omnibuses & when the first came, there was a rush after it while still going on, which reminded me of a lot of minnows after a worm. We saw the cannon on Waterloo Bridge.

Monday 10ᵗʰ April 1848

The great eventful Monday—that might have changed the Dynasty of England, brought civil war into a peaceful country, shedding the blood of thousands, & heaping ruin & misery on millions, by the hands of those who sought to open it but by mistaken means, the great Monday that has shown the mind of the many, the excellent state of the Government, & the vast superiority of England over all the other countries. How glorious will this seem to those who read some centuries hence, that while all Europe was convulsed, while internal discord & civil war raged in all the Continental countries, while Kings were deposed, & governments changed in 3 days, our own little Isle was free & at peace, our Queen sate firmly on her throne, & people felt the benefit of a well ordered government. The mutiny took place at Kennington Common, 20,000 people being present, no procession went to Westminster & all passed off without so much as a single broken head. Feargus O'Connor addressed them, telling them he was doubled up with pain, that his medical advisor had ordered him not to attend, & that on his return he was to have a blister on his chest. But still he was there. The preparations were enormous & apparently out of proportion to the occasion but the event shows the wisdom of it all. All the bridges were guarded by cannon & sand bags to fire from, all the troops concealed in the neighbourhood, 150,000 special constables out besides the police 5,320.

At the Bank besides the usual guard [of] 140, there were a troop of Coldstreams, one of the Royal Artillery, & a Company of Sappers & Miners who ran up breastworks at the corners with loopholes to fire through & piled sand bags all round the top to fire behind. All clerks were armed with muskets, swords & pistols, & the fire engines were in readiness. At all the Banks & public places preparations were made, the post office had 2,000 stand of arms, & some guns on the roof etc. At Draper's Hall, the Clerks were armed well & Mr. E. Lawford came out in full Deputy Lieutenant's uniform. No work was done & the guard paraded the passages all day. A large detachment was sent to Kennington. As the Specials were ordered out Tegetmeir & myself were left alone to do the work of 4. Consequently we were there from 9 am–9-30 pm working incessantly & having no time to think of mobs. We were ordered to sleep there and I was going home for my sword & pistols but the meeting [was] going off so quietly, we thought it was not worthwhile. Alfred went to Woburn Place but I was too tired to follow him. There were 9,000 troops in London today. Alfred & I got a sword a piece & I burnished up my pistols on Saturday in readiness.

In 1812, on the authority of the Duke of Wellington, Major Charles Pasley RE set up a school for training engineers at Chatham. It continues today as the Royal School of Military Engineering (RSME). The first trainees were in action in Spain in 1813 and in 1814. The Engineer soldiers were retitled as the Royal Sappers and Miners.

Photo taken of the April 10th Chartist meeting on Kennington Common. www.bl.uk › ... › Chartists › Historical Sources

April 10th Alfred's E. Lawford of Draper's Hall confirmed: R. and J. R. Miller (agents) to E. Lawford. (clerk), 25 June 1852: Drapers' Hall, London.
www.google.ca/search?hl=en&q=E.+lawford+and+drapers+hall+an d+london&meta

Like many other livery companies, the Drapers' Company is based at a grand building named Drapers' Hall, which is in Throgmorton Avenue. Historically, the Drapers' Company interests were restricted to the woolen cloth trade, in which it held a monopoly, but with the passage of years came an expansion of its commercial interests that eventually spanned the globe.
www.combs-families.org/combs/records/ngland/drapers-hist.htm

Wednesday 12th April 1848

The breastworks & sand bags were removed from the Bank today, but they are in readiness inside at a moment's notice. They say there is to be a large meeting on Friday next, another on Good Friday, & a universal one on Easter Monday, with what truth I know not. Mr. E. Bagehot up. Dined at Wilkinsons' a-la-mode-beef house, & walked to London Bridge. Funds cons. 83¾ opening, 82¾ closing price. On Monday 81¼.

Friday 14th April 1848

Alfred heard on account today from very good authority that there was a conspiracy afoot, for the purpose of setting fire to all the available houses in London. Each man concerned was to carry a fireball composed of rags & tow, soaked in turpentine & pitch & resin, which being of some weight was to be flung through the windows, and over the walls of the Bank etc and from the fact of its being nearly impossible to extinguish them, it is probable they would have answered every purpose of the conspirators. This, in some degree, explains the immense preparations made on Monday last, & the wish of merchants & others in the city to have a standing division of special constables drilled & armed to protect the city during these unsettled times.

After dinner today I took a run to London Bridge, & seeing a crowd looking over I joined them, & saw 12 steamboats coming up the river as full of soldiers as they would hold. They disembarked at the Old Swan Pier, 100 yards from the Bridge, & I had a full view. They were the 62nd lately from India & some other regiment from Gibraltar on their way to Windsor.

They looked exceedingly pretty, especially when they formed in Thames Street, and you looked down upon the bayonets. The very sight of the fellows would scare a mob. A singular thing occurred while I was looking over. A woman who could not see, asked me what was to be seen "Two regiments of soldiers" said I with glee. "Oh is that all" she said & walked on; singular for a respectably dressed girl young, & pretty.

Saturday 15th April 1848

Received a note from Jno Noon this morng enclosing a post office order for £1 to get him a rod & tackle so I stumped down Grace Church Street & bought a beautiful black rod with 3 tops for 12/6, & an assortment of flies, reel and line float etc., & packed it all off by the AG at 4 o'clock. I flatter myself people do not get their commissions often done so quickly in London. The AG this morning bore undeniable symptoms of revelry last night. His head ached, his eyes were swollen & red, & he was thick, stupid & sleepy, he ate not, & sent for bitter ale, & did nothing. When I took a parcel of notes to take with him & told him so, he slowly drew the back of his hand across his forehead, looked up vacantly, then collecting his scattered thoughts, said:

"What? Oh yes. Go & get me a cab", wishing to get me off as soon as possible, but I would not let him rest:

"Will you be so kind as to take this little parcel (the rod) for me?"

"Oh certainly, is there anything else you want to send? Make haste for the cab, or I shall be late"

"No, thank you sir"

"Will you take any cancelled notes sir?"

"No, no not this time, Cab" sotto voice.

"A Hansom Cab sir?" knowing he detests them

"No, not those, a four wheeled one off the stand at Fenchurch Street, or by the Mansion House, sir. Anywhere, anywhere, only be quick."

When I returned with the cab I told him but he did not answer. He was fast asleep. However, a tremendous "Cab Sir" brought him to a state of ---vacancy---.

Alfred heard yesterday that if he passed he was to remain at Lawford's, & everything was settled as regarded salary etc. which shows they have some confidence in his passing. Mem. Bet him 1/ he will pass.

1834 English architect, Joseph Hansom, patented his 'safety cab' known as the 'Hansom' cab. It was a low, two-wheeled, closed carriage, whose distinctive feature was the elevated driver's seat in the rear. It was entered from the front through a folding door and had one seat above the axle with room for two passengers. The driver spoke to the passengers through a trapdoor on top.

Sunday 15th April 1848

As it was a fine day I did not feel inclined to be shut up all day at Woburn Place, & as I had long been wishing to pay Alleyne Foster a visit, I determined to do it today. Accordingly I strolled to London Bridge at 12, & having watched the ships in the river till the time of the train's starting, I took a second-class ticket to Croydon. The ride is extremely pretty, especially about Amerly. There are more diverging branches to this line than to any I have ever been on, & the rails are much worn. I remarked the pipes used in the trail of the atmospheric principle, all along the edge & the stationary steam engines at every 3 or 4 miles which are very prettily built, the chimney being a miniature tower ornamented, & with loopholes all the way up. On arriving at Croydon, I walked to Addiscombe 1 ½ miles off, & found them all at dinner, so having requested the servant to tell Mr Alleyne Foster that Mr. Estlin wanted him, I strolled around the grounds, & inspected the mortars & cannon & mimic fortifications.

Presently I saw a young fellow coming towards me, in the uniform of the college.

"Are you Alleyne Foster?"

"Yes"

"I don't recollect you, were we at school together at Somerton?"

"No"

"And yet you are Alleyne Foster?"

"Yes"

"Joseph Alleyne Foster?"

"Oh no—Allen Foster the other Foster was susticated last term."

"The devil he was, what for?"

"I don't like to tell---"

So my old friend was susticated, & I had come all this way to see a spurious Foster. Provoking. I turned back, & as the next train did not start til 4-15, I amused myself with biscuits & beer, & wandering about Croydon, & at last got home, took a bus to Southampton Row. I thought to get to Woburn Place in time for dinner at 5-15, but found they had done so I pitched into some dessert, & waited till tea, going to St George's in the meantime. Frank & Charles Moline came in the evening, & gave rather a secular turn to the conversation as neither the Dr. nor my aunt (who is gone to Mrs. Augustine's confinement*) were there. My battledores were very graciously received and pronounced to be a very appropriate Phillipena. *This little matter is not intended to come off yet: My aunt's visit for some other purpose.

> *Addiscombe was originally 'Adgecomb" or Adscomb; meaning "Edge of the Coombe". When Elizabeth I reigned in England, Addiscombe was a country estate just a mile from Croydon on the Shirley Road, owned by the Heron family. After the death of the last of the Herons, the estate became the residence of successive benefactors.*

Chapter 7
London Hearths

Monday 17th April 1848

My eyes were greeted today by the sight of Mr. Frederick Stuckey, who came back, bringing with him a whole host of country relations to show them something of London, so he will have a few days more holiday. I must speak to Mr. Sawtell about myself as they require a month's notice here. Alfred heard from Papa stating that Mr. Larkenhead died on Saturday. Funds 81⅝ – ¾.

Tuesday 18th April 1848

Went to the post office, & got Jno Noon's post office order cashed. Called at a chophouse in Cheapside, & fell in with Graham. He asked me to Twickenham on Thursday, & is going to call on Alfred for the same purpose. Looked at some swordsticks in Hoborn [sic] from curiosity, they run from 3/ upwards. Tegetmeir promised me a long, Dutch clay pipe.

Friday 21st April 1848 Good Friday

Could not get Alfred up in time to go to Twickenham at 9, but we got to Nine Elms at 10. We found the Mathews at church, they having given us up. There is a Miss Fothingel staying there, a very pretty girl, but very young & shy. We lunched, & then went to the riverside & took a boat in which Graham & I rowed Alfred up to Kingstone, about 2–3 miles above Twickenham, where one of Graham's sculls breaking, we were obliged to return. The weir was running so rapidly that we were with difficulty able to pass. We returned by rail, & omnibus. There was a young fellow on the train so awfully drunk. He held his head out of the window, & I fancy gave the cleaners something to do in polishing the panels. They inadvisedly shut the window, & consequently we had the benefit of it all inside.

Saturday 22nd April

Got some wood & made a case for my clay pipe to preserve it from breaking.

<u>Sunday 23rd April 1848</u>

Although we had promised Mrs. Mathews to go there today, should it turn out fine, we did not go, notwithstanding that it was a beautiful day. We found the Dr. and Aunt P. returned from Bristol, & Albert better. Sundays spent as Sundays usually are there.

<u>Monday 24th April</u>

Stuckey came today for good. He intends writing to the committee to ask them to let him go into the country. Whether they will agree to it, or not, I know not. First day of Greenwich Fair: bought some Lychees. There was a small disturbance at Trafalgar Square today but of not much consequence.

> *On the first day of the Greenwich Fair, from the Ship Torbay Tavern up to the park gates, the road was bordered on either side with stalls, games, and hand-waggons. These contained goods or refreshments of every description. Mr. Punch, too, sat up the temple of his illegitimate drama at three or four points of the thoroughfare.... ...vendors of spring rattles, who ensured "the whole fun o' the fair for a penny" – speculators in heavy stocks of Waterloo crackers and detonating balls – proprietors of small percussion guns, to shoot with at targets for nuts – kept increasing, together with the visitors, as we neared the park; until the diminished breadth of the street brought them all together in one struggle to get through the gates, like the grains of sand in an egg-glass.*
>
> *It was a great relief to exchange the dust and jostling of the street for the greensward and wide area of the park.... Observatory Hill was the chief point of attraction, and here the great mass of people was collected.*
> *www.victorianlondon.org/publications/lifeandcharacter-16.htm*
> *and festivity only to be witnessed at Greenwich*

<u>Tuesday 25th April</u>

I came down the river by boat this afternoon, & went through the Tunnel. It is much as I expected but longer, & larger. The spaces between the arches were converted into small shops for ginger beer, toys, & numerous other trifles. On coming back I found there had been a ticket for me, for the

Strand Theatre, which was appropriated in my absence by the youngest Sherwood. I dare say the beast was glad enough of my staying away. Stopped on Holborn Hill watching the horses fall & saw 20–30 down.

At the time that the Holborn Viaduct was considered the following rhyme was coined:
All the old horses will jump for joy,
'Twas up Holborn Hill that did them annoy ....
http://www.londonancestor.com/street/str-holborn.htm

Wednesday 26th April 1848

They promised us a smoking party tonight, & Messers Robert, Alder, & Hardwick came in expectation but were disappointed.

Possibly Phillip Harwick. Philip Hardwick, architect, married a daughter of the architect John Shaw Senior (1776–1832), whose son was the architect, John Shaw Junior (1803–1870). In the City, Hardwick executed the offices for Robarts, Curtis, and Lubbock, Lombard Street (1863). The family resided at 60 Russell Square when the 1851 census was taken and then at Cavendish Square in 1861.

Thursday

Received an invitation from Graham to go there this day week to a dance. Went up to Woburn Pl, & found the Dr. poorly.

Friday 28th April 1848

Drunk tea at Stuckey's in the Walworth Road, & went to the Surrey Theatre afterwards. Saw a pantomime there, not a very good one, (Cinderella), & the Bohemians at Paris & another piece. It was not over till very late, & I did not get home till 3 o'clock.

Saturday 29th April 1848

Felt very tired today, but had a delicious warm bath after work, which freshened me up & made me feel splendid. The first regular one I ever had. Had a chat with Tegetmeir's brother, a very nice fellow who knows a great deal, he studied for a surgeon but never went up. He told me he had the pleasure of riding with Miss Ann, Mr. Reynolds & someone else I think he said Dr. William Carpenter. Mr. Primet not returned yet, but I expect him on Monday.

Sunday April 30th 1848

Went to Woburn Place. Doctor not quite well yet. Took a walk in Hyde Park. Went to church etc.: very warm.

Monday 1st May

Mr. Primet returned today. I saw several bands of sweeps keeping up the 1st of May. The early closing the Banks came into force today & I got off at ½ past 4 & as it was a lovely day I ran down to Greenwich by boat (4d). Took a walk with Frank & Louis Moline all over Greenwich Park & Blackheath. The grass in the Park was much trampled by the people at the fair this day week & there was nearly as much orange peel as grass. However, I thought it very pretty indeed. The band of the Maritime School was playing; they play beautifully. The hill in the Park is not as big so Montacute Hill, with the Observatory on the top and numerous old pensioners stationed about with telescopes & ginger beer, & piles of cannon balls looking like oranges, very. As I was too late for the last boat, I stayed to tea. Agnes, Susan, Mrs. M., Mr. M, T & Ls at home. Agnes is decidedly the prettiest of the family. I spent a jolly evening & came home by train.

> *1848, 1 May: On the 1st day of May in London… our own chimney-sweeps employ themselves in the celebration of ceremonies of an … impressive character. A leafy cone, about ten feet in height, and of a sufficient area in the interior* [is constructed] *to contain an adult sweep …. The arch-sweep takes his place. Certain other ladies and gentlemen of the same profession array themselves in fantastic costumes, and with a band of music accompany Jack-in-the-green from street to street.*

> *Chimney sweeps…apprenticed for 7 years, but unlike other careers, most sweeps had no marketable skills at the end of their training because they grew too big to fit in the 9" or even 7" chimneys. They usually worked naked, both to save room and to allow them to slide more easily…. These children suffered twisted spines and kneecaps, deformed ankles, eye inflammations and respiratory illnesses, and were only allowed to bathe a few times a year. An ailment known as "chimney sweep's cancer" commonly appeared on the scrotum from*

the constant irritation of the soot on their naked bodies. Many sweeps were maimed or killed after falling or being badly burned, while others suffocated when they became trapped in the curves of the chimneys. The soot was sold for manure.
www.gober.net/victorian/reports/chldhood.html, www.mustrad.org.
uk/articles/jack_gre.htm

Chapter 8
Ships

Tuesday 2nd May

This is Alfred's eventful day. Harwood called here at 9, & we walked together to Chancery Lane. I left him there, & went to the office by water. He says he has not passed, but as he has answered all the questions, I think there is no doubt but he will. After it was over we took a walk together by the Strand, & on Waterloo Bridge. Bought a Stock. My present (Phillepena) was universally praised. They said at Greenwich they longed to see them, & those that had, & had used them, declared they were better than any they had ever seen. It is one satisfaction to have one's present appreciated.

Wednesday 3rd May 1848

I was sitting writing about 4 o'clock today when Alfred rushed up stairs, very hot, & threw down his hat shouting "Passed". He had just been to inquire, & had ascertained it. He told me first, & then rushed on to Draper's Hall to communicate the intelligence, & receive congratulations. In the evening we went up to Woburn Pl to do likewise. We found the family out at an "Aboriginal meeting" with the exceptions of Edy & Albert, but they returned to tea, & congratulated strongly. Wrote to Aggy, White, Noon, & Stayner. Graham dined with us.

Saturday 6th May 1848

Went with Graham by Steamboat to Nine Elms & met Jem Senior, we then went by the express train to Richmond in 14 minutes. Took a boat there, & rowed up to Teddington & back. A most splendid evening: the river lovely, lots of boats out.

Sunday 7th May

This Sunday was spent very unorthodoxical by me. We (Jem, Graham, & I), took a boat at 9-30 & rowed up to Hampton Court intending to go to chapel there but we were too late as there was a strong current to pull against so we went about a mile up the river & pulled up at a beautiful little island, pulled out our sandwiches, & pulled them in. We then returned to the Court, walked around the grounds & waited till the House was open. The basin in front absolutely swarms with gold and silver fish, many full 1 foot long. The avenue of chestnuts, a mile long, was looking most beautiful being in full blossom. The maze is a humbug, being a little thing made of quickset hedge as high as your head. After we had seen all, we had some ale & ginger beer, & returned bathing on the way. After tea, G & I took a walk on Richmond Hill, & I got a blowing up because we were not back till 10, & they wanted to go to bed.

> *The island is likely Taggs Island now under private ownership. In 1850, squatters occupied the island when a new owner, Francis Jackson Kent, took it over and evicted them. Kent was a Hampton lawyer and property developer who bought large amounts of land in East Molesey (the Kent Town area) for housing.... Thomas (Tom) Tagg had leased part of the island in 1841 from Kent and set up a boatyard called T.G. Tagg and Son.*

<u>*Monday 8th May*</u>

Got up at 6-30, & walked to Kew with Graham & James. We got on board the steamboat, & after waiting half an hour got out again as the paddles would not move, & came in by the Bus. Walked down in the evening with Alfred to St Katharine's Docks & saw a lot of splendid ships.

> *St Katharine's Docks took their name from the former hospital of St. Catherine by the Tower, built in the 12th century, which stood on the site. By the early 19th century, over 11,000 people were living in the insanitary slums of the area and the entire site was earmarked for redevelopment.... To create as much quayside as possible, the docks were designed in the form of two linked basins (East and West), both accessed via an entrance lock from the Thames. Steam engines (designed by James Watt and Matthew Boulton) kept the water level in the basins about four feet above that of the tidal river.*

St. Katharine's Docks in 1828.
en.wikipedia.org/wiki/Image:St_
katharine_docks_1828.jpg

Tuesday 9th

Went with Alfred by the Blackwall Railway to the East & West India Docks. Saw the Seringapatam, 800 tons one of the Green ships about to sail tomorrow, a most lovely & superb ship. Saw heaps of others of all sizes & the 3 tops of the masts & the two ends of the Junk Keying.

The brothers use the London & Blackwall Railway line that originally ran from the Minories (a District and street between Aldgate and the Tower) to Blackwall via Stepney, in east London, England. The East India-Docks are considerably smaller than the West India; and finally, beyond these, stretching from close by the entrance of the East India-docks to Galleons-reach, comes the… Victoria-docks.

The Seringapatam was one of the first of the East Indiamen to be built at the Blackwall Yard. These so-called Blackwall Frigates … were built to look like those well defended ships, with numerous gunports along the sides. …The Seringapatam was built in 1837, 'the first of Green's famous 'Blackwall Frigates' (and) the finest merchant ship of her day.'
www.natgalscot.ac.uk/tipu/tipu341.htm

The Junk Keying (Chinese: "Elder and Brave" The English name is based on Cantonese pronunciation) was a three-masted, 800-ton Foochow Chinese trading junk which sailed from China around the Cape of Good Hope to the United States and England between 1846 and 1848. She is of particular interest, since she testifies to the power of Chinese shipping and shipbuilding at the time of the beginning of industrialization in the West.

Wednesday 10th May

Danced this evening. Mr & Mrs Rosia & Miss Choice here.

Thursday 11th

Went with Alfred in a cab to Paddington. Saw him off in the mail train, & returned to the City in a bus. Very hot, has been since 30th April.

Friday 12th May

Took a walk after work by the west, & had a cup of coffee at Mr. Michaelski's. Heard that Mr. Primet is going to Dover for a week on tomorrow week. I expect to hear of the Alfred's arrival on Monday, have some notion of going down the river tomorrow.

Sunday 14th May

Took a boat at London Bridge, & went down the river to Gravesend. Got there at 12¼, tide against us. About 500 people were in the boat, & no room to sit all the way. There is nothing particular to be seen at Gravesend itself more than the shipping. I walked some way down the river, & lay on the bank eating oranges, & watching the ships coming up & talking to a pilot who gave some information about the Alfred. When the wind is S or SSW, a ship can sail up the Channel, & up the Thames without touching, but if the wind is unfavourable they are obliged to be taken in tow. As I was tired in the evening, I did not go up to Woburn Place.

Monday 15th May 1848

I had the honor of a visit from Albert in the evening to know where I had been. He said James was not so well, but had been spitting blood a good deal.

Tuesday 16th

Took a walk round the Regent's Park with this family, & another short one with Mr. Alder.

Chapter 9
Baths and Bacchus

Wednesday 17th

Went with Tegetmeir, & bathed in the Westminster baths. Mem. Will never go there again. As we were close by we were tempted to go to Astley's, & marched up to the "Gods". Van Amburgh & his beasts are very good. He first has a combat with a leopard, that springs upon him while climbing a cliff, & they roll over & over down to the stage & he shakes it & at last masters it. Afterwards he enters the den with 3 lions 1 tiger 3-4 leopards and some others. The black leopard is very pretty & has a splendid long tail as big as a ladies boa & much softer. The leopard seemed very fond of him. The tight rope dancing was very good & some of the horsemanship & clown tricks. 8 ladies tilted at the ring & Saracens' heads, & fired pistols at the heads, but whether the pistols went off or not, the heads were knocked down.

> *Spurred on by the threat of disease, the 1846 act legislated that there should be at least two classes of baths; that there should be not less than twice as many baths for the labouring classes as for all other*

St. Pancras public baths in the 1840s.
www.victoriantimes.org/ixbin/hixclient.exe?_IXSESSION_=nUlPh17wxec&_ IXACTION_=file&_IXFILE_=illustrations/iln.html

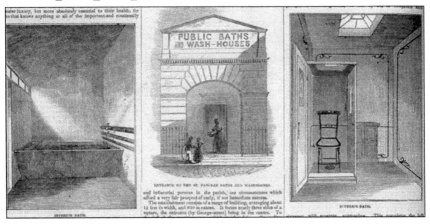

classes together, and that no warm bath, shower bath, or vapour bath intended for the labouring classes could cost more than twopence.

When Astley saw that trick riders received more attention from the crowds in Islington, he opened a riding school in London, in 1768 south of the Westminster Bridge. Astley called the arena a circus because of its shape, and Astley chose it for two reasons. First of all, it was easier for the audience to keep the riders in sight. Secondly, the ring (as the circus was better known) helped riders through generation of centrifugal force, which allowed them to keep their balance whilst standing on the backs of their galloping horses. After a few years, he added a platform, seats, and a roof to his ring. Astley's original circus was 62 ft (~19 m) in diameter, and later he settled it at 42 ft (~13 m), which has been an international standard for circuses since then. After two seasons in London, he had to bring some novelty to his performances, so he hired other equestrians, musicians, a clown, jugglers, tumblers, tightrope walkers, and dancing dogs. This laid the foundations of the modern circus, as we know it today.

Astley's Ampitheatre in London circa 1808.
upload.wikimedia.org/wikipedia/commons/e/e9/
Astley%27s_Ampitheatre_Microcosm_edited.jpg

Thursday May 18th

Went up to Woburn Place: James not so well. Has been spitting more blood, & has been bled. Aunt P has also a bad cold. The young ones had been to Kew Gardens, & had met Graham Mathews there. They went with the Moline Family but I missed them in the boat & had heard nothing of them since they were at Kew. It is supposed that they took Emily home with them or had all got swamped, it is to be hoped not.

Friday 19th May 1848

Received a letter from Alfred & one from Uncle Jem [Senior] to Alfd asking us to go there on Sunday. Primet left today to go to Dover & Boulogne till Monday week.

Sunday 21st May

I went this morning to the Temple intending to cut the Sermon, & go to Twickenham at 1, but I found that they lock the doors after the first lesson. Harwood & his wife were there, but although I pressed against her in the crowd, I did not see her face. She got in, & I wandered about with Harwood. We could not hear a word. When I got to Uncle Jem's I found them waiting although it was only just 3. The house has a splendid drawing room, & staircase made of polished mahogany; the garden is good for so near town with a splendid plane tree in it. I got to the station at half past 9 but the train started as I got up, but luckily there was a special train at ½ to 10 which took me up in ten minutes.

Monday 22nd May 1848

Went to the West End today with Tegetmeir, & ordered my coat. As it was too late for tea, I had a cup of coffee, & played dominos & crib, & I lost as usual.

Tuesday 23rd May

A letter came this morning from Bacchus stating the Alfred would be at Blackwall on Wednesday. A draft was given me today for £25 which someone had to pick up in a shop, payable to Walter Bagehot, so I took it up to him in the evening. I went to Woburn Place afterwards.

Wednesday 24th May

I found by the papers that the Alfred will not be here till next Wednesday, Bacchus having put no date to his letter. As I was at a loss rather what to do, I took a 4d trip to Blackwall & walked about there for 2 hours. I saw the Monarch, in the docks, a most magnificent ship much larger than any there at the time. The Barham and Wellesley being next in size. I went at ½ past seven to tea at Chas Moline's, & Robt Haines'. Frank came unexpectedly in the evening & "Edmund" a friend of C M's so we had a large party. The City was not much altered by the races. The number of vehicles was considerably less, but the people were just as thick. I met an immense number of drunk and half drunk people chiefly with women of bad character, when I was going home from Finsbury at night.

The British ship WELLESLEY (Official No. 308; International Signal Code: HCJN), was built at Blackwall, London, by Richard & Henry Green in 1844. 1014/1102 tons (old/new measurement); 162 x 36.5 x 23.1 feet (length x beam x depth of hold).
The Alfred built in 1845 (1291 tons) for the London and Calcutta run built at Blackwall by Green. See engraving.

The Alfred. Permission granted for use. www.nmm. ac.uk/collections/ greenblackwall © National Maritime Museum, Greenwich

Thursday 25th May

I went yesterday to the top of the monument, 365 steps up. It was very clear, & I had a beautiful view, but I had no time to spare, & so did not stay long enough to please me.

Built to commemorate the Great Fire that devastated the City of London in 1666, the Monument offers panoramic views over London. Standing 202 feet high, the Monument is the tallest isolated stone column in the world. Designed by Sir Christopher Wren and Robert Hooke and constructed of Portland stone in 1671–7, the simple Doric column is topped by a flaming urn of copper symbolizing the Great Fire. The spiral staircase consists of 311 steps to the balcony at the top and you are rewarded with breathtaking views over the city in all directions, as well as (in 2006) a certificate of achievement.

Friday 26th May

I was looking carefully at the Times today, and unexpectedly came upon the name of the Alfred, so at 4-30 I packed up my traps and went, by rail, to Blackwall. There I found the Alfred lying alongside the Monarch, but quite deserted. I left a note with the ship keeper, & went to the Sailor's Home, Poplar, to look for Woolgrove [Bacchus], but found him not, so I went home by a boat to London Bridge, and walked quietly home. When I got there, I found he had called for me about ½ hour before, so I had some tea & in 10 minutes, I saw him rolling along the other side of the street. We then took a walk, & as we were passing Hunter S^t, we called in (at 35) to see Hildebrand, a brother middy, but he was not in. His landlady then entered into conversation, & we found the old man (Hildebrand) had been cramming her tremendously, telling her he had 3-4 parrots for her & lots of things. She had set her mind upon them so, that she had bought the cages. We walked about for an hour, & I saw him to 18 Cecil S^t & then went home.

Sketch of parrots and cage from J. P. Estlin's diary.

Woolgrove alias Bacchus

Later record: OF LIVERPOOL, GEORGE PERCY WOOLGROVE, MASTER, BURTHEN 1149 TONS FROM THE PORT OF LIVERPOOL TO SYDNEY, NEW SOUTH WALES, 24TH OCTOBER 1860
mariners.records.nsw.gov.au/1860/10/040tel.htm

In former times Poplar abounded in poplar trees; its position near the river was highly favourable to the growth of these trees. The inhabitants are chiefly connected with the shipping interest, or are employed in the docks, in Green's and shipbuilding yards. Green, who established the home primarily for the seamen of his merchant ships, paid for it all. Work began in summer 1839 and was probably completed late in 1841.
www.british-history.ac.uk/report.asp?compid=46479
Date accessed: 27 November 2006

This is the Chapel and Sailors' Home endowed by George Green, who built the Congregationalist chapel, and his son Richard. They were both buried in the chapel. The Green company house flag flies on the Home to the right.

Saturday May 27th 1848

I promised to wait for GW after business, but he did not come, so, after calling at several outfitters, I found him at Princes. He then took out my hookah, which differs from what I expected, & gave me two pretty drawings of the Alfred. We then had some tea in the Strand and walked about till dark when the illuminations commenced, most of them were very pretty, and some magnificent; nearly

J. P. Estlin's sketch in his diary of the hookah that he received.

every house in Bond Street and Pall Mall was illuminated. It was late before we had seen them all, & we were very much tired. When I got home I unpacked my hookah, which pleased me much: the part in which the tobacco is to be placed is inferior.

Sunday 28th

Went to Woburn Place in the morning, church, James and my Aunt about the same. Came home at 2, and went to Cecil St. Took a boat from Essex St to Blackwall, had a beautiful ride. We found no one on board & went all over the ship & up the shrouds & down the holds. A most magnificent ship she certainly is. We went on board the Monarch, she is much the same build as the Alfred but was all to pieces, being refitted. We saw an immense number of rats, in every cabin there were 2 or 3 and as the water closets were taken out they could escape us easily through the open pipes, we hit one. There was a large black cat on board, the solitary occupant of that vast mass of timber & he was so delighted to see us, when he heard our voices he ran up "mearrowing" and rubbed against us. He was cut all to pieces by the rats & had not a square inch of fur but had 3 or 4 bites in it. His ears were quite lace & jagged like an old flag fray'd by the wind. We went on board the Wellesley 1100, Barham 1050, & Tartar 800 and as the Wellesley was to sail in a day or two & Green had ordered the keeper not to admit even Mrs. G., if she came, we had to give him a bob. We came home by train intending to go to the Lady Chapel, London Bridge but were too late so we had some tea in the old place in the Strand & walked till it was time to go home.

Chapter 10
Vauxhall, Highbury and Hornsley

Tuesday 30th May 1848

As Bacchus was engaged yesterday, I did not see much of him, but, as they gave me a whole holiday, today, I did. I called him up at 8 as he wished to go to Green's [about] his certificate, which he expected to have at 9, but as he did not get it, we went first to Princes & then to Blackwall to see the Skipper & get it from him. But he was not there, we found Masters, a mid. on board, & walked with him to the other sailor's home, where we met Mac---, Mayhew, Hildebrand, mids.& Daniel & Scott, 3rd, & 4th Mates. Bacchus had to pay a bet of a bottle of wine which we had, & another from Mayhew. We then went to the City, & dined off cold boiled beef, & salad & fell in with Scott, Daniel & Masters again when we went & had a lobster wind up (7/6 between the lot), we lounged about a bit with them, saw 3 of them off, and then started ourselves. We walked to Lambeth & then to Vauxhall for the opening of which we had to wait some time. I admire the gardens very much, the orchestra is very good & one blaze of light the collonades are lighted by different colored glass lamps, & the borders of the paths are marked out by the same, looking like crocuses; festoons of lamps hang from the trees, and all combined produces a beautiful, though rather dazzling effect. In one part is Eve at the fountain, near her a little to the right is Zadock the fortune teller, turning to the right again is Neptune, in his chariot, and 100 yards in front, the slack rope dancing, to the right of which is the ground for fireworks. The Rotunda is near the top of the garden. The principle thing to be seen is Constantinople looking from the Turkey side, with a view of the Bosphorus & Golden Horn on the other side. At the last scene the whole looks one mass of fire with rockets rising, Roman candles wheels of all sorts, & most beautiful fireworks. It is well worth seeing. We were very tired, & hired a cab to the Strand.

During supper as night fell ... each servant touched a match to pre-installed fuses, and, 'in an instant', over a thousand oil lamps were illuminated, bathing the gardens in a warm light that would have been visible for miles around. There was a substantial...building... the Rotunda, built by Tyers as a concert room during wet weather....

'The Vauxhall song', was the first music to have a real mass audience (of over a hundred thousand each season) drawn from all sectors of society, and from all parts of Britain and overseas; the singers became huge stars.

Another account: The Battle of Waterloo was being represented on the firework-ground, and I could not divest myself of the idea that it was a real engagement I was witnessing, as the sharpshooters fired from behind the trees, the artillery-waggon blew up, and the struggle and conflagration took place at Hougomont. The supper was a great feature—eating by the light of variegated lamps, with romantic views painted on the walls, and music playing all the time.... And as the "rack punch"—"racking" would be a better term—was imbibed, until all the lamps formed a revolving firework of themselves, what little sense of the real and actual I had retained, departed altogether. The Mysterious Zadoc, Fortune teller in his Eastern Temple. 1849 www.victorianlondon.org/publications/lifeandcharacter-19.htm

Wednesday 31st May 1848

Bacchus received his certificate this morning, & I went with him to Blackwall, & Green appointed him 5th Mate of the Alfred & 4th next voyage. I had not time to see him to Paddington. When I got to the office I found Mr. Sawtell had given me a guinea ticket to the Provident Clerks

One of several bottles sketched in J. P. Estlin's diary for May 31st 1848.

Life Assurance Company's dinner so I went home, & dressed & was obliged to have a cab to be there in time at 6. I enjoyed the dinner much, & drank a great lot of wine. Mr. Primet gave me a lift in his cab, & as it happened I went all the way home with him, & Mrs & Miss Primet, his wife & sister. As I was tired, it was wet, & I had my best clothes on, & they pressed me much, I went in & stayed there, had a glass of grog & slept on the sofa. Walked in the next morning with Mr. Primet, & never felt better in my life, so the stuff did not do me any harm. Mr. Paul had a bad headache the next morning, & Mr. Tegetmeir was done up "he had eaten too much".

Thursday 1st June 1848

Went to Woburn Place found them a little better. Edy & Emily are going tomorrow to join Albert at Lellack & stay a fortnight.

Friday 2nd June

Went to 36 King St Soho, & paid for my coat. Had some tea, & a game of bowles with Tegetmeir. When I got home I found a note from Greenwich to Alfred which I opened, & found to contain an invitation for next Monday fortnight. Shall go if possible. Met Graham who wanted me to go there on Sunday.

Tuesday 6th June 1848

Received a note from Hancock this morning telling me to be at the Tavistock Hotel at 6. So I toddled up there, & waited till 8, went to 1 Bedford Row, & gave him up, did not see him at all. Mr Primet called in the evening to ask me to tea the next evening.

Wednesday 7th June 1848

Went to Mr. Primet's at 6 & met his mother & sister, Mr. Myart, his mother, and later his wife's sister Miss Standish, & Mr. Someone in the Colonial Bank. Old Mrs. Myart could not speak one word of English but knew a little French. Her son translated into German whatever was said to her.

Friday 9th June 1848

While I was polishing up my hookah, Frank Moline called on me, & having had a cup of tea, I went for a walk with him & rode in the boat with him to London Bridge, and when I got there, he persuaded me to change my 2d ticket for a 4d ticket & go down with him which I did, & having play'd a game of 4 handed chess, Agnes & I against Susan & Frank, I came back by train with Robert Haines having spent a very pleasant evening, the more so as it was totally unexpected. It was raining hard when I returned.

Saturday 10th June 1848

A pouring afternoon. I got regularly wet through, for the first time since I have been in London.

Sunday 11th June

I went to St Paul's this morning at ¼ to 10. The part where the service is held is very small and surrounded by galleries elaborately & beautifully carved: more like boxes at a theatre than anything else. The singing is good, but not so beautiful as at the Temple. The seats, & scaffolding of the charity school children were there, & filled up the interior. The crowsnest on the top is rapidly progressing & adds very much to the height of the dome. I went to Woburn Place afterwards, & saw Con there. James was about the same. I expect Alfred home about Thursday but Woburn Place detachments do not return till later.

Left: Sketch made of the dome of St. Paul's taken from J. P. Estlin's diary. *Right:* St Paul's dome. *Source:* M.and S. Kirkpatrick

Monday June 12th 1848

We had a tremendously wet day, it raining harder than I have ever seen it in London. The water ran over the Shoot at Alexander's & nearly knocked several people down, who thought their umbrellas would keep it off while passing. I took a 3d Bus to Elephant & C & drank tea with Stuckey & took an omnibus home, or rather the omnibus took me home.

Tuesday 13th June

It held up today & was pretty fine. After work I went down to Greenwich by boat. I saw a great number of people looking at something in the water just before you come to the pier, & on coming up to the spot, found it to be the body of a young woman with nothing but a petticoat on. She had been in for some time to all appearances, as she floated high. She appeared to be a very fine young woman & had her hair still done up. It was fair day, but I did not go to the part where the fair was as Frank Moline was not at home.

Sketch from J. P. Estlin's diary for June 13th.

The Greenwich pier was built in 1836 to accommodate visitors for the fair days and weekend visitors from London. This view is from 1850.

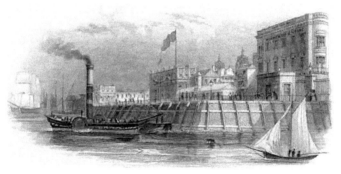

Greenwich Pier.
www.ideal-homes.org.uk/images/greenwich/central-greenwich/pier -01215-640.jpg

Wednesday 14th June 1848

I walked home with Mr. Primet, and we had arranged to go out together with Miss Primet, but a horrid old maid came in, and prevented her going so P & I went to Highbury, Hornsey wood (a small hill with a very few stunted nut & oak bushes), & back by the new river, & Buckingham House (Lunatic Asylum). I got home at 10-30, & found a note from Uncle John inviting me to the Unitarian soiree at the Hall of Commerce, but as I was home so late I could not go.

Hornsey village was mainly north of the road and more concentrated towards the east. West of Middle Lane there were only a few isolated houses.... Farther east the parish watchhouse, school, and workhouse

were grouped together and immediately beyond the first bridge over the New River stood two buildings, one of them apparently the Elms, a large single-storeyed villa that existed until 1939. From: 'Hornsey, including Highgate: Growth before the mid 19th century', A History of the County of Middlesex: Volume 6: Friern Barnet, Finchley, Hornsey with Highgate (1980), pp. 107-11.
www.british-history.ac.uk/report.asp?compid=22517
Date accessed: 26 November 2006

John Bishop Estlin.
Estlin family portrait collection.
Source: Sharon Hope

Chapter 11
London Outskirts

Thursday 15th

Breakfasted early & called at Woburn Place. Saw Uncle John & Albert. Cousin Mary Ann was not up.

Friday 16th

Called at Woburn Place in the evening. I had a chat with Uncle John, in fact, spent the whole evening with him as Albert was busy, and no one else was down.

Saturday 17th June 1848

Stuckey has complied with the order he had yesterday to go to Bristol on Monday, so I shall be left here some time longer. Took a walk in the evening with Bacon & Sheridan & the dog. Met a friend of Sheridan's Herr Von Toll, who is a ventriloquist, he made some bird chirruping in his handkerchief & the dog jumped about & tried the reach it. Then he went away, and imitated some cats in an area, and Hector barked again, & kicked up such a row. When he made a big dog, Hector put his tail between his legs, & ran away. This was the greatest compliment to his skill he could possibly have paid to him.

Sunday 18th

Went to Woburn Place. W church, dined with Emma & Albert, the latter has a rheumatic attack.

Monday 19th

Took my carpet bag to 51, dressed there, and then went down by boat to Greenwich by myself, that lazy fellow Alfred, taking it quietly in the country all this time. I got there punctually at the time, & found only Robert Haines arrived; it seems he wants to get an army situation, & Anna Moline says her greatest wish is for Robert to wear a moustache. The company consisted of

Anna, Agnes, Ellen, Susan, Frank & Louis Moline, 2 Miss Pontifix, 2 Misses B---, a tall young man and his sister, Mr. Haines, Walter [Bagehot], a Mr. Day & myself. Most of the people went early, but I stayed & just missed the last omnibus so I stopped a little longer had some more dances, & walked home. Got home at 3¼. Very jolly altogether.

Tuesday 20th June 1848

Met Hancock at Covent Garden went for a long walk with him & into the lobby of the House of Commons.

Wednesday 21st June

Dined at Billingsgate with Tegetmeir & went up the river to Chelsea. I walked back & found Alfred had arrived & was rather tired.

Thursday 22nd June 1848

Alfred & I took a boat and went down to Blackwall, where we strolled about & I took him over the Alfred, she is in dock now & dismasted.

Friday 23rd

Called at Woburn Place & found the young people returned but not my aunt. Jem about the same.

Saturday 24th June

I ran down to Greenwich today as I had promised to take a walk with Frank, & I had heard they expected me. I found all the young ones at home but Ellen. We had some chess, & a good deal of laughing & fun, & I returned & 10-1/2.

Sunday 25th June

Alfred did not feel the thing at all today, so we took a walk, & after some time, found ourselves at Gravesend. We saw several sea steamers come in, & one landed a number of troops. We saw also a number of horses landed from an Ostend boat.

Monday 26th June 1848

Forget what we did today but recollect clearly having a glass of ginger beer with Alfred near G. Inn Lane.

Tuesday 27th

Called at Woburn Place, they all leave tomorrow for Lea near Blackheath. James about the same.

Wednesday 28th

I went up to Holloway in the afternoon with Mr. Primet to see a cricket match between Holloway & Queens College, in which Holloway beat.

Thursday 29th

I got an octagonal piece of deal, & made a stand for my hookah covering it with velvet & ornamenting it with gold thread.

Friday 30th

Took a walk with Alfred, & had the most delicious glass of ginger beer inconceivably splendid.

Saturday 1st July

Left here at 8 o'clock & worked all day, going without dinner, & got home at 11, rather tired. However we got all our balances right & if I go early on Monday I shall get it up close.

Sunday 2nd July 1848

Alfd & I went down to Twickenham today, we met Ellen & Graham walking out so we turned back & walked until dinnertime. There was an ancient lady, Mrs Fussell who knew Papa some 60 years ago, & an old maid very acute as to nose, who gave herself out to be 20. She made a squash & put it away to eat at tea. Ellen & G found it out, & put an immense lot of cayenne pepper & salt in it. She ate it out of spite tho' she coughed all the time. We found a splendid seat on the top of a weeping larch, & had some fruit there. Returned via rail & omnibus.

There were Fussells living in Bristol when Alfred, John Prior's father, would have been there.

Monday 3rd July 1848

Called on White at Mr Clare's, & saw Mr, Mrs & Miss Clare, I wonder if she is to be Mrs White.

Tuesday 4th July 1848

As usual very busy today, & shall be more so tomorrow. Felt out of sorts today & an inward pain in the stomach from climbing the tree at Twickenham—hope only a bruise. Bought 16 prints for 2s " The Bottle" & " Drunkard's Children" by Cruikshank. Put the crowning touch to my hookah in the shape of a covering for the snake. Mr. Aiken paid us a visit from Bristol.

May be Mr. Peter Aiken owner of a cotton factory in Bristol.

George Cruikshank, caricaturist and illustrator (of Charles Dickens'
Sketches by Boz and Oliver Twist) produced two narrative series
of prints that were morality tales advocating temperance. The
Bottle (1847) and The Drunkard's Children. A Sequel to The Bottle
(1848) were a series of prints reproduced from etchings by means of
"glyphography," an inexpensive form of graphic reproduction.

Thursday 6th July

Received a note from Frank Moline asking me to go down there to play cricket, so I called for White, but found he had gone into Herfordshire for some days.

Friday 7th

Went to Greenwich by myself, & found Mr. Thompson there: we all went up on Blackheath & played cricket. Emily, Susan & Mr Moline came up for a short time. Edy, Con and Albert came over in the evening so we had quite a party. We were too late for the last train, and were obliged to take the omnibus, Mr. Thompson got out at the Old Kent Road & I walked with Charles to Finsbury & thence home.

Saturday 8th July 1848

We were invited to go to Lea this evening, but because it rained in the day Alfred would not go, although it turned out a very fine evening with blue sky & no rain, in fact it stopped raining at 5-20 & we were not to go till 7. Very provoking. I would have gone by myself if I had felt certain of its being so fine. They had a fine evening there, & danced on the green & were very jolly.

Sunday 9th July 1848

This has been the worst Sunday as regards weather we have had this year. We went to St Andrews in the evening as it held up a little.

Monday 10th

I had a visit from Frank Moline at the office, who asked us to go down there this evening so I told Alfred, & at 5 he came across but had to go home first and dress, so I waited for him till ½ past & then went down. We found they were gone on the heath, & so went up there, but did not find them, so we strolled on to Lea and saw Aunt P & the Dr who told us Con & Edy were up there, so we walked back, & found them at last. We, and Edy, Susan M & the men, went to G. & R. Haines, Anna & Con went to Lea. We came back with Chas Moline.

Wednesday 12th July

Went down to Greenwich, & had a bathe with Louis Moline, saw none of the family but him. Bathed in the Ravensbourne.

The Ravensbourne flowed to join the Thames at Greenwich and the latter stages seemed industrialized in 1837 maps.

Sketch of swimming in the Ravensbourne from John Prior Estlin's diary.

Thursday 13th

Saw White, who has been ill, & who had a blister on at the time; he fell down fainting this morning as he was getting up, & so, I suppose to strengthen him, put on a blister. He has taken the school at Turnham Green.

Saturday 15th July 1848

We went down to Greenwich, called at Nelson St, & walked up with them to Lea. Had a good game of cricket in the field behind the house, & afterwards a game of prisoner's base with the ladies viz Edy, Susan & Emily Moline. I found when I

Sketch from J.P. Estlin's diary for July 15th.

arrived at Greenwich I had left my handkerchief behind, & so was obliged to buy one, for which I paid 1/9.

Sunday 16th July

We walked to Waterloo Bridge, & took the 1-15 train to Richmond where we wandered about the park until 6. The Park is 8 miles round, & is very pretty; indeed the parts least frequented being the most beautiful. We took 6d of buns with us, but had nothing more to eat till we got home at 10. We saw a body taken up at Waterloo Bridge. Some poor victim of self-destruction probably.

Monday 17th July

Alfred went off today on an excursion of business to Herford, & thence to Crediton by Exeter, & is to return on Wednesday. Went to Billingsgate, & bought a lot of shrimps for tea, & saw an immense lot of pineapples just come in.

Tuesday 18th July

Went home with Mr. Primet and had some wirtleberry pie & cream, both from Somersetshire. On dit. Robert Haines has got his appointment and is going to be married soon, & go out in the Autumn Emily most probably accompanying him. The Irish are beginning to break out, having broken in a prison or two.

Thursday 20th July 1848

Went up with Primet by 3d boat to Putney to see the races. Mr. Sawtell hindered us for some time so that we were very late, but we saw 2 or 3. The river looked very pretty covered completely with boats. We saw a steamboat with its paddle knocked in and a lighter barge sunk in the middle of the river. I saw one of the wager boats upset & immerse 2 fellows. One eight oared cutter is 50 feet long. I saw one which must have been considerably more. We fell in with Charles Luce. He is rather a jolly person fond of good living and a joke.

These barges were known as lighters because they would draw up next to a ship and take off goods to lighten the load. Lighters were large vessels with no motor or sail. They were moved by the force of the tide. The lighter man merely steered the barge using enormously long oars.

Friday 21 July 1848

Went with Tegetmeir to the Public Baths at Euston SQr, & had a delightful warm bath.

Saturday 22ⁿᵈ

Received a note from White asking me to buy him a watch, & not to go much beyond £2. After work I went down Fenchurch St round Aldgate Pump, up Leadenhall St, Cornhill, Poultry Cheapside St. Paul's Churchyard, Ludgate Hill, Farrington St. Fleet St., & Strand, looking into all the watchmakers' windows, and calling at some, taking notes all the way. I looked into 30 odd windows, & at last fixed on one for £2-2, in 58 Fleet St which I bought, & left my own to be cleaned. I then walked to Marbledon Pl, left the watch, and a note for White, & came home.

Sunday 23ʳᵈ July 1848

A most beautiful morning: Alfred & I walked down to London Bridge, and went by boat to Blackwall. There we saw the Alfred & Monarch all done up. The Monarch ready for sea (she goes to Gravesend tomorrow), & the Alfred fitted up, but without ballast, or cargo. Ten days ago she had not a mast, or rope, on board. We then went to Gravesend by the Brunswick, it of course, came on to rain about 6 o'clock, & we came back in it. The Agincourt, 1,000 tons, was lying off Gravesend. Coming back an old man of 45 would jump about to the polka tunes in the rain, when the water was an inch deep on deck, & consequently wetted himself thoroughly, & drenched us. We saw a young lady whose upper face was perfectly beautiful, her nose & mouth not being so good spoilt a most lovely face.

John Prior's sketch in his diary-one of the ships at Blackwall.

This last week has been without any facts worth recording, more than the Irish Rebellion. Smith O'Brien is at the head of some thousand men, & is dressed in green & gold. He is outlawed, & has a reward of £500 offered for him. I dined today at Billingsgate with Tegetmeir. After dinner, we sat outside on the balcony looking at the shipping, & I left my umberella [sic] on the table; while we were outside a man came in & cabbaged it, & sold it to a French Captain of a smack who was off while we were there.

From the 23rd to the 29th of July 1848, O'Brien, Meagher and Dillon raised the standard of revolt as they traveled from County Wexford through County Kilkenny and into County Tipparary. The last great gathering of Young Ireland leaders took place in the village of The Commons on July 28. The next day, O'Brien was in The Commons where barricades had been erected to prevent his arrest. His local supporters—miners, tradesmen and small tenant farmers—awaited the arrival of the military and police.

Chapter 12
Outings and Alfred

Sunday 30th

We went to Twickenham today via rail from Waterloo Bridge. We had a boat, & rowed up above Teddington, & had a splendid bathe. We came home, made a tremendous dinner, & took a walk to Strawberry Hill with Ellen.

The Walpole family owned the gothic castle Strawberry Hill. In 1846, Frances inherited Strawberry Hill. Then, in 1847, she married the elderly Liberal MP, G.G. Harcourt, and became a leading Liberal hostess. In 1855, she decided to restore Strawberry Hill and turned it into a place for the great political receptions of the time.

Monday

Had a note from Jno Noon saying he had gone to Queenswood in Stockbridge, Hants.

Tuesday 1st *August 1848*

It rained tremendously in showers, most of the day, but at Greenwich it was finer. Anna Moline was married to Robert Haines today by Con in Lea church, from the Dr's house at Lea. Agnes, Ellen, Susan, & Emily Moline Edy & Miss --- were Bridesmaids, & all dressed in white. It all went off as these things usually do, except that the Bride would have a quadrille before she left. They went to Warwick for the tour. We dressed as usual in the City, & went by rail taking our boots in a bag, which was of immense advantage, as it turned out, & got there (being obliged to walk from the Terminus) just after they sat down to Dinner/tea/supper a nondescript meal. Soon after, the dancing commenced. The schoolroom was lit up, & evergreens put against the walls, & all was decorated with flowers evidently the work of skilful women's fingers. We did not keep it up half long enough, but broke up at ½ past eleven. We imagined it would have been later & so stayed after the last train, which obliged us to walk home, which we did after changing our boots again.

Wednesday 2nd Aug^t

Wednesday 2nd Aug^t

I took a "bus' to Turnham Green this afternoon & called on White. His house is larger, & better than I expected, & I think there is every prospect of his getting a good school there. His sister Elizabeth is with him. A very nice little body & rather pretty, who takes the honors of housekeeping. I slept there.

Some 20 years later, J. P. Estlin sends his two boys to White's School. Turnham Green is a public park situated on Chiswick High Road, Chiswick London. It is separated in two by a small road. Christ Church (1843) stands on the eastern half of the green. On the south side is the old Chiswick Town Hall.

Thursday

Thursday

Breakfasted with White & his sister, & came to town in the omnibus.

Friday 4th Aug^t

Friday 4th Aug^t

A very busy day. Met Bacchus at Cecil St & took him to pay a visit to White whom we found with a couple of architects making improvements. Had some grog, & came home.

Saturday 5th Aug^t

Saturday 5th Aug^t

Met Bacchus at the Docks went with him, Meridith & Daniels to the Sailor's Home in the carriage, dined there, & came up in the evening half price to the Olympic, saw Monsieur Jaques & some other thing. Alfred was at Woburn Place.

Sketch of Bacchus in his sailor's uniform from John Prior's diary.

Sunday 6th Aug^t

Sunday 6th Aug^t

At 4 o'clock this morning I was rather startled by Alfred's rushing into my bedroom shouting "Get me some brandy, something has given way in my heart & I'm dying." So out I turned, waked the women, he going straight into their room, & walked him downstairs, we were some time finding the brandy, during which he was jumping about and not knowing what he did. I sent the servant for Mr. Bridges, but she mistook it for Dr. Prichard & went there one of the others going for Mr. B., during which time he was running about half wild, when suddenly he came along the passage with a glass of brandy in his hand saying to Miss S. "go for a doctor yourself", then he stopped short, held up his hands, let the glass fall and staggering backwards would have fallen had I not caught him in my arms, when to my horror he turned as stiff as a log of wood, so much so that when I laid his head on my knees his heels touched the ground and no other part. He then was seized with convulsions, foamed at the mouth and kicked in the same manner a dying rabbit does, this in a few minutes subsided, & he opened his eyes with a wide vacant stare, pushed me off, played with his nightshirt & trousers (all either of us had on) punched me hard in the side, got up, and began beating me with his fists, knocking me down, and not saying one word but grinding his teeth in a most frightful way. I, at last, got him into a corner, & clenched his wrists which I held till they brought a man to help. He knocked the man down, & cut his nose open against the fender, upsetting the fire irons, breaking a chair in two and knocking the table to the other side of the room; then he dragged us both through the passage, down 2 steps & to the back door where I again got him in a corner.

He looked vacantly at the latch, but seeming to despair his head dropped heavily on my shoulder & I carried him into the parlour, & made him drink some more brandy. He then opened the window himself & lay down. In the struggle he had trod on the wine glass, & cut his foot, & he played with my foot with his toes making the blood ooze out at each movement still not speaking a word. Just then Mr. Bridges came and ordered a mustard plaster, which greatly revived him. He asked him his age, profession, whether married, to all of which he answered, "I don't know". By this time the Dr. had arrived, & I carried & helped him up to bed, where having had some ether & other medicine he felt much better. During the day, he improved much, but I did not leave his bedside till the evening or rather morning at 2 o'clock.

It is unlikely that this attack was one of mental illness as it appears not to have happened before and does not happen again—at least during John Prior's diary keeping. As the reader will see Alfred recovers, and later continues his studies, practising law in Somerton for many years. Holding such a position would be difficult with mental illness. It is possible that Alfred had a case of botulism since convulsions are part of the symptoms. It is also possible that he ate poisonous mushrooms or fish while dining out that brought on halucinations.

Wednesday 9th Augt

Alfred has got better up to this time, but still frightens himself very much, which keeps him back. He was well enough to spare me, so I went and dined with the officers of the Alfred who sail tomorrow morning. I came up to town with Woolgrove & left him at his cousins. I then called at Chas Moline's but he was from home. I got back at 10 & put Alfred to bed.

Thursday 10th Augt

I got up this morning at 5 o'clock, and walked down to Fenchurch St, but found the Blackwall trains did not run till 8 so I toddled on to the East India Docks on foot, about 8 miles in all. I passed the City Proof House while they were proving a lot of muskets. They fire them in threes so that if any one hangs fire, they may not come near till it is off. I found them very busy in the ship, and after having a jolly breakfast at the Sailor's Home, saw them off. They warped the ship into the lock by means of hawsers fixed on shore, & passed around the capstan. The sailors deferred till the last minute, & while the ship was moving out, there was a regular scramble, one man being left behind. The crowd was immense, & having given & received three hearty cheers, the steamtug towed them down the river. We waved our hats to each other as long as in sight, and then I went to the dull city while my heart was all the time with the splendid ship, & her gallant crew.

> *Proof is the compulsory and statutory testing of every new shotgun or other small arm before sale, to ensure so far as is practicable, its safety in the hands of the user. It involves the firing through the barrel of a considerably heavier load than is customary in the shooting field, thereby setting up pressure and stress on barrel and action much in excess of the pressure generated by standard load cartridges. Such pressure should, and is intended, to disclose weakness in guns, whether new or used. Proof was necessary to protect the public against the many unsound arms then being made and sold, which not only endangered the public but, indirectly brought discredit upon reputable gunmakers.*

Saturday 12th Aug[t]

Alfred better, I dined at Billingsgate and we 3 had a 4½-pound salmon & 5 large soles. We took a long walk and had 6d worth of Surrey a duel, assassination, & suicide.

Sunday 13th August 1848

The Dr. and Aunt Prichard called this morning, & soon after we went in a cab to Waterloo Bridge & thence to Twickenham. Mrs M. seemed very well, pleased that he [Alfred] should be there, & he thought he felt better already. Livingston Hastie called this morning. He is by no means improved and looks fast. I came up early & went around to Woburn Pl but they were all gone to bed although it was not eleven o'clock.

> *William Livingstone Hastie married in 1849 but died in 1851 at age 27. The use of the word fast in this case refers to irresponsible, or reckless behavior, especially refers to deceitful when it comes to women.*

Monday 14th Aug[t]

I promised Graham that I would try & get a holiday after 2, and go down with him to the Islesworth regatta, but as it was so awfully wet I did not think of it for a moment. I went to 17 Fish Street Hill to see if I could learn anything about Capt June, the man who bought my umberella [sic] and am to call there on Thursday next.

Tuesday 15th Aug[t]

I went tonight with Sherwood to the Principe's & saw M. Herrman perform some juggling tricks, which were very amusing, one in particular. A boy stands on a table near the wall, & is covered by a frame of wood, in a minute M. H. takes a gun, and fires at it knocking it over, and the boy comes in with the flash behind him. I also saw the suspending trick.

> *Principe's stood on the site of the Royal Circus, which opened on 4 Nov. 1782 and continued in use until 1810.... It was Richard Shepherd (who succeeded Alfred Bunn in 1848 and remained at the theatre until 1869) who established its reputation for rough-and-tumble melodrama.*

Wednesday 16th Augt 1848

I left the office at 3 'clock today & went with Graham to the Richmond regatta, we took a boat, & rowed about during the races. We saw 2, 8-oared, 2 pair-oared, & 2 scullers matches. It was very wet, & we were obliged to take shelter under the bridge part of the time. A 6-oared boat crew came back to town in the carriage with me, & most of them were drunk, one dropped his hat as the train was starting, & left it there, another lost his ticket, & they all sang & hallowed to an awful extent.

Thursday 17th

Took a walk with Harwood, & went home with him for an hour. His wife is at Bristol. The Nashes have taken him up again.

Friday 18th Augt

Went down with Graham, & 2 friends of his, & Tegetmeir to Billingsgate, and made a tremendous dinner. We had a game of bagetelle & bowles afterwards. It is very unsatisfactory for I won 5 games of bowles, and lost 2, and yet I had to pay 1/ & receive nil. I shall not go there again.

Bagatelle is an indoor table game related to billiards, the object of which is to get a number of balls (set at nine in the nineteenth century) past pins (which act as obstacles) into holes.

Chapter 13
Taking Leave

Saturday 19th Aug[t]

At dinnertime today I went down to Custom House stairs, & took a boat to be put on board the City of Boulogne where I saw Capt. June, to whom the man sold my umberella. He is a very jolly fellow, and let me have it again. Must be more careful of it in future.

Sunday 20th

I went to Twickenham today, and got there in time to breakfast. We went to church, & afterwards took a walk. After dinner we had a row, & met the Youngs on the water with whom we bathed. Returned in the evening by the train.

Tuesday 22nd

Stayner and his sister Eliza came up today, & I went to Mad. Tussaud's with them. It is worth seeing, & has a good band of 3 pianos, a harp & 2 violins.

This may be James Stayner of Illminister a stockholder and manager in Stuckey's Bank in 1850. He appeared to be a Trust Treasurer for Illminister for 1846. This incident is further evidence that John Prior was involved with banking at Illminster, prior to coming to London. Stuckey's bank also had a branch at Wells.

In 1835, Madame Tussaud ended her touring years, and set up her attraction on its first permanent site in London's Baker Street.

Thursday Aug[t] 24th

I went down in the evening to Greenwich, & found them very busy. I helped to paint a box & stay'd to dinner. Afterwards, the bride came in, & also Edy & Albert. They made me cut 24 handkerchiefs etc. I returned with the Prichards.

Saturday 26th Augt

As arranged, I walked out towards White's to meet him on the road; I overtook him (for he turned back) at Hammersmith, and played 7 games of chess with him all of which I won. When we were going to bed I saw on the wall a Cardinal, [Spider] the beast's legs stretched 5 inches or more and were thick & very hairy, his body about the size of a filbert and of a lightish brown color. I hit him with the poker & burst him, but after that he ran right across the kitchen until I settled his hash.

Sunday 27th Augt

I took a bus from White's to Twickenham, but found them at church. For further particulars see last Sunday.

Monday 28th Augt 1848

Alfred returned from Twickenham today but not for work. We went up to 7 Finsbury pavement and called on the "newly married couple". We found Anna up to her eyes in packing. She, however, found time to give us some cake & wine.

Tuesday 29th

We went down to take leave, & found at large party assembled at Greenwich. Alfred had promised to go up to Woburn Place so we went there, & did not stay at Greenwich. The Doctor ordered him to go into the country on Thursday.

Sketch from John Prior's diary for Tuesday 29th.

Wednesday 30th

Alfred got leave from his Superiors to go into the Country, so in the evening we packed up all his things in a most masterly style.

Thursday 1st Sept

I saw Alfred off at Paddington today, and got back at 11. It was a beautiful morning, but in the evening at 6 o'clock, we had some tremendous thunder & lightning.

Saturday 2nd Sept

I had promised White I would go over there tonight, but I found Mr & Mrs Clare were to be there so I wrote to tell him I could not go, & it was well I did for a tremendous billious headache came on, & I was obliged to go to bed, and resort to the usual remedies.

Sunday 3rd

Got up at 1 and after dinner went to Belitha Villas. Met John there & drank some wine. They are going to the Isle of Man next Saturday. Came home with John [possibly Senior].

Belitha Villas were built (c. 1845) in Ilslington as Italiante pairs.

Monday 4th

Hard days work. Packed up Alfred's remaining togs in a box to send him tomorrow.

Tuesday 5th Sept

William Sherwood came over from Jersey today. I like him very much from what little I have seen of him.

Wednesday 6th September 1848

I went this evening with Primet to a friend's, who is a clerk in the Southhampton Railway at Waterloo; we drank tea with him and then went to the Vauxhall which is reduced to 1d now. We heard some good singing and music. The Ethiopians with "Bones" & Juba who is an extraordinary dancer, exceedingly active, & kept up for an immense time. We walked all the way home.

Quote from the Illustrated London News, August 5th 1848: "The Negro Dance is a reality. The "Virginny Breakdown," or the "Alabama Kick-up," the "Tennessee Double-shuffle," or the "Louisiana Toe-and-Heel," we know to exist. If they did not, how could Juba enter into their wonderful complications so naturally? How could he tie his legs into such knots, and fling them about so recklessly, or make his feet twinkle until you lose sight of them altogether in his energy. The great Box immortalized him; and he deserved the glory thus conferred. www.londonancestor.com/iln/juba-vauxhall-gardens.htm

Thursday 7ᵗʰ

Went over to White's this evening, & won 6 out of 7 games of chess.

Saturday 9ᵗʰ

Took a walk with W. Sherwood, & in the evening he played at tricks with cards of which he knows a great number.

Monday 11ᵗʰ

Walked in the evening with Wm Sherwood, & called on a friend of his with whom we had some grog.

Wednesday 13ᵗʰ Septʳ 1848

I had a visit from White today, he had accomplished a feat for which I did not give him credit; he had broken the Thermom. I gave him.

Friday 15ᵗʰ Sept

Went with Wm Sherwood to the "Marrow bone " theatre & saw Mr. & Mrs. Keely.

Sunday 17ᵗʰ Septʳ

I walked with Sherwood to London Bridge at 8 to see him off by boat for Herne Bay, & finding it was an excursion day, I went with him. We breakfasted on board. I had a delicious bathe out of a boat, & a good dinner, & got home at 11.

Herne Bay was a newly created Victorian town. The town still displays its Victorian roots, particularly along the seafront, with the Clock Tower (erected in 1837), the sunken gardens (refurbished in recent years) and the bandstand next to the pier. The iron pier which replaced a wooden one, was laid low by a series of violent storms in the late 1970s. It was once the second longest pier in the country, after Southend in Essex. All that remains now are the Pavilion, attached to the land, and the pier head out to sea.

Tuesday 19ᵗʰ Sept

W. Sherwood went today with his patient. He brought him here, & he had six fits. After tea he always gets up & wipes his hands on his handkerchief & asks for a piece of paper with which he scrapes them.

Saturday 23rd Sept 1848

Nothing particular has occurred worthy of record. I went today by the 5 o'clock Bus to Turnham Green, & had some games of chess & crib: in the morning we took a 2d ride to Chelsea and then to London. I left him [assume White] at Hungerford Bridge, & went on to Greenwich, where I found them just at dinner, so I dined with them, & took a long walk after, & went to church. Had a chat at White's with a man who used to be a great deal with the Marquis of Waterford.

Monday 25th Sept 1848

Had a letter from Mr Tegetmeir stating that he will be back on Thursday which will enable me to go on the Saturday following.

Wednesday 27th

Had a letter from home saying I might ask Frank Moline into the country, so I dispatched a letter to him, telling him to come up here on Thursday evening, sleep in Alf'ds bed, and go on with me on Friday morning which I hope he will do. I walked up to Primet's, & got a hatbox to convey Alfds headpiece in, and called at Andrew's lodgings.

This completes John Prior Estlin's London diary.

Part III
Prairie Winds
1880–1911

Sharon M. Hope

The Boundary Commission Trail Map: Northern Boundary
Survey 1872-1876.
Source: www.mhs.mb.ca/docs/mb_history/19/
boundarycommissiontrail.shtml

Introduction

In Britain, a long period of depression starting well before 1881 and lack of employment contributed to English emigration that peaked in the 1880s. Many immigrants went to the United States. Canadian politicians became nervous watching the US immigrant tide moving west. Through Sir John A MacDonald and the Ministry of Agriculture, Canada launched an intense campaign to populate the west to insure sovereignty.

In 1881, immigrants responded to Canadian promotional materials and the assurance of free land registered for $10.00. By 1882, a stream of both British and experienced Ontario farmers were arriving in Manitoba to take up homesteads. Upper class gentlemen were not encouraged to come, whereas Canadian agents targeted lower class European farmers, used to a harsh life and hard work. Professionals such as shop keepers, and teachers were specifically asked not to come.

Following instructions from the government, the agents minimized the risk of frost, grasshoppers and gophers. They did not explain that soils of the Souris plains were less drought resistant based on the soil organic matter content, than those of the Red River Valley. The land was advertized as an agricultural paradise, with an invigorating climate and soil so fertile that crops sprang up. Agents stated that there was an inexhaustible source of hay, water and fuel. In southern Manitoba, it was true that some fuel aside from buffalo chips existed and that there were sloughs but no one mentioned the alkali water. According to the claims, supplies could be obtained easily in the nearby towns. In truth these towns were usually days away by ox cart. The concealment angered many settlers, who turned south to the United States.

As immigrants continued to arrive in southwestern Manitoba, Sir John A MacDonald determined that a land office was necessary and G. F. Newcomb was appointed. In 1881, the provincial boundaries expanded to take in the lands of the western Souris plain but on March 12th 1882 the government withdrew land in the Turtle Mountain District, placing most of it in railway reserves. This was particularly hard on those who were already crossing the country, with the expectation that land was available. The alternative for settlers was to take a chance and "squat" on railway land hoping that they would be allowed to stay.

Settlers that persevered lived on their land in tents until their houses could be raised. They planted crops as quickly as possible. Those that knew carpentry constructed their own furniture consisting of tables, chairs, and bureaus. It was not an easy life. One difficulty was the lack of eligible women. According to Norman Wright, at one time in the Brenda and Arthur municipalities there were 188 single men and only 25 single women. Distance to markets and product prices were also barriers to success. Men had to haul their crops to Brandon and then received low prices in many cases. When the railway finally arrived to Boisevain and Deloraine, these trips were shortened considerably but the price of wheat and freight charges continued as sources of contention.

In the 1870s, England living conditions were not always ideal. Some Somerset towns were not healthy or progressive. About 1880, there was sickness in Burnham and Highbridge due to contaminated water and sewage problems. Typhus, disordered stomachs, and ague frequently occurred.

The owner of Clarence House in Burnham, one of the leading seaside hotels down the road from the Estlins, complained that the smells were driving visitors away because sewage was draining directly onto the beach. Mrs. Dupuis, the wife of the local vicar and a good friend of the Estlin family, had the vicarage well analyzed. When she found it contaminated, she arranged for water to come from a spring at Brent Knoll.

Burnham on the Sea, where John Prior Estlin settled, had little paving and attempts to build a full esplanade were slow because the owners of the seaside properties were given the responsibility for construction. The roads were muddy in winter, dusty in summer; when John Prior arrived the town council was still naming the streets. In 1876, there were only two gas street lamps in Burnham. It was pitch-black at night even in relatively good weather.

Although trade was driving most of the town's growth, Burnham was slowly becoming a holiday destination; there were donkeys to ride on the sandy beach where one could swim and the bandstand and park were starting to have entertainments.

The Estlins lived a typical Victorian domestic life where having 5-6 children was common. Like most families, they embraced the concept that one strived for success through hard work, and that one had community and family obligations. The Victorian man believed it was his role to be the provider and breadwinner. Failure or reverses in business were serious because they struck down this image. Fathers were usually strict but gave a series of gifts at Christmas, birthdays and other special occasions. They insured that the children, particularly the sons, had skills to provide properly for their own families in due course and achieve independence.

Mothers ran the household and represented the moral compass in the family. Usually Victorian children saw little of their parents but the Estlin family was an exception because the children spent time with Prior and Emily. The Estlin children declared that they were close to their parents, but it is difficult to know if present day family ties would be equal to their own. The Estlins had a cook at least (whose last name was Hooper) and a general servant. This was probably slightly less than the typical number of servants for their position in society.

Victorian leisure experiences were visiting, sewing (for women), walks, boating, bicycling, music, scrapbooks and dancing. The Estlins indulged in many of these pastimes. Except for being a closer-knit family and well educated, the Estlins were very typical of middle class English immigrants. We encounter John Prior and his family about 17 years after the completion of his London Diary.

Chapter 1
English Life

John Prior Estlin established two offices in the brick and tile business; one in Highbridge and the other in Burnham, Somerset. Financial pressures began almost immediately after his marriage because he wanted to provide properly for his wife, Emily. Her family, the Goodlands, were prominent in Taunton and doing well in the coal shipping business. Prior, who loved Emily dearly, knew she was accustomed to a comfortable lifestyle.

By the late 1870s, the family consisted of three boys and two girls. Emily Maude or Birdie was the eldest child, a kind, nurturing soul by all accounts. When Alfred came along next, he was named after his uncle and grandfather. The Estlins commissioned a pastel portrait of Alfred as a small boy. He was playing with a ball, his hazel eyes looking slightly upward, and his brown hair quite long. He wore a dress, which was customary.

After Alfred's appearance, Charlie was next, a steady, reliable fellow like Birdie. Euty, the youngest brother, claimed that Charlie appeared naked as a child one Sunday morning, on the wall that separated the adjacent yard from the Burnham churchyard just as the church service finished. He was severely punished. Charlie, it seems, wasn't a perfect angel.

Euty was clever, a bit of a storyteller, and a good musician but he didn't always realize the potential of various ventures he launched. When he was younger, he lost things and daydreamt to the point his brothers and sisters teased him.

When Mary Katharine or May, the youngest arrived unexpectedly, she got quite a bit of attention. After all, the rest *"were virtually grown up when I was born."* [1] May always had a strong will and exercised it; perhaps Prior doted on her for that reason or because she was the last child but May confessed that she was his favorite.

The family moved frequently, always renting good-sized estates that gave them space for the children. The estates that Alfy and Euty remembered best had "splendid views of the ocean and ships..." One had *"a cobbled backyard that led to the servants' rooms, and the kitchen—it also had a large kitchen garden with a high wall."* Alfy the eldest boy recalled that *"... Besides the garden, the property had a lot of meadowland, a piece of rabbit warren, and a pond well stocked with fish on which a large flock of ducks and geese flourished. We also kept a flock of chickens, a couple of cows, a few pigs, and a pony and trap as we were two miles from Town."* [2,3]

At first, the Estlins lived outside Burnham in places like Edithmead that consisted of a few houses, and then in Brent Knoll, a slightly larger hamlet. These locations had fresh air, cheaper rents, and the opportunity to grow fruit and vegetables. It was the healthy country living that Prior loved but eventually they moved to town. Tregunter House, the Estlin home next to the

Current photo of Tregunter, Burnham, Somerset. Marine House in far background.
Source: Sharon Hope – Photo sent from Somerset

churchyard in Burnham, had polluted water because the graves next door were only four feet deep. The drainage from Tregunter went straight into a ditch combined with that of other cottages who shared privies.

Prior had many interests ranging from natural history, mechanics, and agriculture, to politics, sea going vessels and public health. A well-educated fellow and skillful with all kinds of tools, he became an excellent shot as well as a keen sportsman.

The Colony, Burnham as it was when the Estlin family lived there. Emily Estlin in foreground.
Source: Estlin family collection, Sharon Hope

He was accused of shooting a neighbour's cat when the family lived at a place called the Colony. The cat was bothering the chickens and the enraged owner next door took the execution of his cat to the police. However the neighbour could not gather sufficient evidence to have the police take action, so he posted rewards of sizable amounts to have information about the matter brought to him. He thought that by making the incident public, Prior would be shamed into a confession but he very wisely never responded. Since no one in Burnham would help the man by supplying information, he received neither compensation nor retribution.

Eventually Prior became *"Commanding Officer of the 4th Somerset Rifle Volunteers. ...I* [Alfy] *also joined as soon as I was old enough and...won the rank of Lance-Corporal and the crossed rifles—the Marksman's badge."* [2]

The Volunteers had exercises, practices and various dinners. In addition to his military pursuits, Prior enjoyed the theatre, and entertainments. Although he did not engage in these latter activities as rigorously after his marriage, he still wrote letters to the local papers, poems, and participated in a few social events. He joined the Burnham Amateur Rowing Club and eventually became Chairman of the Board of Health. Prior was friendly with the Chadwick and the Board families in Burnham; the heads of these families were both advocates of public health.

Burnham Militia Muster. *Source:* Estlin family collection, Sharon Hope

Above all, Prior was a meticulous recorder. He began a scrapbook in which to keep his published letters and other newspaper clippings. In this book, he noted such details as his weight annually and subsequently wrote down the weight of his wife and each child as it arrived. Although it is doubtful that Emily wished her weight recorded for posterity, science won out and there it is. He continued these types of records over many years documenting among other things, daily rainfall for Burnham and the yearly expenses for each child.

"My youngest brother [Euty] *and I* [Alfy] *inherited his mechanical ability; ...our workshop...contained a turning lathe and all the necessary carpentry tools which we learned to use under our father's tutelage...."* [2]

Charlie on the other hand, had his father's eye for detail, organization and record keeping. All the children played an instrument, sang and/or acted in amateur theatricals from time to time, except, perhaps Charlie. The whole family loved literature and read a good deal. As you might imagine, they had a happy, lively life.

Except for May who was too young, they attended boarding schools. The Estlins for generations believed in quality education for both girls and boys. Professional and upper middle class families sent their children away to school, but traditionally only boys received full education. Birdie and Alfy went to a school in Lancastershire at Salford. One of the Chadwick girls near Birdie's age was an assistant there. Alfy remembered distinguishing himself by fixing a plumbing problem for Mrs. Moore, the head, at age 11, and she offered him a shilling much to his surprise. Birdie and Alfy were keen on skating at school during the winter.

Euty and Charlie first went to a school in Bristol run by a Dr. Hargrave, who was a Unitarian minister. Euty gleefully reported that he observed men climbing into the servant's window of the Prichard's house next door at night and that image seemed to be a much stronger memory than what he learned. Adults who finally received this information were shocked by the incident.

Estlin school photo – note the man in clerical collar.
Source: Estlin family collection, Sharon Hope

Later Charlie and Euty went to Cheswick School near Hammersmith where Euty trapped rats that frequented the place. Euty, who declared he was the youngest student in the history of the school, suffered from stomach disorders. When he was forced to get up at night and make his way to the lavatory in the basement, he had to avoid a large dog tethered to a newel post at the bottom of the stairs on the main floor. According to his description, he had some fine scars on his legs from passing by. The headmaster was a Mr. White, an old friend of Prior's who saw a lot of him in London when he was working there.

Although Prior liked animals and took pride in his garden, his first concern was the family. He took a great interest in all the children, writing to them while they boarded at school, or when they visited relatives. When he travelled away on business he always wrote his wife. No item was too small if he thought the children had an interest. He jotted the match scores down on a postcard for Charlie after he went to work in Brentford and asked after his nosebleeds; he sent hampers of apples to the children at school. He described May's 6th birthday party of little ones as "[a] *Magic Lantern show and buns.... Sundry dolls and presents for the dolls house but I think she likes the books the best...."* [4]

Baby May provided many amusing anecdotes. Emily wrote: *"We have some trouble with baby May—she will dig in the parsley bed for a baby boy most obstinately, Today she pulled up some radishes which were old and cankered so when she came* [in] *she gravely said, 'I'm afraid my little brother will be worm eaten'..."* [5]

May rode donkeys on the sandy beach a short distance away from the house, saved her money for skates and thoroughly enjoyed life.

"Living as we did by the sea, boat building was our chief boyish interest." [2] In the spring of 1880, Prior, Euty and Alfy built a 20-foot boat called the Foam that they enjoyed very much. On August 7th, Mockridge, the brickyard foreman, Prior and Alfy took the boat from Uphill to bring her

Current photo of Marine House, Burnham with the Round Tower just visible; church behind.
Source: Sharon Hope–Photo sent from Somerset

over to Burnham, and were driven to Portishead by a gale that blew so hard the spray went right over Marine House Round tower where they lived.

The bathing machines on the Burnham shore were broken or run right into the sand dunes. In the same gale the lifeboat went out to save a crew of seven from the schooner Brune. The family stayed up all night worrying about the three, until Euty finally had to go to Uphill to find out what had happened. Prior and Alfy sent a telegram when they could, but somehow it didn't reach Burnham. The three of them went without food for 14 hours, lost the mizzenmast, and had an injury to the rudder. A steamer passed close by, but didn't respond to their signal for help. A passing Gloucester pilot in the Sarah took them off, although they still had difficulties because the towrope broke several times. The pilot was commended for his bravery at the town hall. At the ceremony, Captain Smith the pilot, broke down and couldn't say anything, but they had a splendid reception with rockets after. A piece appeared in the local paper and the trio had a picture taken.

Left to right: Mockridge, brickyard foreman, John Prior Estlin, and Alfred B. Estlin. *Source:* Estlin family collection, Sharon Hope

On leaving school, Alfy entered the brickyard business. Since trade was slow, they decided to sell the second office at Highbridge. Through connections, Charlie secured a position as a clerk in Brentford quite close to Hammersmith and his former school. He began work there in February 1880. Since he was the first to break away from the family, his mother instructed him on appropriate behaviour with annoying frequency. There was a flurry of letter writing as he took up his position, with messages about Prior's health and the business. Emily wrote: *"I am very glad you have comfortable lodgings...I hope you won't find the pickles and jam have run over everything...Papa is rather stronger but he won't gain much strength until this business is settled.... [however] there is nothing settled at Highbridge ... Papa has four offers of a thousand...don't let Fred lead you into dissipation...."* [5]

There were numerous pubs in Brentford and Emily may have become aware of this. In June 1880 she wrote: *"...hope you do not exceed two glasses of porter a day...."* [5]

Charles Prior Estlin, age 19.
Source: Estlin family photo collection, Sharon Hope

Prior didn't bother with admonitions. *"...I wish someone would stand us as I would like to see you in...bachelors lodgings [rather than boarding] but tin is no new thing...Nothing has turned up for Euty yet and we are trying in all directions...he must go somewhere as he is doing harm to himself here ...."* [4]

In May of that year, there was little more to report except that trade was still slack. Alfy gave a speech at the Rifle dinner and Euty's rats, that he persisted in keeping, had young. In July, Prior commented in his letters that if he were not so short of cash, he would go and hunt up some of his tile customers. It might *"...do me more good in body and I hope in pocket..."* [4]

Like most Burnham families, the Estlins took holidays in places like Dunster, a sleepy little hamlet in the Somerset countryside. When they vacationed for a prolonged period, they sublet the house in Burnham. Since the town was becoming holiday place, there was an opportunity to make some money rather than leave the house empty. At first Dunster seemed fine. Emily, known as the Mater to the children, went up in the third week in August 1880 to look at lodgings. The town, which lay in a valley but surrounded by high hills, was beautiful with many walks. Euty and Alfy went for a time. Prior, who stayed for a week, went to Washford to fish. Birdie, May, Emily and Prior walked over to Minehead about three and one half miles, and came back by train. They took May to the museum where she developed a fear of a mummy and a stuffed wolf. According to Birdie, Emily toddled up and down the hills at an amazing rate. Prior went back again in the fall from Burnham, but by October circumstances changed. His health was poorly again, and he had to stay in bed. The weather was diabolical, the chimney smoked and the cooking was dirty. Prior did recover the use of his legs, however.

As Prior's health declined, Birdie often acted as a surrogate parent sending hampers to Charlie at Brentford, and inquiring about getting his boots made. It was Birdie who told Charlie that Baby May had fallen on the front steps, and almost bitten her tongue through.

That autumn, Emily wrote to Charlie that she thought Papa's legs didn't swell as much, but the weather was against him; Birdie also reported in October that Papa was very poorly, but now better. Prior still took an interest in Council affairs, and was chairman of the Liberal Association.

During the year, Charlie, in particular, began spreading his wings. He went to a fancy dress ball in early February 1880 in Burnham at the Troods, family friends, and danced until 6 am; he went to the Pavilion from Brentford until 3 am and played football at Turnham several times. He met his pal Fred Chadwick who went with him to the Alhambra, and the Gaiety. Before starting work, Charlie managed to see Buckingham Palace and the Prince and Princess of Wales, as well as the Lyceum; just after he started work he dined with his former schoolmaster Mr. White. Much of his nightlife he did not divulge to his mother or even to his brothers and sisters until many years later. After not coming down at Easter, he did his family duty coming down to Burnham later. When he did, Euty asked how his girl was.

Euty, who was sailing a small punt he'd worked on around the brickyard ponds, also had an interest in girls. Alfy noted in a February letter to Charlie that Euty had been courting all day. He went to a dance later in the year in a pair of Charlie's trousers, and a tailcoat lent by their family friend Mrs Chadwick. Alfy commented that many of his old flames also turned up at this dance, which he said was a bit embarrassing.

Birdie was the only one of the siblings to have a formal understanding or engagement in England. The man's name was Harold Hayes Harker, a civil engineer, who was working with the Somerset and Dorset Railway. He planned to go to Brazil to work on the Railway there and after he settled, was going to send for Birdie. He expected it would be several years. Harold, who sang lustily in the choir, became Hon. Secretary to the New Somerset

Emily Maude Estlin and Harold Hayes Harker. *Source:* Estlin family collection, Sharon Hope

Liberal Association that Prior chaired. Harold first went to Essex to be godfather to one of his little nephews; later he went on to London to be with his family before he immigrated to Brazil. Prior mentioned to Charlie that he might run into Harold in London since he was there inspecting machinery that he expected to take out. Birdie and Harold continued to correspond after he left for London. She wrote to Charlie as well hoping that her brother would look Harold up. Prior remarked to Charlie in one of his letters that he might find HHH changed. Charlie, however, did not become a friend to Harold in London.

Chapter 2
The Crossing

The year 1881 did not bring any greater prosperity, or better luck to the family.

The quandary remained: *"What to do with the boys?"*[2] Everyone discussed it at great length, including uncles and aunts on both sides.

First it was suggested that Euty and Alfy leave for New Zealand where there was a cousin who could find positions for them. However Emily did not approve of having "the boys" so far from home. In those days there were few steamers, and the trip would have taken six weeks. She may have been afraid she would never see them again. The family hoped that Cousin Mary, Uncle John's daughter, who was fairly well off and took a great interest in them, might help Euty, or even that Charlie could help him.

Emily felt that Charlie deserved a raise by this time, and wanted to see if Mr Neill would be willing. For Euty and Alfy, nothing turned up. Prior even considered sending Euty to Telegraph School.

At this point fate intervened *"...the Glasgow Bank failed, which caused the suspension of the Bank with which my father did business."*[2] When faced with bankruptcy in the brickyard business, the family, except Charlie, who was secure in his position, decided to leave for Canada. The decision to go to Canada was prompted by several books and pamphlets that promised, among other things, viable farming in Manitoba. One book in particular called "Newfoundland to Manitoba" had an impact. On Sept 21st Mr. Board, Prior's solicitor held the first meeting with the Estlin's creditors at the George and Railway Hotel in Bristol. By that time the die was cast.

The Estlins busied themselves gathering all the things they thought they would need for a new life. *"As soon as the final decision was made we had a sale, disposing of most of our surplus belongings. ...We did not realize what a Canadian winter was, so the clothes we bought, although warm and serviceable, were not adequate for our needs."*[2]

They did acquire a good supply of blankets that proved invaluable. *"We took one small rifle, my father's double-barreled* [sic] *breach loader, a long barreled duck gun, and a revolver* [later referred to as the blue nosed revolver], *as well as all the ammunition we were allowed by regulation. We also took an ample supply of fishing tackle, which was of no earthly use on the prairie in those days."*[2]

Estlin family taken about 1878.

Back row, left to right: Emily Maude, Eustace Senior, Alfred Bagehot, Charles Prior.

Front row: John Prior, Mary Katharine, and Emily Estlin (nee Goodland).

Source: Estlin family collection, Sharon Hope

They took as many tools as they could, but these were very heavy, and the baggage weight was limited. Just before they left, they all went to the churchyard to visit the grave of the little brother who died nameless, only a day old. He fell between Birdie and Alfy. They didn't know when they would be back, if ever.

"We arrived safely in Liverpool, put up in a hotel and went to bed tired with all the preparations…. We were up early the next morning, seeing about our luggage, and looking over the docks filled with strange looking people from all over the world. Boats and ships were loading and unloading, busy little tugs running here and there…." [2] Having spent the day roaming about Liverpool, where they saw their first electric street lamp that sparkled evilly with a blue light, they finally went back to the hotel. Here the Estlin siblings joined their Mater and prepared to board the steamer, which was to sail at 9 pm.

J. P. Estlin, Emily, Birdie, Euty, May and Alfy boarded the Sardinian at Liverpool on Oct 13th 1881. Charlie saw them off from the pier. They took the Sardinian because the original ship that the family booked passage on, the Parisian, was "commandeered" by the Marquis and Marchioness of Dufferin. The Marquis had been appointed Governor General, and the couple required a ship for themselves and their retinue. The departure was delayed somewhat due to a workers strike because the crew did not wish to work on the 13th. As a result, there was no time to clean, or fumigate the vessel, because it was in a hurry to leave once the worker issues were settled.

The Estlins arrived at the vessel in good time, found their berths and deposited their luggage. The 4,349-ton Sardinian of the Allen Line was a smaller ship than the Parisian. It was about 400 feet long and 42 feet wide. The ship had both sail and a very noisy engine with a single funnel. New technology came into effect about this time to control pitching and rolling but no such technology existed on the Sardinian. The ship had provision for

The Sardinian.
www.theshipslist.com/pictures/
sardinian1874.htm

180 saloon, 60 intermediate, and 1000 steerage passengers. The family was accompanied, as it turned out, by a number of other immigrants including Russians who were traveling steerage. According to the advertisements for the Sardinian, the intermediate passenger berths were placed on the upper passenger deck, the steerage being located on the upper and second passenger decks; both classes were to be supplied with cooked victuals of the best quality.

The women's cabin was 16x20 with 16 bunks all around the four sides of the room and a long table in the middle where they had meals which were very poor. The food was mostly corned beef and rice pudding. Other passengers have described having up to 30 persons to a cabin on the Sardinian, so the Estlins had it better than some. The weather immediately became stormy, and most people were seasick into tins that hung on the sides of the bunks. Emily was not seasick but she had neuralgia.

"We boys and the Pater were good sailors, and enjoyed ourselves, getting acquainted with fellow passengers, and the ship's officers, and watching for passing ships...." [2]

They got to Derry the following night, where the ship took on a few passengers. *"All the time, however, the wind kept rising and the waves increased in height. This was made evident to us by the pitching and rolling of the vessels that passed us, and that we passed (our boat was so big that at first we hardly felt any motion), but we soon began to roll ourselves. By nightfall we were making pretty bad weather of it, so tumbled into our bunks and slept soundly. Breakfast next morning resembled an athletic competition more nearly than a meal. The dishes, which swung on chains from the saloon ceiling, had a habit of depositing their contents down your neck or into your lap, anywhere but into your plate. The plates were gyrating about the table on their own account, being kept from falling off by the raised edges, [which were] used only in heavy weather."* [2]

The next night, they *"...had an interesting time trying to keep in our bunks. When the ship rolled on her beam-ends, all loose items, including our boots, and clothes etc chased across the cabin floor, back and forth in a never-ending procession.*

"The steward of the men's cabin had a couple of upper bunks unoccupied, that he used to keep spare crockery in as well as the brackets that held it. These, of course, pitched across the cabin, landing in the occupied bunks on the opposite side, much to the annoyance of the occupants. My brother and I were, fortunately, not opposite the invading crockery, and found by putting our knees up and pushing with our hands against the bottom of the bunk above, we could keep from rolling out." [2]

When the covers on the ventilation shafts came off the women's cabin, the ship's carpenter eventually nailed canvas over them. Before he did, the cabin floor accumulated at least a foot of water. Birdie didn't find her shoes for a week because they were on the floor under water but she was too sick to need them. Several kennels sat beside women's cabin each with a large dog chained to it. The dogs, kennels and a lot of crockery all went to one side of the ship with frightful crashing noises. In the night when the storm was at its worst the stewardess for the women's cabin fetched the interpreter, a tall blue eyed Swede who looked embarrassed. A very stout lady in the next bunk but one climbed out backwards and rushed into the men's cabin next door to fetch her husband.

Despite the bad weather Euty maintained his father looked happier than he had in years. Euty felt Prior's heart had been broken by his business failure. The trip on the Sardinian, however was Heaven compared to what the family faced next.

Chapter 3
Point Edward

As the Estlin family neared Quebec, the width of the St Lawrence astonished them. Soon they could distinguish the shoreline, then hills, and finally, the little homesteads. Emily and Prior were in front when they disembarked to go to through Customs. As they moved along, a man grabbed Emily's earring but Euty grasped his wrist and pulled it away. They landed at Quebec on Sunday Oct. 24th and the train, which was drawn up by the dock, left about 12. Changing their money for dollars, the family procured food because there were no such amenities on board. According to Alfy, the carriages that they were packed into would not have been used for pigs in England. Officials called them Emigrant Cars. The cars had hard slatted seats, innocent of cushions, lining the outer edge of car and two people could sit in each seat. When the family protested the situation, stating that they were entitled to first class travel, those in charge told them this was the only accommodation available, so they had to make the best of it.

Alfy stated it was a great hardship for Emily and the girls *"…who were accustomed to all the comforts of an English home, to sit on those hard benches, night and day, among all kinds of people, with dirty, crying children running up and down incessantly."* [2]

Much of the country they passed through was burned over from brush fires, and not particularly attractive. The family spent 2 days and nights without a chance to lie down or wash. They stopped for a few minutes at refreshment stations; at other times they stopped an hour but could get nothing to eat. The Estlins had to take the steamer for Duluth at Sarnia, but they found, owing to the weather, no steamer would sail before Friday. While on the train, Prior seemed ill, shaking and shivering, so the conductor wired for a doctor to meet the train at Point Edward, a major transfer stop. Dr McLaren, who met them there, said they must get off because their father was very ill. There were no hospitals, so the family went to a hotel. They got a "rig" to transport him because, at that point, he was insensible, and couldn't stand. The Doctor advised them that Prior, who was extremely ill indeed, could not be moved. Dr McLaren gave Prior some 'physic', but as he was leaving, he called Euty and Alfy out, and told them that their father was going to die—the confinement and suffering in the cars had made his legs terribly bad, bringing on dropsy. The Doctor came 3 times that day, as well as once the following day. Nothing passed through Prior, who had a high fever. However, his temperature abated eventually, and he regained his body.

The family could not go on from Point Edward by steamer to Winnipeg because they had to provide their own beds and provisions. With this delay, the Estlins did not have enough money to do so, because they had wired money to Winnipeg. They were doubtful if they could get any more money until they arrived there. Alfy wrote to his uncle in England: *"We are in better spirits today, but I am afraid at the best it will be a long time before the Pater is well enough to be moved...we are 5 days and nights journey by rail from Winnipeg, and 8 or 9 by water...."* [6]

The country, which was very fine, had a neglected air and every place the Estlins visited seemed dirty. Point Edward, the Canadian railway terminus, was a town where many of the residents were employed by the railway itself. The village population, when they arrived, was about 2000. The town contained stores, sawmills and large immigration sheds.

Since there was no lodging house in Point Edward, the family continued to stay at the hotel. It was a little wooden building, where they had 3 rooms that were quite comfortable, as far as bodily wants were concerned. There were 3 meals, 6:30 breakfast, 12 dinner, and 6, tea or supper. They paid $3.50 a week each for board and lodging, but every meal they missed was taken out.

Euty, who got a job helping to build a house, received a dollar a day, which made him very proud. The entire family was anxious to get on to Winnipeg since the people in Point Edward thought it a Paradise, and labour was, they were told, very scarce indeed in that town. Alfy explored about trying to get some work in Point Edward, but did not meet with any initial success. Emily, Euty and Alfy had not been in a bed since they left the ship because they had to be within Prior's call. Since there was no bedroom nearby, Euty slept on 5 chairs and Alfy slept on the piano, which was a large one and quite comfortable.

While they waited for their father to get better, the boys tried to learn more about the Point Edward region. The residents caught fish by the ton there; the family could hardly believe it. Six men with a seine could catch six tons a day easily in Lake Huron. There were plentiful wild ducks but the boys couldn't get at their guns to shoot any. The country around was magnificent and the weather was like an English summer but cold at night. They were sure that they would like Canada when they got settled. The family was obliged to give Prior a bath of ice; one blessing was that they could get any amount of it for the asking. Milk was 2 1/2 d a quart and one could get ⅓lb of the best baccy for 5d and the best cigars for 2½d each. Coal was almost unknown; all the stoves and railway engines burned wood or lumber as people called it in Canada.

By November 2nd, Prior was slowly improving, but the family expected it would be a week or more before they could leave Point Edward. An abscess formed on his bad leg that the Doctor talked about lancing. *"One bright morning the family decided to take a walk, [so] I volunteered to stay with the patient. After chatting for a while, he went to sleep so I thought. But hearing him give a deep sigh, or gasp, I went over to prop him up. He died in my arms without speaking again. The doctor called it angina followed by ship's fever or typhoid."* [2]

Chapter 4
Moving On

It was the 12th of November, the Estlins were homeless strangers and Prior, their leader and guide, had been snatched from them. It was a dire situation, but the village residents were kindness itself. They took the family into their homes, and did everything possible to help. *"I have often heard it said that the Canadian people are the kindest, and most hospitable in the world, and we can vouchsafe the truth of this statement. From the time we landed until we settled on our farms, and long afterwards, we received the greatest kindness and most helpful advice that could possibly be given."* [2]

Meanwhile Charlie, on receiving a wire from his father about the safe landing at Quebec, went about his life in complete ignorance of the catastrophe. Aunt Clara asked Charlie if he had news, because she had seen from the papers that the ship had arrived safely. Several relatives invited Charlie to spend Christmas.

Now the family had the agony of contacting loved ones in England and the difficult process of making decisions, with no homesteading experience in rural Canada. When Charlie was first informed of his father's death, he wrote from Brentford saying that a telegram had reached Edward Bagehot, a relative looking after his father's affairs. It read: *"Father dead please inform friends."* [7] Charlie hoped it was all a mistake, but *"I saw too plainly that some dreadful change must have taken place…. If Alfy wants me to come out, I'll do my best to join you…."* [8] He went to Richmond to be with family for a few days, and later visited Burnham.

As soon as Charlie received a full account by letter, he replied that Mr. Sutton, his superior, was letting him stay away as long as he liked. Charlie wrote: *"… You cannot imagine how I long to be with you all as it was so dreadful to think… I should never be able see him again, although I see him so often waving to me from the Sardinian…. When we all strive together we shall be sure to succeed in the end…."* [9] When relatives and friends abroad heard, or suspected that the Estlin family had no funds, they responded. Much appreciated money, advice and condolences poured in from various parts of Britain and even from New Zealand. Edward Bagehot promised to help Charlie with clothes, and provide him with a ticket for the trip out to

Canada. Although Prior had insurance, and various relatives in England struggled to obtain it for Emily, it would be many months until that issue was resolved.

Prior had told the Doctor that he was a Mason. That proved one of the first pieces of good luck. The Masons helped immeasurably during the family's initial stay in Ontario. They took care of the funeral and burial expenses. Prior was buried in the Sarnia cemetery. The clergyman, incidentally, was a full-blooded Indian named Mr Bearfoot. Those in the Masonic Lodge advised the rest of the family to stay for at least the winter, so they rented a small cottage in Point Edward. The boys borrowed some tools, because their own had been checked as far as Winnipeg. These tools gave them the opportunity to make furniture. Alfy remembered that a particular chest of drawers that travelled out with them to Manitoba, served them well for many years.

The Masonic Society and Mr Treen, their next door neighbour, offered to find the boys work. Mrs Treen taught Birdie to keep house. The family had always had servants in England to cook and clean, so they were ignorant of many domestic matters, and their Mater, Emily, was not expected to take these chores on. Birdie, for example, had not kept household accounts before, but became expert as the years went by. She was still in touch with Harold Harker; her letters first went to Britain and then out again to Brazil. They were very costly indeed to send.

The Treens had two girls 13 and 8. The 8 year old became a good friend of May's. She spent a great deal of time at the Treen's house. May, who was seven when the family left England, felt her father's loss keenly because they had been close and shared a fondness for ships and the sea. Doctor McLaren also was very helpful, forever finding jobs or introducing the family members to people whom he thought it would be useful for them to know. When the neighbors found the boys could use carpentry tools, they got quite a lot of work that brought in welcome dollars.

One morning the Estlins did not get up at their usual time because it did not get light. *"As time went on, it became nine, ten and eleven o'clock. At that point we became uneasy so we dressed to go outside. It was as dark as night but no one knew why. Consternation reined supreme. Someone recalled Mother Shipton's prophesy that the world would end in 1881. Many people who accepted this explanation went into churches to pray or wandered the streets disconsolately. Some even forgot to go home for dinner. We were not among any of these groups. We simply accepted this phenomenon among the many that we had encountered since we left England."* [2]

When about 5 o'clock the family saw the sun struggling to shine through dense clouds of smoke, they found it was the coincidence of a total eclipse with the thick black smoke from bush fires in Michigan. The eclipse took place on Nov 21st according to the Farmers Almanac. The Michigan fire, called the Thumb fire, which started several months earlier, covered a million acres in all with the loss of 500–1000 lives. There were no agencies to fight the fire so it dragged on, reduced in activity.

The family all wrote as frequently as they could to Charlie—even Baby May: *"Sis flirts with the drugstore man. I have a nice little kitten with a white tip to its tail and its name is Spot Tail... The Doctor gave me little cup and saucr [sic] with remember me on it. I hope you enjoyed your veset [sic] to Burnham. Mama sends her love she hopes you are coming out to us soon."* [10] Charlie wrote back in early December saying that Edward Bagehot suggested March as the best time for him to come.

When Christmas came it wasn't as bleak for May, who was still a child, as it was perhaps for the rest of them. The church had a Christmas tree, and everyone in town must have sent her a present. Alfy advised Charlie at Christmas about the crossing. He gave any tidbits of news such as the fact the family had gone to Sarnia on Christmas Eve to look at the shops and to get dinner. *"Our Xmas was not very bright. Xmas is not kept up much—New Year's is the day. Gentlemen go and call on their lady friends where they have refreshments and generally come home as full as tics [sic]. Illustrated came all safe and we were charmed to have it. ...Take a few things to eat at odd times with you as I expect you will spew considerable. Birdie says lemons are good. ... get a top bunk.... Try to wear all the new things once or twice as they will charge duty on them if they have not been worn...."* [11]

The need for the boys to have good paying jobs to earn as much as they could, still hung like a sword over their heads. But even so Alfy asked Charlie why he couldn't leave before the middle of March. Alfy felt desperate to resolve their situation. He explained to Charlie that he was trying to get a job as timekeeper in Swifts Meat Packing plant in Chicago. He planned to board down there, but this job never materialized. In terms of the village life, Alfy enjoyed the lack of snow and the chance to go skating but the responsibility for the future of the family weighed heavily on him. He was the eldest son, but people like Edward Bagehot did not recognize his new role. He complained to Charlie regarding his arrival date: *"...I shall write to Mr. Bagehot myself shortly, but he will only write the Mater and does not answer my letters...."* [11]

The chief topic that winter was when Charlie would come, because when he did, Alfy could leave the girls and his mother in Charlie's care, and travel on to the prairies to find the land necessary on which to homestead. This seemed the most sensible plan when they consulted with their new friends. Despite the family wanting to be together, they recognized that Charlie could do more good by staying at his position in England, and earning what he could until spring. It would be shear folly to venture west in the winter though the family initially had wanted to do just that. They had, at that time, no sense of what the journey west would be like. Their new friends insisted that they proceed cautiously. The Estlins had no money to go back to England, and no future to return to. The decision had been made to make a new life in Canada.

Fortunately the family made an important ally who was going west in the spring, and who was patient enough to take the boys under his wing. It was Doctor McLaren who introduced the family to the Merlins, William and Annie who had a little girl.

Merlin, who was about 30 and from England, had a partner, Albert Latham, who was living in Emerson. Merlin wanted to go out there to buy his outfit and then move west to homestead. This was a wonderful chance for the boys to accompany him, and they gladly accepted the invitation to come along. It relieved their minds of much uncertainty.

On January 15th 1882, Alfred asked Charlie to bring the Engels bulldog revolver and a charcoal filter for Merlin as well as any seeds he could find. He also told Charlie that he could get 5–6 dozen oysters in Point Edward for a shilling. Charlie replied that they were to be sure to save him some because he would be there very soon.

In the country around Point Edward, there was quite a lot of bush so the boys supplemented the larder with the odd rabbit and partridge. *"One or two trips to the famous St. Clair flats, where the St Clair river joins Lake Huron, produced some wild ducks most of them species new to us; we only knew the mallard and the teal."* [2]

Alfy joked to Charlie that he and Euty were going to take lessons in butchering. Alfy became a rare hand at drawing, cleaning and dressing fowls, turkeys and rabbits. *"Euty who was always more interested in sea fishing than I, went poking along the shore of Lake Huron where he soon made the acquaintance of one of the chief fishermen, who often presented Euty with a 'mess' of fish which was most appreciated at the cottage....*

"We settled into the life of the town working at what ever we could get to do. One job was pumping the water out of a sailing vessel that had been laid up for months. We started at 7 o'clock in the morning. The pump was a big iron one made for four men so it was about a full load for green boys whose muscles were not accustomed to heavy manual labour. After we pumped

away for an hour or two, the man who employed us thought the pump should be oiled. We took a rest while he greased it. It certainly helped [the situation] quite a bit but it was such a grueling job that we were very tired by 10.30 when the man came back to inquire how we were doing. When we said the water did not seem to be going down very much, he replied, 'Oh that's alright. Come down below and get a lunch'. We accepted gladly, having a cup of coffee, captain's biscuit and cheese. This little break helped us immensely, so that we were able to go on pumping till dinnertime, when we got a good rest. After dinner we went back and finished the job by five o'clock.

"By that time we were aching in every joint. We decided then and there— we would not make pumping out bilge water our means of livelihood. We were paid $1.00 each for the job, considered good pay at the time." [2]

As time went on, the Estlins were accepted into Point Edward society. Euty, who was a talented musician, played several instruments, and Alfy could play the violin. Birdie, who like the rest of the family was fond of theatricals, was quite an accomplished actress. As a result, they all were kept busy helping with charitable entertainments.

As the winter drew to a close, the family had more detailed discussions with Merlin, who was to shephard the boys out to the west. He read the boys letters from his partner Latham that made them anxious to start. The family was united in one single thought and, despite all the hardships they experienced later they did not deviate from the original plan which was to seek land in the west and farm.

Chapter 5
Emerson

By the time Alfy left for Emerson, he knew that the family's new friends in Point Edward, such as the Treens and McLarens, would look out for them. Charlie too, was due very soon. In early March, the Estlins received a letter of credit in Point Edward on the Bank of Montreal for approximately 185 pounds through Edward Bagehot. This was sufficient to move ahead with their plans. Euty had obtained a job with the Grand Trunk Railway in the town, by this time, so he stayed behind initially, while Alfy went up to Emerson alone with the Merlins. Merlin, who was a big fine man, broad shouldered, and strong, had a very even temper. He was in business in "The Point" as his partner Albert Latham was, in Emerson. Latham ran a two-storied gents clothing store there. In1880, Latham had registered for 320 acres somewhere near Emerson.

Alfy and the Merlins left so hastily on Saturday March 11th that when the time came, Alfy did not have a moment to say goodbye to Birdie. He was not even sure if the others who had come to see them off, jumped safely from the train. They got into first class, but it was rather crowded and the roadbed was rough, so they did not sleep at all. *"The baby fared the best, sleeping like a top; the little beggar was as jolly as a sand boy throughout the journey."* [12]

After reaching Chicago at 8, they took a bus across the large, dirty city. While waiting 2 hours at the Chicago and Northwestern Depot, they got washed before having a comfortable breakfast. Alfy recalled the next cars were splendid (1st Class), with plenty of room, and there were two very nice men going to Manitoba that provided congenial company. Just to be on the safe side, Alfy took out insurance for 5 days for $1.20 for the train trip.

On Sunday, when the group arrived at St Paul, it was 6.30 am so despite the fact they were very tired, they had to wait there until 8 that evening. The city was filled with such magnificent buildings, and so clean. The station was impressive, in fact all the buildings were. They were so high, 7, 8, 9, or 10 stories, mostly of cherry red, hard, close natured brick. All kinds of food were dear there; beef was 18 cents a pound. They went over the Mississippi Bridge that morning, which was about one half mile long, and 100 feet above the frozen river. St Paul was cold, the ground was white, but the sun finally came out. There were several sharpers and pickpockets on the

No. 3014   Date, *Mch 10* 18*82*
Station *No. Edward*   Train *S. peel*

THE ACCIDENT INSURANCE CO. OF CANADA.

$4,000.. . .   FIVE DAYS.   . . . $1.20

The purchaser of this Ticket, whose name is written on the back hereof, is hereby insured for 120 hours from the time of starting of above numbered Train of the Grand Trunk Railway, in conformity with the Terms endorsed hereon, for the sum of $4,000, in the event of death—and $20 per week in the event of totally disabling injury by accident occurring to him while travelling on a Railroad, Steamboat on inland water, or other public conveyance within the Dominion of Canada or the United States.

A. T. GALT, President.
EDWD. RAWLINGS, Manager.

N.B.—As an extra security the Assured can, if he choose, sign on the back of the counterfoil for registration.

Alfred's insurance ticket Point Edward to Emerson.
Source: Estlin family memorabilia, Sharon Hope

train, some of them going to Manitoba. As a precaution, the travelers kept one person awake all night, sleeping in twins. Alfy met several people who had lived in Manitoba for 10 or 15 years; they all spoke well of the Estlin's intended destination, the Souris and the Turtle Mountain District. Alfy and the Merlins hoped to reach Emerson the next day.

It was dark when they got off the train, *"...the blackness of the night lessened slightly by a couple of oil lamps on the station platform. A stiff breeze was blowing, while snow was falling, as [Merlin guided us] to a long box-like arrangement on iron runners with low sides drawn by a pair of horses. ...After we were pretty well frozen stiff, we inquired of our driver what we were waiting for, and he said 'the train from the north' in a tone that said as plainly as possible, 'another English greenhorn'."* [2]

The train from the north finally arrived and the man piloted the sleigh a half-mile to the town, where they all alighted at Latham's door on the main street. The travelers soon forgot about their ordeal when they were inside with a good fire, supper all ready, and a friendly chap who gave them a warm welcome. After saying grace, Latham dished out the food he had prepared.

The town of Emerson, which lies on the east bank of the Red River, near the International border, was a thriving town. It had *"...several thousand people, three or four hotels, stores, drinking establishments, entertainments, implement warehouses, lumberyards, and everything necessary for outfitting the newcomer."* [2]

It was busy with real estate offices, banks, churches, a school, and every possible service for its growing population. It even had a mayor, Council and several policemen. West Lynne was opposite on the west bank of the river, connected to Emerson by a bridge.

The next day, Alfy headed off to the Red River to water Latham's yokes of oxen. Latham had a pony as well. Alfy liked Latham very much; he was a very energetic little fellow. The ice on the river was 3 or 4 feet thick, yet Alfy didn't feel

Photo of Albert Latham's store in Emerson. Photo by Alice Maude Hope taken in 1967. *Source:* Sharon Hope

the cold that much. No doubt the air was drier than Point Edward, and accounted for how he felt. Sleighs were the main mode of transportation in Emerson, Alfy noted, and there was just enough snow to make some good sleighing.

The following day, Merlin and Alfy spent 14 hours in St Vincent, the United States border crossing about two miles away, waiting for their stock. The town started as a fur trading post and was a huddle of a few buildings, and the railway station. When the stock came, the animals were all alive and in good condition. Unfortunately, that could not be said of the human immigrants because Mr. and Mrs. Merlin and Alfy developed bad colds and sore throats. Alfy still did not have his baggage, or the furniture, but he continued to hope for its arrival. He wrote to Point Edward: "*... we will just have to shake down the best we can. Today it is colder, but the sun is out; the air is as clear as crystal. Tuesday night we had about three inches more snow so sleighing is now splendid, we are going out for a sleigh ride this afternoon with Latham's pony.*" [12]

Latham was a bright-witted fellow, who had a nice musical tenor that he indulged nonstop. Whereas Merlin was large, Latham was short, slight and quick, with sharp features. He was a good cook. *"Whether Latham was making flapjacks or washing dishes you would hear 'Shall we gather at the*

River, the be-oot-tiful, the be-oot-tiful River', or 'Oh where is my bo-hony tonight' issuing from the kitchen." [2]

Because the store had plenty of room, Alfy and the Merlins decided to stay with Latham, reducing the workload by dividing the chores. These tasks consisted of getting water, cutting wood and running errands. Alfy hoped this consolidation would defray some of the high costs of living in the town. The price for water, for example, was dreadful at 25 cents a barrel.

First Alfy and Merlin cleaned the stovepipe, and then found a place for the pigeons, since one of them had escaped already. Alfy wanted Euty to know that the men who brought the pigeons up liked to show off the boys' prizefighter. The men had also tamed the rabbits so that the animals would drink out of a mug with a lip and cover. Alfy and the Merlins enjoyed watching the rabbits taking a sip. Alfy assured the Point Edward family that he didn't lose "the coin" [money] and he only had some pastry, a bit of cake, cheese and biscuit left after the trip.

After a short time, Alfy decided to go up to Winnipeg to find the family's belongings that had been there since the previous fall. Emerson was now going to be their centre for heading west. *"I arrived in Winnipeg after a few hours on the train and went to the officials to locate the baggage.... The baggage rooms were crowded to the roof, cars without number stood unloaded in the sidings but the baggage man observing that I was a novice to this scene, took me to the freight sheds where there were the same endless array of... merchandize... trunks, packages and bundles. I gave up all hope of ever finding our boxes but after a long hunt we located them and arranged for shipment to Emerson. By this time it was getting toward evening, so I wandered some half-mile up the town and tried several hotels for a room."* [2]

There were none.

Finally, driven by hunger, Alfy entered the Brunswick Hotel, where many travelers stayed, had his supper, and sat down in the billiard room to smoke his pipe and watch the games. *"When closing time came, I told the proprietor I had to have a bed. He assured me every bed was full, ...but he said if I would sleep on a billiard table, he would make me a shake down."* [2] Alfy consented, and so passed his first night in the Metropolis turning over and over all night long on a billiard table.

The next morning, when the hotel people began to move about, *"...I got up and did my ablutions in a very uninviting washroom, ... attempting to dry on a roller on the back of the door."* [2]

Since the roller appeared to have been in service for a month or more, Alfy had to examine it carefully before he could find a place on the inside where he could risk putting his face. After a good breakfast, he decided to walk around the city for a bit before leaving on the train.

Winnipeg consisted of one long street called Main Street that seemed to run from the station in a southwesterly direction. It was 132 feet wide, and filled with substantial buildings. There were a number of cross streets a short distance away that were also built upon. The city had about 15,000 persons, which was almost double the population from the year before. Most businesses were real estate offices and everyone seemed to be selling it. The other businesses appeared to be drinking shops and about sixty of them lined Main Street alone. These shops, no doubt, supplied the needs of the residents of the many hotels. The hotels put up short-term visitors like Alfy, and also provided homes to businessmen who could afford it. The dirtiest of dirty immigrants lined the streets, where everyone seemed to be grumbling about something. It seemed a city of hustlers, women of ill repute and speculators.

The fact that Alfy had not got the luggage down to Emerson as yet, perhaps colored his frame of mind, but he did not like the place. *"There had been a lot of snow that was piled up in large dirty drifts. All the accumulated garbage of the winter was scattered about, and shocked my sensibilities. … Of course it was the worst time of the year in this climate."* [2]

Oxen drew most conveyances; loads of hay and wood seemed to predominate. There were a few passenger conveyances and heavy sleighs drawing merchandize. The oxen though, wallowed along at the same pace in the slush with empty sleighs or full loads. Alfy left for Emerson.

Winnipeg in 1882. Permission for use, Glenbow Archives.

Chapter 6
Flood

On March 23rd the snow was about eight feet deep, and everything froze. There was one half inch of ice on the water about 3 feet from the stove. The weather was so bad that the waterman could not come so they had to melt snow. Wood was $8 per cord, and one had to keep piling it on all the time. Alfy had not had his clothes off since he left Point Edward, nor had on a collar, but he found neither of these details a great hardship. Mrs. M. was continually groaning over her cook stove; Latham invented the one she used. It was a sheet iron box with two holes on the top and a sheet iron door that was a great work of art. The stove, which burned three times as much wood as any other, would not bear the weight of a full kettle. The fire would go to the back of it just where it was not wanted. You could only cook one thing at a time.

Alfy was becoming more accustomed to the farming chores. The oxen, which were doing well, knew him now and looked out for him to drive them down to drink. However his clothing was not sufficient for the weather. He needed to get another muffler because the plaid red and black one he brought from Ontario was not nearly enough. Mr. M amused them by announcing to Mrs. M. that he was going to get some chamois leather for her to make a covering for his rooster's comb and lobes, because the frost affected them badly. There was not much to do while the weather was poor but read. Alfy read a good book of Latham's "Ocean to Ocean" written by one of the surveyors for the CPR.

Alfy told the family not to fret, that they were very well off where they were because dozens of people were going back east disgusted with the cold and not being able to get lodgings.

Emerson had terrible weather, very cold, and more snow. Latham got stranded in Morris for a week, before he went up to Winnipeg. He found out that everyone must physically go to the land office to take up land at Turtle Mountain. Following his trip to Winnipeg, Latham and a chum of his, a good fellow called Frank Main, whose farm was near Morris, decided to go out together to pick out locations. Frank had preempted his farm four years ago, and sold it for $4,000. Frank was going to go out with Merlin, Latham, Euty and Alfy. Alfy did not go on this prospecting trip; he trusted Frank Main and Albert Latham who had years more experience than he did.

Alfy instructed the family: *"Don't ship anything or start until you hear from me; there is no necessity for Euty to leave the Grand Trunk till I tell you when you are to start. Charlie can do all the packing."* [12]

Then Alfy gave the latest news: *"Latham let the oxen out this morning for 'a run' as he said, …he had two hours work finding them, and only got them back at 10 tonight. The Merlin's baby had the measles but is almost all right now. Six of the pigeons are sitting. I have a dorg [sic], a scotch collie pup such a little beauty 2 months old and very sharp. I call her Kitty. Frank Main gave her to me and she sleeps with Jack in the yard. I have a ride nearly every day, Latham broke the pony himself, but she has never done any work, so you can imagine what she is like."* [12]

Merlin and Alfy chaffed Latham about unsubstantial carpentry. The stable he built with his own hands fell down, killing one of his hens. After a day or two, Alfy and Latham began rebuilding it. The two had a tight day with axe and shovel. Fourteen hours of leveling the yard, breaking up the frozen ground, and then rebuilding the stable was no joke. The hen they had for dinner the next night.

Charlie arrived at Point Edward about March 22nd. As a result, Alfy was anxious to know if Charlie had learned anything about the insurance business because it made a significant difference to the family's plans. There was no news. Finally Charlie wrote saying the vessel he travelled across in was very small, only 2300 tons, and rolled heavily. They had little cabins that took 4, and meals in a very fair mess, where they could sit all day if they wished. The ship had 60 intermediate, about 300 steerage passengers, and very few saloon individuals. There was a good evening concert that he enjoyed very much. According to Charlie, he didn't "cast up his accounts" until they had been at sea 5 days and then the stink made him "spew" after that. All the officers were very nice, except the 2nd mate who was a devil. *"There is a dance at the Treens tonight, and Birdie says the usual set are going, but I don't know who they are, doubtless you do…Treen says he will find a job for me."* [13] Charlie took on chores at Point Edward immediately, cleaning out the workshop in the cottage and placing the stove there as well as obtaining more wood.

In Emerson, it started to freeze again. The snow melted a little but lay deep on the prairie. On April 3rd, Alfy decided Euty might as well come up as soon as possible. Alfy thought he might be going on to Brandon either ahead of Euty, or the two of them might go together. They could build a shanty there for about 150 dollars. The carpenters had struck in Brandon, so Alfy thought it might be an ideal time for the two of them to obtain good paying jobs. They should be able to make at least $4–$5.00 a day since the carpenters were getting $8.00. Then the rest of the family could join them. Alfy told the family to buy a cook stove if possible, ship it up, and to pack everything ready to go.

Merlin and Latham, being in the clothing business, were having difficulty in obtaining a supply of collars. With the large increase in men moving west, the variety of entertainments available in Emerson, and the good hotels, collars were a popular item in the store. Merlin thought that since Euty was coming up from Point Edward shortly, he could bring along the collars they needed. Moreover, Alfy was anxious to accommodate them, after all that Merlin and Latham had done for the family. Alfy knew though, he would have to get Euty to sneak them across the border through customs. In a letter to his mother, Alfy gave Euty details:

"...Merlin wants you to buy 4.5 dozen stand up collars at $2.00 for 25 at the following sizes, 15, 15.5, 16, and 16.5 and 1 dozen celluloid cuffs. You can get them at the 99-cent store in Port Huron. Throw away the boxes and put the collars in your coat pockets and pack them in your trunk. Don't forget as they have been very kind to me...." [12]

Euty arrived on a Wednesday morning about eleven; he nearly missed the stop, but when he looked out, as luck would have it, he saw Emerson on the board. He managed to pass the collars by taking out his eatables, making a display on a vacant seat, and then putting the collars under them. He did this just before he reached St Vincent, where the trunks were examined.

Around April 15th, Alfy telegraphed the family not to ship the goods. Latham woke him at about 3 am calling from outside. Latham and Main went to the Turtle Mountain Land Office, and found that people had crowded there in swarms taking up land without ever seeing it. All the land within 30 miles of timber was taken up. They went on to Brandon, and then came back by rail two weeks before Alfy and the Merlins expected them. In Brandon, there was no lumber and hundreds of people were living in tents. Dozens of men in all trades were out of employment, so the boys decided not to go there.

Whole cars of stock had been starved for lack of feed or frozen to death. The destruction of baggage and freight was appalling. The snow blockade prevented things from being sent down from Winnipeg, and one could not get even the smallest items. There was no ink to be found in Brandon nor could the people get coal or oil. The boys heard that over five million feet of lumber was being sent there from the States.

On Monday, Alfy went to see how things were in Winnipeg. Although he got Euty's baggage, there were 1000 tents with people living in them. He couldn't get a bed, and had to sleep in the corner of the printing office on a pile of tents, paying 50 cents for the privilege. There was no lumber in the city, and there were hundreds of men out of employment. One of Euty's boxes (the toolbox) had been opened, and his rug had been stolen, otherwise his things came through safely. The revised plan now was to start from Emerson on May 1st, taking all their accessories, and go west to find land. In addition to other provisions, Alfy wanted to buy a wagon, 2 yoke of oxen, 2 sets of harness, 2 ploughs, and 20 bushels of oats for the oxen.

Charlie wrote to Alfy again about Euty's portmanteau after his younger brother had arrived in Emerson, saying that the family in Point Edward was not all surprised Euty lost something, *"...the last thing I said to him was to get it checked at Chicago but parting with his Polly, I suppose, was too much for his nerves. I did not get it checked through to Emerson because I thought he had his rugs in it, and might find it cold in Chicago when he could have got them out...I don't see much of the Empey girls; I don't pay them enough attention so they don't care for me, my affections are bestowed further down the street. Ahem!! ...."* [13]

Euty retorted in his return letter: *"...my portmanteau turned up, we got it very easily...I will tell you how I came to miss it so he* [Charlie] *need not think I was lost in thought of Polly Laurie.... If he were leaving I'm sure he would lose his head parting from his dear Emily...When we got on in Chicago, the baggage man came through and sang out 'Have any of you got your baggage checked to Chicago?' I said I had a portmanteau, and he took my cheque and gave me a different one...."* [14]

At the same time that Alfy and Euty were trying to organize in Emerson, Birdie was writing various contacts around Point Edward to ask about items the family might need later. She wrote Edward Small in Detroit asking questions about the wringer machine that they had got for the cottage, and coffee grinders. Concerning the wringer [he replied], *"...it is considered a better machine than all the others...Mrs. Treen did not see the type I sent since we had none in stock over there... We have coffee mills at all prices 35–45 cents and upward to 60 cents...I would recommend the 40 cent* [type] *rather than the more* [expensive] *or cheaper machine...."* [15]

Before the boys could proceed with any action in Emerson, however, there was a serious setback to their plans. The Red River had risen 60 feet since thaw set in. The whole town was threatened. One day Alfy saw that Merlin, Latham and an older man, a Mr. Stovin, whose boys also wanted to go out with them, appeared excited. Latham said Stovin was worried. There had been a terrific blizzard that raged for 3 days and 3 nights covering everything with deep new snow. Finally, it turned to a heavy rain. This caused a rush of melting snow into the Red River. The mouth of the Red

River in the north was still frozen. Stovin, who was on his way back into Emerson, *"...found the water rising so rapidly that the creeks were flooded. He knew it would be impossible for him to get home except by water. As his farm was on low land, and since both he and his son Will had been away, they decided to buy a boat to get home at once."* [2] They did so paying, Alfy believed, $27.00 for it. They arrived safely, but it was the last Alfy saw of them for many days.

The boys would walk down to the bridge every day to watch the ever-increasing flow of water rushing by. The next thing they knew water was seeping into the town cellars. Now that they had seven inches of water in the kitchen, and the level was still rising, they were obliged to live upstairs. On April 17th, people lined the banks of the river near the new Emerson bridge to watch the water rise. About six o'clock, a large field of ice came floating down, carrying away the swing portion of the bridge that was composed of wood and iron. After the bridge floated a short distance, it went to the bottom. The bridge cost $40,000 to build. One bridge in Winnipeg went costing the same amount. The railway bridge in Winnipeg that cost $200,000 had been damaged to the extent of $40,000.

Loss of the Emerson bridge was a serious problem, but not without a solution. Some enterprising soul built a scow and established a ferry. Although it was slow and could not take large loads, it did provide an essential service. The ferryman, Duncan, was a character. He was a burly Highland Scot, good natured and obliging. He was courting a girl, Elsie, in West Lynne and had proposed to her again and again. For whatever reason, Elsie would never say yes. Finally Duncan made up his mind it could not drag on any longer. Fortifying himself with libation, he wended his way to Elsie's house and called:

"Elsie will ye marry me? Will ye marry me Elsie?"
No answer.
"Elsie if ye don't like my style ye can plumb go to hell."
They were married shortly after." [2]

If the situation for immigrants was bad before, Alfy wondered what impact these new developments would have. There were on average from 500–1000 people outside the Winnipeg post office all day; it took three hours waiting to get a letter. When Alfy thought of the thousands who were on their way with very little money, brought by false reports, his blood boiled. There was no work for these people when they got there. He was very thankful that they did not go to Brandon.

Alfy still had not heard of their trunks but continued to hope they could obtain them. He expected he could cope with Euty's clothes but boots were the worst problem. If he didn't receive his trunk before they left, he would have to buy a pair of long ones.

The boys made arrangements with the others to pay half the food costs. Alfy slept on a lounge with a great coat over him while Euty and Latham (who were immense allies) occupied a mattress on the floor. They had 30 bushels of loose oats in one corner of the room, as well as the " beds", the table, chairs, and a little gas stove on which they would cook. They were as happy as kings and made as much row as a lot of schoolboys.

They expected to find the kitchen stove underwater the next morning so Alfy had moved the food up out of the way. He informed the family in Point Edward *"...I shall have to get a boat to post this later. The Post office is an island. Merlin has just come down, stood on the bottom step and washed his hands. When we are finished washing in the morning, Mrs Merlin gets Euty up, taking him by the ear to insure he does the same. I think about having a wash over in the kitchen tomorrow morning. I think it best to stay where you are...."* [12]

When the water rose to 2 feet on the floor of the store, they went down the stair as far as they could to mark the level on the doorjamb of the stairway. In this way, they could see if the water was rising or falling. The water rose at the rate of 6 inches a day for a week.

Emerson, Brandon, and Winnipeg now were all flooded. Traffic was carried on by boat. The boys determined to build a skiff immediately. *"We bought some clean pine boards from the lumberyard, some nails and screws from the hardware, and got out our tools."* [2]

Euty and Alfy started to build the boat on a Tuesday and finished her on a Friday, although they had to stand up to their waists in water to do so. They initially tied the boat to the ceiling of the store's lean to kitchen and then later moored it outside.

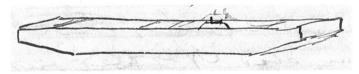

Alfy and Euty's boat sketched in Euty's undated letter.
Estlin letter collection. *Source:* Sharon Hope

The Merlins, Latham and the brothers had 18 loaves of bread in the house and lots of other supplies so they felt they could hold out for a while. People were struggling about the streets. The streets were graded and the water was up to 6 or 7 feet deep at the edges. People got some rare duckings at times. Alfy couldn't think what the poor people living in tents were doing. The boys were obliged to keep both the dogs and the wood on the top of the next building. Jack looked in the window and bestowed kisses on anyone going out there. The water was still rising but they hoped the rain kept off. The incident was keeping them back terribly.

It was quite impossible to take Emily and the girls when Alfy and Euty left, because the women couldn't live in a wagon as the boys were going to do. Alfy wrote to Charlie: "...*you will have to get a job and stay with them ... we will have to send for them...it would not have done to leave Euty there for several reasons....*" [16]

The trunks finally came in good order. Alfy, who felt that two months in the same clothes was long enough, was looking forward to a fresh set. On April 27th, the boys started to build a shanty where the Merlins and Latham could put the goods out of the store, and Mrs. Merlin and the baby could live until autumn. Everyone was thinking of moving in.

To fetch water from out of the store window, they tied a rope to a bucket and lowered it; they just threw the slops down the stairs. There was no bread to be got now but they still had a fair amount in stock with the initial 18 loaves. The water was still rising but not as fast. The boys both kept well; they had no colds, in spite of continual wet legs and feet. Alfy thought his mother should have heard something about the insurance by now, but he reduced both the number of oxen and implements that he was going to buy as a precautionary measure. The puppy, who was growing quickly and turning into quite a handsome dog, got in the bad habit of stealing eggs for a time. She carried off no less than four one Sunday.

Euty paddled about in the flat bottomed dingy. He secured a lot of good wood, a barrel of coal oil, and Alfy got a walking stick, a new tap, sundry clothespins, books, boxes etc. Alfy and Euty planned to go duck hunting on the 27th, but a gale came on with such a torrent of rain that they decided to delay it until evening. There were hundreds of ducks around Emerson, and they fancied one, but they didn't know how to cook it.

They built quite a nice shanty for the Merlins on Park Street, with three windows in the front and one in the back, 3 rooms with the kitchen in the middle and a bedroom on each side. There was a shed for wood and fowls on one side. Euty completed the fittings, doors and windows. The water now was about a foot above the counter in the store, but in the yard it was up to one's neck. The boys commented that it was amusing to see the different things floating about such as cordwood, tables, chairs, lumber and barrels by the dozen.

Steroscopic view of Emerson in April 1882. Permission given by Manitoba Archives.

Most of the sidewalks on the street were wide and built of new two-inch longitudinal planks. Initially, all the sidewalks floated free about the streets and then headed down the river. However, the city fathers and police quickly anchored them in place so people could walk on them, as long as they only went two at a time. Pedestrians were continually stepping off the walks and getting a cold bath. One young man, a Dr. Byers on his way to Winnipeg, was hurrying up town for refreshment when he turned the corner of a sidewalk too quickly, and went in up to his neck. The boys rowed up in their boat to fish him out. A group of well-dressed bank clerks were hurrying back to work. They had to pass an intersection where the sidewalks were level with the store cornices. They were all in a close group when they turned the corner, only to drop into twelve feet of water. What a sight!

Armed with their trusty boat, Alfy and Euty collected an ample supply of wood which they piled on the slanting roof of the shed which served as a landing place as well as a place to dry all the flotsam and jetsam they collected. The boys took out a window to make an improvised door to their dock. Because they were mobile, one of their first jobs was to go down to the Post office and fetch the mail that came up from Grand Forks, Dakota by streamer, because all the trains had stopped. This generally occupied the best part of a morning because so many people wanted a lift to someone's place and back, or some other errand done. The boys cheerfully toted people about, or executed their commissions; they had nothing else to do.

"One morning when the water was at its peak we were pulling down to the Post Office as usual when we saw the Post office coming to meet us. We

rubbed our eyes and looked again but there was no mistake. There it was with the sign Post Office still on it. When we 'went aboard', and inquired the reason for this unseemly behavior on the part of a sedate Government building, we found there had been a high wind blowing in the morning when the mail boat had come in, and she had bumped against the building loosening it from its foundations, and it had floated downtown." [2]

The Post office was transferred to the Station that stood on higher ground back from the town. The small steamer continued to come up the river to deliver mail by proceeding right up the main street.

The river was wild. The stream, which was miles wide, had a swift current. People came from outlying districts in boats. Whole lumberyards, haystacks with a solitary cow on top, fences, and icehouses floated away downstream. Toward Winnipeg, thrifty people living along the river contrived rope and cable booms and set them out to capture the floating objects. One day, as the boys watched from the front windows, a house gently floated by upside down. Mrs. Merlin consoled herself with *"Well if we can live in this we can live in anything."* [2]

Some days when it was fine, Alfy and Euty took the boat beyond the town limits. One morning, they were surprised to see countless trunks and boxes floating downstream. They watched them for some time, but there did not seem to be any end to the procession so they went home to dinner and reported the strange occurrence. *"We found that a lot of baggage cars have been left on the sidings to the south of us, and the water had washed out the roadbed overturning the cars. The roofs had come off, spilling the baggage into the river and the pieces had floated to the north into Canada without regard for custom regulations. We went out again after dinner and found the same thing going on. We caught a few trunks and tried to open them but most were locked. One or two that were not locked we opened, but there was nothing of value in them, nor any identification marks so we sent them on their way."* [2] Alfy supposed the Railway companies paid for them eventually.

Euty declared that people would hardly believe that you could not get in some stores except by boat, and even then, could not get in under the tops of the doors. There was one man drowned in Emerson. Ironically, it was the man who sold water at 25 cents a barrel. They joked that he could not get enough of it. The pigeons hatched, but because the boys were obliged to put the hens up the same room, the "brutes" of fowls killed the young pigeons. The rabbits also "hatched out". Again, the boys did not have their boat at the critical time and could not attend to them, so the gentlemen rabbits thought it best to make a meal of the young ones.

By this time, the water had gone down 6 inches but the level was still 4 foot 6 in the store. They were all tired of being cooped up in the place. There was no meat of any sort in Emerson, but by this time, the bakers had rigged up ovens on their roofs so now the castaways could get plenty of bread. The boys, Latham and the Merlins, could get tinned stuff, cheese and butter. Since the fowls laid a few eggs, they did pretty well. They had no writing paper nor could they get any. By April 30th, there still were no letters from the family in Point Edward. Alfy continued to send off regular letters to them. He was getting anxious about not getting any letters and couldn't think why they didn't receive something.

Alfy told the Point Edward family: *"...Don't delay sending the money. ...I hope Charlie has got something to do by this time. We all keep well but shall be very glad to get to dry land again; it is cold and damp living over water. We shall plant vegetables directly we get on our land...the house is our great bug bear though, most likely we will build it of logs... It is now 3 weeks since I had a letter...."* [12]

Finally Alfy received the following telegram: *"Western Union Telegraph Office Iroquois Ont. 1/5 1882 received at Emerson Care of Latham and Mailer* [sic] *Letter 19th received will stay here you go on. How we send money? Emily Estlin."* [17] It was a great relief.

Chapter 7
Getting Ready

The weather improved and the swallows came; Alfy heard a ringneck that reminded him of England. The water was going down slowly week-by-week. Alfy reiterated to his mother that he needed $350 dollars for equipment and supplies. He knew that he would have to spend a total of $450 or $500 and he wanted to put aside the balance for timber that they might use later for the house. The boys' plans were quite open since they didn't know what resources they might actually have to hand. Because the party expected to have some shooting for Prairie Chicken on the way out, Merlin ordered a gun from Hines in Sarnia; he was very proud of his new purchase.

Alfy, Euty, and the others were still working on the outbuildings for the shanty, such as the fowl house, but the appearance was good so they were all anxious to move in. Euty made Mrs. Merlin some kitchen things such as knife boards and shelves. The place had taken longer to finish than they expected, given the extras. They used to get up at about 5, and work until seven; they ate like horses. Latham claimed that he wanted 5 meals a day.

About this time, the boys lent their boat to a man to go home and though he promised to return it, he had not done so by the time they needed to feed their animals. After not feeding the rabbits in the morning, Alfy and Euty finally drew lots to see who should wade out and feed them in the evening. Alfy drew the prize. The water was very warm so it was not the unpleasant job he expected.

The final group solidified to go west: *"Frank Main who was Irish, medium build, was married to an English woman Sarah. He had a farm about 14 miles north of Emerson [near St. Jean Baptiste] where he had been for some time…. He was apparently doing well because he had a lot of stock, and a good-sized grain crop. Then there was Frank's brother Tawm [sic]. He was a year or two younger than Frank and Frank always treated him as if he had committed some crime, so that if he did not behave himself and do what he was told, he would be given up to the police. Fortunately Tawm, was a retiring disposition, and always did do what he was told, so nothing serious ever happened. We never could discover any reason why he should be so treated. He only asserted himself in one instance, and that was he would not drive oxen. When we started on the long trek, he insisted on taking his team of horses and feed for them, much to Frank's disgust.*

"The next member of the party to be introduced to us was William Simms, a relation of the Mains who worked for them. He was a quiet inoffensive man from Ontario, well accustomed to life in the new country. He was to take up a homestead of his own, a great opportunity for a man with no means but with a wife and family. He was to be the cook and general factotum of the party.

"Last but not least came the [Stovin] family. The old gentleman was a typical, bluff Englishman, a professional man who had been in the country some years...." [2]

Stovin had been an architect, surveyor and planner of early buildings in Winnipeg while his family lived near Emerson. As his family grew in numbers and stature, he wanted to move west, where all the children could obtain homesteads. *"We got along well with the gentleman who introduced us to his two boys, Will and Joe, who would be joining us. Will was the eldest, eighteen or nineteen, while Joe was much younger probably twelve or thirteen. The intermediate boys stayed at home to work the farm. The gentleman used to come in often to sit and smoke his pipe, telling us stories, thumping his fist into the palm of his hand while exclaiming 'By gad sir, I soon showed him'."* [2]

The plan remained to start direct from Emerson with Merlin and Latham's 2 yoke of oxen, a pony, Frank Main's 2 yoke of oxen and 1 yoke of steers, and the Estlin's 1 yoke of oxen and the accompanying wagons of course. In writing to Point Edward, the boys stated again that it was no place for the women living in a tent for three months and it would be absolute madness to attempt it. Alfy had seen plenty of tent life since coming up. It was all very well to talk about it in theory, but the practice was totally different. In June, the group expected 25 wet days, coming straight down, *"real soakers, none of your drizzles."* [16] It would pretty well kill them. The women had no idea of the roughness of the country. Alfy fancied that he knew something about it when he started from Ontario, but now he felt he did not.

Alfy wrote: *"They call me 'the immigrant' because I wear Papa's huge boots and my hair (until tonight) has not been cut for over two months. Shaving is not indulged in; my teeth are cleaned only when I can get something to do it with. I certainly am an object but I can't help it. My trunks are at the Station and there they must stay until we get into the new shanty.... However, when ...I darned a pair of socks a few days ago, Mrs. M. was most complimentary...."* [12]

When Alfy and Euty finally heard from the family, life appeared to have carried on in much the same fashion as when they were there. Charlie had been invited to an assembly to be held at the G.R.T. Dining Rooms under the auspices of the Point Edward Syndicate Club, the invitation obtained through the Treens no doubt, since Mr. Treen was on the committee. Dancing, they heard, began at 9.00 o'clock. The boys were very glad to hear Charlie had a job. They felt Charlie would not have been able to contribute that much coming west with them since the boys only had one yoke. Now he would have a chance to get acclimatized before he came to this land of "rich food" as Alfy put it, where the boys lived on canned salmon, bacon, bread, and applesauce.

When Emily mentioned Prior's gravestone at Sarnia in her letter, it brought a flood of emotion. Alfy missed his father a great deal, particularly since he came up. [I] *"... felt so many times if I could have only asked him what to do. ...I was going wild with doubt and uncertainty, not knowing and having no one who could really take in all the circumstances."* [12]

Merlin and Latham had been most kind, and Alfy talked things over with them before doing anything, but the boys' mentors did not know everything so they could not fully advise him. Acting on Merlin and Latham's suggestions, however, saved the Estlin family hundreds of dollars. If the brothers had gone west earlier, their cattle would have starved because, at the beginning of May, there was not enough grass on the prairie to feed a rabbit. The trees were just budding; experts said it was a backward season.

The government had stopped immigration but people in Brandon were still starving with money in their pockets. Since the boys could not get meat in Emerson, one could only imagine how terrible it was in Brandon. There were over 6000 people there at that time and fodder could not be bought.

On May 11th Alfy wrote that the draft for $300.00 had arrived. The water was off the streets now and things were getting back to normal. He tried to respond to all the questions the family had. Well-meaning persons were advising them in Point Edward, but people there really did not have a true or current grasp of the situation. He tried to explain that the family must have wood available within a days travel because he didn't fancy not having a plentiful supply for the winter. All the land near water was taken up in the Turtle and Souris Districts as well. Alfy advised not buying another lounge or *"I will be at my wits end how to put the stuff you bring in the wagon, it is far from being a railway car. E and I will have to cut and contrive to get ours in...."* [12]

The boys had 25 acres to break, vegetables to plant, hay to cut, make and stack, firewood to get and cut, a well to dig, as well as providing the walls, roof, doors, and windows of a house, and they would have to bring the wood, tarpaper, and shingles from Brandon.

While Alfy was writing his May 11th letter, Merlin came in to offer a mackintosh that was too small for him but fitted Alfy very well. Alfy claimed it was A1 for working in wet weather. Alfy felt that his friends were so kind, Mrs. Merlin washed and darned all their clothes while Frank Main offered him some potatoes (Early Rose) for planting and seeding. Frank said they were the best in the country. During the flood, Euty and Alfy *"picked up some capital buckets, a splendid basket, a packet of grass seed, and a wash board all of which we plan to take west."* [12] On May 12th, they moved into the new shanty, but couldn't leave for the west until there was grass on the Prairie.

Time passed slowly now. As the brothers prepared, the mosquitoes came out in swarms; it continued to snow from time to time, but it melted quickly. Alfy and Euty couldn't find any wagons or oxen in Emerson, but they bought two straw hats with wide brims, a butcher's knife, some mosquito net, and tick that Mrs. Merlin kindly made up for them. They decided to get a tent to sleep in on the way. The boys also planned to buy a Prairie Stove, which was basically a portable box made of sheet iron with a door in front, and a stovepipe. It stood on a couple of metal legs. One of Latham's oxen died which was a heavy loss for him. It cost more than 100 dollars and now the other was almost unmanageable without its mate. Latham acquired another pair of oxen near the end of May.

Euty's trousers wore out so he modified a pair Charlie had given him with considerable success. He completed this project under Mrs. Merlin's supervision. Euty now wondered if the rug he said was stolen was ever in the toolbox. He remembered trying to see if it would fit, but now he was uncertain if the rug was actually packed. He wrote Emily about it and gave her a mixture of other information. The town was building a pontoon bridge over the river. The boys heard that the kind baggage man who helped them find their luggage had drowned. Apparently he got drunk and drowned in an inch and one half of water. He left a wife and three children. The boys also heard news from time to time of Harold Harker, Birdie's intended, in Brazil. His descriptions of an upper class life and servants made them slightly envious. He seemed to the boys to be a "little king". A young man that they knew in England, Walter Wake, came to see them on his way home. He had been up at Winnipeg more than a month and had only been able to get four days work. All that time he'd been living in the Immigrant Shed.

Chapter 8
Gathering the Train

Since the party had very little room to assemble the cattle and wagons, Euty and Alfy moved to a vacant lot north of town in the shelter of some poplar bluffs. There was a good well close by. The boys pitched their tent and set up camp with their stove and bedding. Latham drove his huge yoke of oxen over; the sight of the little man driving them was amusing because he didn't come up to their shoulders. At first the boys thought the oxen were strays, until they heard Latham's high tenor voice saying, "Gee Buck". *"After Latham pointed out all* [the oxen's] *fine qualities, which we dutifully admired, we tied them up and fed them some hay."* [2]

Latham had bought a wagon; he and Merlin collected their belongings, and bought others. Alfy and Euty helped move these items to the camp. Every day the boys did the rounds of the barns, looking for a yoke of cattle for themselves. The brothers required a well-broken pair, and these were not plentiful. Most of those for sale were either ranch cattle, or unbroken steers.

Alfy and Euty were very discouraged by their lack of success in finding oxen to go west. One day, when they were telling Frank about their problem, he proposed to sell Jack and Tom to the boys because he had steers and could get along without the oxen. The oxen were not only in their prime, but Alfy knew how to handle them. This was an ideal solution, so they struck a happy bargain; Jack and Tom became the brothers' property.

Things moved along quickly now. Alfy and Euty conveyed Merlin and Latham's wagon to the spot near town. They purchased their own wagon, a set of harrows, a breaking plough, cross cut saw, rope, nails, and all the things that Frank advised them that they would need. Euty made their own tools serviceable.

Around May 14th, Frank Main said his farm would likely be dry enough in a week to start spring work, and it would help him to be ready sooner if Alfy would go out there. He also thought the experience would be good for him, to gain a little insight into farm work like ploughing and harrowing. Since they couldn't start until the Mains and Stovins had finished their seeding, Alfy was only too happy to oblige. It was arranged that if the weather kept fine, he would go out the following week. Alfy watched the weather closely and was very glad when Merlin and Latham thought it would be all right to leave. On May 23rd leaving Euty at Emerson, Alfy got on the old sidewheeler for the trip downriver toward Morris feeling free at last.

Red River Steamboat. Permission granted for use, the Glenbow Archives.

The trip was uneventful except for a difference of opinion between the mate and one of the crew, a large Negro. *"...When the mate gave him an order, he refused, whipping out a sheath knife and springing toward the mate, threatening to kill him. The mate, coolly drew a revolver from his pocket, and told him to put away the knife and obey the order. His determined appearance convinced the Negro that he was not bluffing and the black man slunk away like a whipped cur. No one seemed to take any notice of the affair. Soon after this occurrence, the boat arrived at my destination."* [2]

When Alfy disembarked, Frank was waiting for him with a pony and buckboard. It was four wheeled with a spring seat, made of five or six strips of hickory about 8 feet long and five inches wide, fastened to the axles. *"I don't know how the name originated but rather suspect that it was derived from the similarity between riding it and a bucking bronc."* [2]

Frank drove Alfy up to the "Store" where Frank had to get some things, introducing Alfy to the proprietor, Peter Parenteau, a man of some standing in the District. Shortly after they loaded their stuff, they arrived at Frank's farm. Here Alfy met Frank's wife who was very nice. After Tawm greeted Alfy with a few words, the children came out. They all had supper consisting of good wholesome farm fare; eggs, pork, splendid homemade bread and butter, lots of potatoes, milk and cream, which was a very welcome change from the boys' monotonous diet of canned salmon and slap-jacks on which they had been subsisting. After supper the men went out to do the chores; feeding the horses and cattle, pigs and calves, milking the cows and bringing in the wood and water for the morning.

When they got to the milking, Tawm quickly grabbed a stool and was hard at work filling a pail. *"Frank jokingly said to me 'Here's a pail for you,' but when I said, 'Thanks which cow will I take?' Frank was so taken aback that he didn't know what to say. Finally, somewhat dubiously, Frank assigned me a cow. When I finished and stripped her off properly, I could see that I had made a good impression on both Frank and Tawm. We had all learned to milk in England. This incident, and one or two others like it, earned the goodwill and hearty cooperation of our friends that we valued so much."* [2]

The next morning Frank called Alfy about 5 am. He and Tawm had been up for an hour or so, feeding all the work animals. They had only to milk, wash and have breakfast. Alfy managed to milk two cows while the others did three or four, but he received strong praise. Then they began the spring work.

"Tawm, [who] had a pair of horses, ...did all the harrowing and dragging, while Frank sowed with a bag of grain slung over his shoulder, flinging out the grain in a semi circle in front of him. I was given a yoke of huge red oxen.... ...I watched as Frank put the yoke on the 'off' ox first, (the one on his right), and then told the 'nigh' ox to get in its place (the one on his left), which it meekly did, just the same as harnessing horses.... I found 'gee' meant right, and 'haw' meant left, wanting them to stop was simply 'whoa' followed by 'haugh', a... short grunt which seemed ... effective. After Frank had yoked the oxen and provided me with a whip, he called Tawm and told him, ' Better hitch to the plough for a while, and let Alf harrow to get used to driving the oxen, then he can take the plow.' Old Jack and Tom, ... my charges,... were well broken and very 'handy'. Frank showed me how to guide them by throwing the whiplash gently over their necks, and shouting 'gee' or' haw' as the case may be...."* [2]

Alfy got along quite well with that part of it, but his feet and shoulders suffered from trudging all day on the soft ground and lifting the heavy harrows in order to clear the stubble. The fine black dust seemed to get into every pore and coated his lungs. *"Well, you get used to anything if you stick to it, so just when I thought I could worry through it, Frank told me to hitch onto the plow, which I gladly did. He showed me how to hold the plow and the oxen knew all about it."* [2] Once Alfy had a nice damp furrow bottom to walk in, and very little dust, he got along well.

When the Stovins and Mains were finished crop preparations for the coming year, the entire group left for Emerson. Alfy and the Mains were ready when the Stovins appeared at the Mains' farm in the morning. Will, the eldest, was driving a pair of mules with Joe, his younger brother, sitting in the back. Frank drove a wagon drawn by oxen, and William Simms rode an Indian pony. *"Simms drove a pair of steers as well as two or three cows and heifers that Frank had taken out of his herd to provide milk for the party. Later, we were thankful for this."* [2] Tawm Main had his wagon drawn by a team of horses, followed by a big Montana ox pulling a Red River cart.

These carts are "... *built entirely of wood kept together by wooden pins for pegs and tied where necessary with 'shagganappi' thongs, which are strips of rawhide that are very strong and durable.*"[2]

The Red River cart is famous for two things: first its ability to go though soft ground without sticking in the mud, and secondly the noise it makes. The wooden axles grinding on the wooden hubs make a hideous squealing, and a train of these carts can be heard for miles. This one lived up to its reputation because the group never had to hitch anything on to help the big ox out of the mud, and the noise it made was seldom equaled.

When the party headed out toward Emerson and West Lynne, Alfy proudly brought up the rear driving Jack and Tom, excited to be starting at last.

After reaching Emerson, Alfy told Euty to take their new team and wagon to the store to fetch final supplies. Euty, who had no experience with oxen, and no reins, had to use his voice to guide the oxen. The nigh ox was a "Muley" and Euty had no idea of what words to use because he had not been schooled by Frank, as Alfy had. The result was that Euty went to the store desperately hanging on to "Muley's" great ears much to the amusement of various bystanders. Since the oxen knew their business, they scorned the feeble attempts of the driver, reaching their destination without his assistance.

In the early evening, Duncan transported all the dismantled outfits on the ferry to West Lynne, while the oxen and horses swam behind the scow. By this time, the mosquitoes were a terror and Alfy's hands were twice their natural size. After making camp and insuring that everything was comfortable, they left Euty and William Simms to mind the place while the rest of the party had one last overnight in town. After Euty rowed them over, he returned to the bivouac. The others were taking the ferry back to West Lynne in the morning.

Grassy cottonwood meadows on the Red River's western bank-near West Lynne 2011.
Source: Sharon Hope

Euty crawled into his rugs under the wagon, (buffalo robes were between 5–6 dollars a piece) placing the family's big blue revolver under his pillow. All would have gone well except that the flood had driven the local Indians out of their usual camping ground. The voices of the men could be heard late into the night calling from one point to the other among the great elm trees which bordered the river. When at last the voices died away, Euty dozed off.

When the moon came out, it shed a sickly light through the trees. There was a stealthy movement about Euty's rugs. He awoke to gaze into the face of the ugliest squaw he had ever seen. Euty maintained that sleep, the strange light, and the unfamiliar surroundings made him disoriented. All he could think about was the fact that his friends were far away across the river. Impulsively, he reached under the pillow for the revolver and poked its nose into the face of the intruder. The face promptly withdrew; he heard moccasins padding rapidly away as she made good time down the path among the trees, back to her own people.[18]

On the same evening, while Alfy was going into town for a last night in Emerson, and Euty was lying under the wagon, the "Misses Estlin and their friends" were attending an Assembly in Sarnia at the Firemen's Hall—18 dances were listed; festivities began at 8.30. Such entertainments now were quite foreign to the boys.

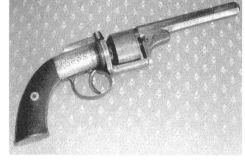

The Estlin blue-nosed revolver.
Source: Sharon Hope

On the next morning, June 1st, Alfy jotted a quick note to his mother before he took the ferry back to West Lynne to get breakfast. He declared proudly that he had learned to plough. *"Just off for the far west, everything straight. I've been very lucky, got a cheap yoke of cattle and have paid for everything and have $260.00 left. Is that not good? I am glad to hear about the insurance but don't count on it...I will write you once or twice along the way. We are late starting but we got a 12x8 tent big enough for 5 or 6. I am just going to get a bottle of brandy as I know if you were here you would not let us go without it...."*[12]

The final party consisted of 4 yoke, one odd ox, 3 wagons (including a buckboard), 2 carts, 12 head of cattle, mules, cows etc, dogs, 7 men, and two ponies. The party took their first breakfast together in the open air, before watering and feeding the animals. The Commission Trail was only two wagon tracks that stretched between sunrise and sunset. They followed it for 21 days only stopping for meals, nights and the search for land. Frank gave the order to pull the driven cattle out first, the horses next, then the mules, the big ox and cart after them, then Merlin and Latham's wagon, and finally, last but not least, the Estlin boys. Alfy was teamster, and Euty and the pup were in the wagon. As they pulled out, the last thing Alfy could see was their boat lying on the riverbank by the end of the broken bridgehead.

Chapter 9
Commission Trail

The Boundary Commission Trail, about 500 kilometers in total length, followed not only the paths taken by buffalo and natives, but the routes of early explorers, fur traders, hunters, missionaries, and the Northwest Mounted Police. In 1873, the International Boundary Commission selected it for their principal supply route as they surveyed and marked the 49th parallel as the border between Canada and the United States. Now it was the route for hundreds of prospective settlers, like the Estlin brothers, coming west to seek land close to the Canadian border.

It was a beautiful morning, with a warm sun and cloudless sky. Everyone was in good spirits, particularly Alfy and Euty. The prairie was just beginning to show green, the birds were singing, and there were wild ducks on the small ponds. Since the leading teams had the responsibility of picking the trail and avoiding soft places, their oxen trudged contentedly behind following the others. Soon Alfy climbed up beside Euty to enjoy the boundless prairie with glimpses of different animals, the occasional jackrabbit, red fox, or gopher. Everything was interesting to them. As soon as they saw the front teams stopping, they realized it was dinnertime. They all unhitched, helped to make a fire and examined all the loads to insure that nothing was likely to drop off. Just as they finished the check, *"...we heard William Simms shouting, 'Grub pile!' He did not have to call twice.... During the course of our journey, Simms received many compliments for his culinary art. After the meal, we washed the dishes, packed them carefully, and then had a smoke to allow both the animals and ourselves a good long rest. Then we hitched up and got underway.*

"About the middle of the afternoon, we saw something approaching on the trail, which as it neared us resolved...into a train of Indians with carts, some light wagons, and a lot of ponies. They were coming back from a buffalo hunt, and were going to Emerson or Winnipeg to sell their skins. Of course they stopped and had a chat. Tawm and Frank who talked enough of their language to make themselves understood, told them all the news especially about the bridge going out. When they saw that my brother and I were much interested in their skins, they unpacked one, and spread it on the prairie floor. It was a magnificent buffalo hide, in perfect condition, which would have made an ideal covering for a large room. I have never seen such a large

one since. ...When Frank queried 'How much?' the old chief held up his two hands up with fingers extended once, and then one hand, meaning $15.00. Such a skin would have easily brought $150.00 only a few years later.

"Unfortunately we had no money to spare, or I certainly would have bought that robe for our bed. After this little break, which helped to pass the afternoon, it was almost camping time." [2]

The boys learned from their traveling companions that they should always carry wood shavings forward from one camp to the next to insure a campfire and that buffalo chips were a good substitute for wood when there was none.

After supper, the party prepared for the night. Initially it wasn't cold, so they made up their beds under the wagon to save the bother of unloading, and putting up the tent. "However, before morning, it grew so cold that white hoar frost covered everything forcing us to put up our tents. I shiver yet when I think of that night and getting into frozen clothes, covered with frost in the cold grey dawn." [2]

They travelled on until they came to a Mennonite settlement. It was so novel that they stopped for a look at the sod buildings with their outdoor clay ovens where bread was baked. The ovens were fueled with flax straw and badger brush. The stable and house were built under a single roof. A Winnipeg reporter described the Mennonite houses as built of mud and sticks, with straw or hay thatch. He saw walls of delicate lilac, dull red window sashes and grey shutters.

The brothers poked around as long as they could, bought some fresh eggs and then climbed on the wagon again. That evening they made a comfortable bed in their tent. The next morning, the party was up early, fresh and eager for another day's travel. When the group stopped for dinner, "... we asked Frank about a thin blue line that appeared on the horizon. 'Pembina Mountain' he replied, 'but it's a long way off yet.' And so it was." [2]

On a long journey, it is slow travelling with oxen as a team, because one can only cover twenty to twenty five miles a day under good conditions, and with moderate loads. On the other hand, the train that the Estlins joined had very heavy loads, and a spongy, or soft road in places. In one 24-hour period, for example, the party completed only six miles. The train lumbered along, the men sometimes walking, sometimes riding alone, or accompanying one of the other loads. They watched the blue streak on the western horizon gradually broaden. Finally, an object caught their eye coming from the northwest.

"At first we couldn't make out what it was. Although not on a trail, it moved fast.... In a short time, the object transformed into a pair of horses *drawing a good looking rig, with two men in it. The horses were sleek and full of life; the men appeared well dressed, with good coats, and comfortable robes. They drove right up to the front rig and stopped. We, of course, all stopped and when we walked up to the rig, we found one of the men had climbed out and was shaking hands with Frank."*

[Frank turned to introduce the man:] *"'Boys shake hands with Hugh Sutherland. He's running for Member at the next election and wants you to vote for him. Me and Tawm is goin' to and you'd better too as he's on the right side.' Frank and Tawm were strong Orange men and Torys [sic] of the most consistent type. ...Mr. Sutherland assured us that if we did not vote for him the country would go straight to the dogs, but that if we did, it would flourish like a bay tree. Moreover, a railroad would be built right to where we were going to settle....*

"But we knew nothing of Canadian politics. Our family on both sides were Liberal in the Old Country, but when we told Frank... he said politics out here was just the opposite to [what it was in England]. ...I was never able to verify this statement, my own experience being that if a newcomer was a Liberal at home and came out to Canada, his political leanings did not change. Be that as it may, we voted for Hugh Sutherland...." [2] The Estlin family remained Tory for a very long time.

As Alfy and Euty journeyed toward the blue streak on the horizon, they noticed the poor oxen laboring harder and harder. They found to their surprise they had actually climbed the mountain but the grade was so gradual they didn't notice it. It was more of an escarpment than a mountain, and the top was almost flat. Here the boys found a variety of vegetation new to them: aspen and birch, burr oak, high bush cranberry and red osier dogwood.

In contrast to the climb up, the descent was quite steep. *"Frank came back and told us all to put our drags on. We hadn't the faintest idea what he meant, but we found that by keeping quiet and watching our friends, we could conceal our inexperience.... ...we waited until we saw the others getting out their logging chains and winding them two or three times around one hind wheel of the wagon.... This action was necessary when teaming with oxen because there was no breeching on the harness usually used on the prairie and this simple device enabled the oxen to make the descent safely and comfortably. The long uphill pull had tired the animals, so when we got down the hill, we camped early...."* [2]

The next day the party forded a river, [the Pembina], that was considered good for both water and fish. Although it was usually a smaller stream, the high water this year made it both deeper and wider. In order to test the depth and soundness of the bottom, Frank arranged to hitch Tawm's horses ahead of the Stovins' mules for the first trip over. It proved to be a safe crossing, because the bottom was hard, and the water not too deep. Tawm rode one of his horses back in order to take his own load through. Then Merlin and Latham started over. Alfy didn't know whether the oxen did not like the water or the driver did not curse them sufficiently, but the wagon came to a halt midstream in four feet of water.

"First Tawm offered to hitch his horses ahead of the oxen, but Frank wouldn't have that. He said, 'Them horses would be too quick for the oxen. Even if the oxen pulled at all, which I very much doubt, they would not pull together.' Then Will Stovin suggested he would hitch the mules to the load, but this did not suit Frank either. 'No them damned donkey feet are too small'." [2] After giving it more thought, Frank reached a solution. He decided to take Jack and Tom from Alfy's load, put a yoke on them with a logging chain and then make it fast to the end of the pole.

Once hitched, the well-trained oxen knew what to do. As soon as Frank said, *"Get up Jack, Tom"* [2] they threw their whole weight against the yoke, and the load moved. As soon as Merlin's oxen felt the load ease, they stepped up too. In no time, the load reached the dry bank. Frank returned to take his own load across with the big ox, and the Red River cart tied on behind. Meanwhile Alfy and Euty were unyoking Tom and Jack and re-hitching them to their own wagon. Although the boys were pleased with their oxen's performance, Alfy wasn't confident about driving the heavy load into the river, and then up the steep bank on the opposite side. Luckily Frank was already wet and he offered to drive them across. Alfy gladly handed over the responsibility. Because this activity took up the whole morning, and Frank, Merlin and Latham were wet to the skin, the party unhitched for dinner on the far bank rather than continue on.

The Pembina River-crossing 200m from foreground. *Source:* Sharon Hope

Chapter 10
Land

As the party moved further west, the country became rolling with frequent large sloughs and creeks. Using their hands, the boys drank water the colour of weak tea from the sloughs they passed. The burn't grass from the previous fall wildfires coloured the water; the wrigglers added zest to the drink. *"We noticed that the deep ruts in the old trail ran almost straight through these deep sloughs and watercourses yet we often had to detour around them. Sometimes we had to walk a mile or two to find a crossing place. When we asked Frank what the explanation was, he told us the trail was made in a season when all of these places were dry. Because the trails were anything but dry now, our progress became slower and slower. The hard hauls with frequent doubling up, were wearing out our teams which became discouraged, and stuck in places that they might have gone through easily just the week before."* [2]

The train plodded on until they saw a small rounded hill on their right called Pilot Mound. Although it developed a town on its slopes later, what interested the group then was a wide slough full of water with no way of getting around it. This time instead of waiting until the wagons stuck, they doubled up first. This solution proved highly successful. Since the poor animals appeared worn out due to the hauling of the past week, the boys suggested to Frank that they should wait there until morning. Ducks were flying around them in flocks and they reasoned that the teams could rest while they went duck shooting. Frank quickly agreed because they all wanted a rest. Unpacking the guns from the wagons, the group spread out around the slough. The boys were all wet through so they waded into the weeds where they had some excellent shooting. Because the ducks were relatively unaccustomed to hunters, the men got all they could eat in no time. The hunters took the ducks back to camp where they plucked and dressed them, before handing them over to Simms the cook who served up a wonderful dinner. After eating heartily and thoroughly enjoying the change in diet, they all went to bed early. The party was up the next morning well rested, ready to start.

At Crystal City, located close by, men were excavating the foundation for a flourmill. There was a blacksmith and general store. The Hon, Thomas Greenway, Premier of Manitoba who owned and operated a large farm

Pilot Mound. Permission given by Stan Milosevic.

there, had a great influence on the growth of the town. The 1880 map of the area advertised much unoccupied land so Alfy and Euty decided to go to the Dominion Land office, not only to inquire about land locally but to ask about land further west at the next Land Office, near Deloraine. Alfy intended to notify the family of what they found. After a short look around the settlement, they resumed the trek until they arrived at the Land Office that was situated in a nearby ravine.

Sheltered by oak and poplar trees, the picturesque log building sat on the bank of a creek. A Dominion Agent and his assistant ran the office. They had topographic maps of every quarter section in the district serviced by the office. *"Every British subject who was of age, provided he had $10, could obtain a homestead entry of 160 acres with a further privilege of buying or preempting an adjoining 160 acres at $1 per acre when he had performed his homestead duties. These duties consisted of building a habitable house, not less than, I think 12x16, and breaking up 5 acres each year for three years. At this time he must have resided for at least six months out of each year on his homestead and have fifteen acres under cultivation when he made his patent...."* [2]

A Government Inspector looked over the land and if he found that all the duties had been properly executed, the homesteader got his "recommend" which was a certificate that his patent would be issued in due course.

"As soon as the homesteader received this certificate, he could mortgage his homestead for about $400 and pay for his preemption (which was usually done). He could use the remainder of the money to buy stock and equipment.

"The officials at the Land Office, who kept a record of all homestead entries, explained the land system to us. One-mile square contained 640 acres. A township was 6 miles square and contained 36 sections. The rows

of townships were numbered from the international border northward. The north and south rows were called ranges; homestead entries were only granted on even numbered sections, the odd numbered sections were reserved for railway building, sections 11 and 29 were school allotments, and section 8 and three quarters of section 26 was ceded to the Hudson Bay Company. This land system, once explained to us made perfect sense because all sections were posted." [2] By finding a corner post, any person would know exactly where he was in the vast expanse of prairie.

After Alfy and Euty made their inquiries, Alfy scrawled a postcard from the land office. It was Tuesday June 13th 1882: *"Made good time no mishaps, we shan't go near Brandon unless we can't get land, have had lovely weather, and enjoying company very much. Good shooting and lovely country but land all taken up. Will write again from the Turtle Mountain Land Office which we should reach on Sunday* [June 18th] *more time then."* [12]

The boys' load was the heaviest of all so Frank suggested that they take the spare yoke of steers that were being driven with the cows to hitch them in front of Jack and Tom. It sounded all right so they accepted the offer. No doubt it helped the oxen that were beginning to flag, but there was a negative aspect. The steers, which were unbroken, had only been driven a few times, so Alfy had to walk beside them to pull and push them as necessary. He had to walk all day, in all weather and terrain. Alfy was supposed to be an experienced driver, comparatively, so he didn't expect Euty to spell him off. They struggled along better when the road was reasonably good, but when they came to muddy portions, the boys had to take the steers off and hitch another team. The steers did not understand how to pull hard. In all, Alfy thought the steers were more bother than they were worth, and did more harm than good. According to Alfy, the incident that finally broke up the steer combination happened near LaRiviere's homestead.

LaRiviere, a Frenchman or halfbreed and former fur trader, had a large ranch, a good set of buildings and fences built of poplar poles. He ran a stopping house and had a reputation for having sold the Indians alcohol in the past; the place was named Wakopa, meaning "White Father". It was a good agricultural district with a large supply of timber.

On June 16th, the party was travelling along well because the road had been dry for a period, when they came to a fairly steep descent, a sharp turn and a deep creek. It had a stony hard bottom, but rather rough. A poplar pole bridge, floored with round poles, crossed the creek. Alfy had the lead rope for guiding the steers while Euty and the pup walked beside the oxen. *"It's a good thing they were, because when the steers felt the load off them on the downgrade, they started to run and cut the corner short on the bridge. I managed to hold on to them and keep my feet. The old oxen tried to make a proper turn, but the steers' pulling nearly crowded them into the creek. The wagon with two wheels on one side of the bridge and two wheels in the air, turned completely upside down with all our worldly goods inside…. The wagon box plunged into four feet of water. It fell so heavily we thought it was smashed to smithereens. Guns, ammunition, groceries, flour, syrup kegs, bedding and clothing sank to the bottom of the creek."* [2,3] It was a sorry sight but no time for lamentations.

"After we took the wagon off the box, we pulled it up the bank. Then the four of us got into the creek again and with one of us at each corner, lifted the wagon box. Two more stood in the water on the downstream side to prevent objects released in the process from being washed away and lost. As soon as the box was clear of contents, we carried it up and put it back on the wagon. Next we took the heavy stuff and repacked it in the wagon." [2,3]

Euty removed his lower clothing and waded into cold water so that he could search for objects on the bottom. *"With shivering legs and frozen toes, I fished in that miserable creek until nearly perished while the older members of the party amused themselves throwing pebbles at my bare anatomy."* [3]

Alfy and Euty took some time drying their clothes and cleaning the guns, but Alfy didn't think they lost anything. They had most of their perishables in cans for protection against damp and mice. The flour bags had a half inch caked on the outer sides but the inside was all right. *"The most unfortunate thing of the whole upset was that in repacking the stuff we accidently packed a five-gallon can of coal oil or the lantern or both against the bags of flour and not withstanding the one half inch caked flour on the inside of both flour bags, the coal oil or kerosene soaked all the way through both bags and as there was no more [flour] to be had, we were forced to eat it. Fortunately it is quite harmless but [there is nothing]… more sickening than the ever-recurring flavour of it at every meal. Only the ravenous appetites induced by our open-air life and the fact we had nothing else enabled us to eat it."* [2]

Chapter 11
Nearing Journey's End

On June 17th, the next day, the party stopped in the afternoon after crossing nearly twenty creeks. The rain soaked down and everything was wet through—the rugs, clothes, and groceries. They were about 18 miles from the Turtle Mountain Land Office near Deloraine. Alfy was afraid they would be short of sugar and salt with the wet but they would make do. The tent, that was only 7 by 12 feet but sleeping the six of them, leaked so the beds were wet. It was terribly cold. Alfy vowed to put up two tents that night. *"...We had a good square meal today here and are in a house which is a great comfort as it is terrible weather... We shall make the land office if fine tomorrow, if not, Monday...."* [12] [Since Alfy mailed this letter he might have done so at Desford which opened a post office in May 1882 and lay between LaRiviere's and Newcomb's Land Office on Turtlehead Creek.]

With good weather, they had done well to that point. They had travelled about 200 miles through the Turtle Mountain District. The land was glorious but lumber was dreadfully scarce. All but the railway land was taken up. They met dozens of people going back unable to get land. These reports did not improve the boys' spirits. The party decided, however, to go on until they got land, perhaps past the Souris where they would camp. At that point, three of the party on ponies could look up land. They heard all the land at Moose Mountain was taken up but they wanted to confirm the news through someone who lived closer to the location. The boys also considered going toward Birtle north of Brandon if other avenues failed. They knew that Indian land was not open for settlement. Alfy even thought they could cross the border and take up in Dakota a few miles from the boundary near LaRiviere's homestead. Alfy hoped they wouldn't be driven to such extremes, but they all wanted to settle together and were willing to go as far as the Rockies if necessary to achieve it.

Since the boys left Emerson, Alfy had not passed one night with dry feet. The "mosquiters" were terrible, so that their necks, ankles, wrists and hands became dreadfully sore. Mrs. Merlin had kindly made the boys a bed tick and some bags to go cover their heads to keep the 'skeeters' off, but the boys didn't find them until the day after the wagon overturned.

The brothers could see the Turtle Mountain in the southwest but, as they travelled, the creeks and coulees became even more numerous. Since the creeks all ran from the Mountain in a northerly direction, they crossed the Commission Trail. These creeks were full of water due to melting snow, and there were only occasional temporary bridges. Travelling became very slow and difficult; the group had to hitch two sometimes three teams onto each wagon in turn, pull it across, and then go back for the next one. In one particularly bad place, they hitched all the teams to one badly mired wagon before they finally got it out. That day they made only six miles in a twenty-four hour period. All day long they were lifting and pulling at the wagon wheels; unloading and reloading wagons, hitching and unhitching; lugging whiffle trees and logging chains. At night when they lay in their wet clothing, the ground did not rest their aching muscles.

Camping near a slough a little later than usual, they laid out the bedding after a hasty evening meal. Then they gathered to light their pipes and swap yarns. Between the camp and the dying light there was a ridge and the horses, cattle and ponies were quietly feeding along this ridge, making a fine silhouette against the darkened sky. Suddenly a cry sounded over the evening air. 'Clunk a clunk' like an old wooden pump. There it was again, 'clunk a clunk'. Whether the other members of the party knew what it was or not, the boys did not. Alfy and Euty retrieved the shotgun from the tent intending to murder the animal whose weird cry got closer and closer as they neared the slough. Suddenly something fluffy moved in the dead grass, another rustle in the grass. Alfy raised the rifle and shot at close range. They both ran forward to secure the kill but there was no sign of a kicking animal in death throes. Farther ahead the fluffy tail reappeared, so they rushed forward, fired another shot and then a third. By that time Euty was trying to smother his laughter. "What's so funny?" Alfy asked. Then the truth came out. The Indian pony had a long leather rope fastened to his neck to catch him easily in the morning. This rope had a knot that had become unraveled so as the pony moved along cropping the grass, the rope-end ran over the prairie. The cry, it transpired, came from a bird not familiar to them. The boys unloaded the gun shame-faced and headed back to camp hoping no questions would be asked. [18]

The boys knew that the Turtle Mountain Land Office could have as many as seventy people waiting to be served and occasionally those who arrived early in the morning had to wait until late the following day before their turn came. The office was at Turtlehead or Whitewater Creek, as it was known originally. It was located near the junction of two trails and therefore a popular place. The terrain surrounding it was mixed grassland and oak scrub. A Mr. Newcomb and his assistant ran the office.

2011 Turtlehead Creek Crossing. Former land office location 500m to left. *Source:* Sharon Hope

Their departure from the land office was prompt, on Monday June 19th, because there were no openings at all. The land had been withdrawn from the market, much of it placed in railway reserve. Alfy wrote to his mother *"…can get no land to take up, so are going to Moose Mountain to try there— everything going all right, am anxious about land, shall take up Rw land if we can't get it at Moose Mountain."* [12] Alfy posted the note at Deloraine, a hamlet close by that consisted of a post office and store run by a Mr. Cavers that had opened only a few months earlier. Later it expanded to include a blacksmith shop, boarding house and flourmill.

When the party had driven the wagons a mile or so from the Land Office, the Stovins turned south to their homestead in the Turtle Mountain. The old gentleman entered it the previous year, getting the location probably from a friend who was going to locate close by. Although it was quite common to enter "sight unseen" to quote the vernacular, this practice could be risky and seldom turned out satisfactorily. After saying goodbye to the Stovin boys and their mules, with many good wishes for their welfare, the rest of travelers resumed their weary journey.

In leaving the Turtle Mountain behind, the country grew flatter. Everywhere, as far as the eye could see, were patches of white on the prairie green. These were the remains of buffalo and the bones piles were sometimes only a few feet or yards apart. So numerous had the herds been, that as they travelled in search of new feeding grounds, their hooves dug hollow trails sometimes nearly a foot deep. These trails crossed and re-crossed each other over the plains like lines on a map. At intersections there seemed to have been battles caused by one herd trying to break the line of another and pass through. Later on, when the railways came, the settlers were not slow in taking advantage of the bone piles for fertilizer. Gathering the bones up, entrepreneurs shipped them away.

The group camped on the west end of the Turtle Mountain region at Tom Ritchie's homestead. He was very busy but made the party welcome. Ritchie gave a wonderful account of the location. According to him, it was excellent land, with lots of timber, fruit and game in the Mountain. Naturally the group was impressed with his enthusiasm so it was agreed that they would stay a day or two to look over this paradise. They found his description quite accurate. They drove up into the Mountain, going up the west side that slopes more gently down to the prairie. When they neared the top they obtained a wonderful view of the surrounding country.

The Mountain was covered with timber, particularly poplar with some white birch, oak, ash, and scattered elm and maple. There were a lot of wild fruit bushes, wild pea vines, even hops as well as much grass in the low places. The vines of the hops were so thick that it was hard to pull them apart. There were small lakes and ponds teeming with ducks as well as plentiful rabbits, partridges and prairie chickens.

"In later years when the timber had been destroyed by uncontrolled cutting and burning, the government opened the western portion for homesteading. Some French and Belgians settled there. They had nice farms and were very successful. The rainfall is more abundant, and the higher altitude protects the crops against early frost, so these farmers were able to get good crops while their prairie neighbours suffered from both drought and frost. It appears to be the rule in new countries that the pioneer seldom reaps the full result of his toil but the man who follows him falls heir to it." [2]

After leaving the Mountain the brothers looked over the prairie to the west. There were many varieties of wildflowers growing for miles, like a colourful carpet. From the farming perspective, they discovered good black loam with clay subsoil, a few round ponds and some stones. Since the land was so desirable, the brothers felt sorry that none of it was available for homesteading.

Rising early the next morning, the party made a good start, wishing their newfound friend Ritchie goodbye and good luck. Although there were still some sloughs, the trail had improved now that the train was past the Turtle Mountain with its ravines. The trail continued for several miles until suddenly they arrived at a wide ravine filled with water and low bare banks. It was known as Blind River. Drawing the wagons up together, they sent a scouting party to look for the best place to cross. The scouts reported shallow water with soft alkali mud spots and a deep dip in the middle that became shallower again toward the far bank. By doubling up immediately, the train made it through all right but *"the water was so deep in the dip that the oxen had to plunge and half swim to get across, and we had to tuck our legs up on the wagon seat to avoid getting wet."* [2]

After traveling about a mile further, the group arrived at the east bank of the Souris River, which was full and about a quarter of a mile wide. It looked so forbidding that after gazing at it in the deepening twilight, they decided to postpone surmounting it until the following day. Down on the flat, the boys saw a log cabin and a man moving about near it making his meal. Expectant Indians hovered comfortably about the man and between them there appeared to be an excellent understanding. This was Walter Thomas who, as Alfy discovered later, had suffered several narrow escapes from death that included being lost in a blizzard, and losing his arm when he accidently blew off his own hand with a rifle. On the far bank near the trees, a store could be seen that belonged to Alf Gould.

The flooded Souris River crossing from top of the slope, 2011.
Source: Sharon Hope

They went back to the wagons to set up camp. The party decided to wait to be taken across in the morning by ferry to find their way to Moose Mountain [now in Saskatchewan]. It was June 21st 1882, exactly twenty-one days after leaving Emerson. A man appeared while they were smoking and chatting around the tents. Visitors were important because they often imparted priceless information to homeless wanderers like themselves so the party listened attentively. The visitor, a gruff Englishman who had settled in a sod house, owned a blacksmith shop and store quite near their camp. He told the group there was quite a little settlement, Alf Gould, the Elliots and, of course, Walter Thomas whom the party had seen.

Mr Gerry told them that a man who ran a scow across the Souris, would, no doubt, visit in the morning. Then they heard that all the land within 80 miles of timber was taken up. The party immediately became discouraged, not knowing what to do.

They discovered the next day that the cost of the ferry was high, $7 for a load or around $70 for the outfit. This added to their disappointment. They knew too that the crossing would be an onerous process. The loads would have to be taken off and then on the other side the wagons would have to be reloaded after the animals swam across. At this point it all sounded like a tall order. The travelers had neither spare cash, nor the time for a fruitless search. They wanted to get some land broken up for a crop the next year, the sooner the better.

As it turned out, the Souris represented the western terminus of the train's journey. After talking it over in camp for hours, the party decided unanimously to seek out land reserved for railway purposes. As they turned back from the Souris River, they met another party coming to the crossing. The men told the new arrivals all about the costs but they opted to go on. Theirs was a smaller party so perhaps they made a better deal.

The wagons travelled back a day's journey stopping again at a homestead. When the potential homesteaders explained their decision, the man very kindly offered to show them where there were 3 or 4 choice sections of Railway land not on the market. They decided to take a chance on getting their squatters rights recognized. [The homestead was likely Tom Ritchie's since he took up land in 1881 very close to where the family eventually homesteaded].

After unloading a wagon, Tawm hitched his horses to it and the whole party set off, taking lunch, coming back after dark. This routine went on for several days because it was often necessary to see a choice more than once. Eventually everyone located to his satisfaction. No one attempted to grab the best land. The boys were given the benefit of the older men's experience with full and free choice on the boys' part. As a result, settlement began with an excellent feeling of good will.

Frank squatted on one section and Merlin and Latham on another. Tawm Main and William Simms stayed with Frank. They located later on abandoned homesteads. Euty and Alfy had a half section. Merlin and Latham were about ½ mile north while Frank was a mile or so northwest of them. Packing their wagon, the boys picked their way to their new home by following the wagon tracks made while prospecting the property.

The government had reserved railway land by the foot for whatever company built a railway through southwestern Manitoba. There were thousands of acres of it. The Southwestern Railway Company had the charter to build the line. They had issued a notice to any one who might squat on the land saying he or she would have the land at the price they settled on when the company got the land themselves.

All the land for miles and miles was squatted on, so the boys didn't think they would have any difficulties in getting their claim recognized. The brothers thought they could make the first payment, and then sell the claim if they liked for perhaps as high as 2 or 3 thousand dollars. Meanwhile, the boys were looking around for sections that were taken up nine months ago that the owners had neither lived on nor improved. They intended to apply to have the entries for at least two half sections cancelled, and their names entered for them. Alfie and Euty felt if successful, they could turn these preemptions into homesteads for Charlie, their mother, or themselves.

The land absolutely enchanted the boys with its birds, butterflies and flowers. The railway ½ section, a magnificent piece of rolling prairie, lay about 2.5 miles from Turtle Mountain where there was abundant wood. The land was twelve miles from a store and Post Office; 14 miles from a sawmill, and there was a limekiln and sand pit nearby with a blacksmith on either side of them. They believed the location excellent, the country like a picture. Although the boys' outdoor work was only just beginning, they were burnt black as halfbreeds already. The Estlin's land was Section 15-2-24 W about 7 miles from the International border. Alfy hoped "the Mater" wouldn't be disappointed that the family did not have homesteads. "...*I was very* [disappointed]," Alfy told her, "*but rather than to go on to a place that wouldn't grow wheat and was 30-40 miles from timber, I would have gone back to Ontario....*" [12] It was imperative for the boys to have crops the next year.

Chapter 12
Building A Home

Alfy and Euty pitched the tent carefully on a dry knoll, placing the boxes inside to make a bedstead or table as the need arose. All the items that did not fit in the tent, sheltered under the wagon box. After cleaning the grass off a spot, they placed the stove on it. As soon as they unloaded, Alfy dug a hole in the bank of the slough for water to seep into because water was a high priority.

The next day, the boys were up with the sun. Euty began searching for something to bake bread in; later he simply baked once a week at either Frank Main's or Merlin's place. While he got the breakfast of fried bacon, biscuits, and tea, Alfy went to fetch the oxen. *"They had wandered off, which was customary, about one half mile and were deep in the middle of a slough feeding. They disregarded my attempts to get them out with verbal assaults. They were so unconcerned and unresponsive that I waded in up to my knees to drive them out.*

"Tying them to the wagon until after breakfast, we hitched them up, then taking a chain, several ropes, the axes and some food, we wended our way to the Turtle Mountain to get dry wood for our fire and poles to build a pen for the oxen. As we climbed the west side, we were amazed and awed to behold the limitless expanse of prairie stretching away to meet the sky in every direction. It was awe-inspiring. Only a small black spot of newly broken prairie could be seen here and there, a white tent or a log or sod building to break the evenness of the view.

"...After a short rest from climbing the steep hill, we looked about for a place to get our load. Soon we found a patch of poplar that had been killed by a fire a couple of years before. We attacked this with more vigor than success. Our axes had never been ground.... The warmth brought out the mosquitoes, black flies and bulldog flies in droves. The load we managed to collect was not an imposing one. We mangled off half a dozen green poles and twenty or thirty small dry ones. Glancing blows from our axes scored our boots. We loaded the poles, tying them with the rope and chain, then struck off for home leaving the flies in the bush but taking the mosquitoes with us. ...We had the pleasure of these insects not only all the way home, but for the rest of the season. We felt quite proud of our load of poles until Frank came over, ...looked at the poles,... and squirted a stream of tobacco

juice on it. He remarked, 'Ye didn't go all the way to the Mountain and back for that did ye? Why I could wheel it all in a wheelbarrow. Looks as if beavers chawed it off. You'd better bring your axes over on Sunday and we'll grind them.'" [2]

When Alfy and Euty took their axes over to Frank's, they became familiar with the bane of Ontario boys existence, "turning the grindstone". *"If you've never had this experience you can thank your lucky stars. In those days, axes weren't finished at the factory, as they are now because they were apt to chip with rough transportation. When an Ontario axeman started to grind a new axe, woe betide the unfortunate boy who turned the handle. It took hours to wear the hard tempered steel to the required thinness. It was a great relief to finally hear the blessed words 'I guess that'll do' and see the hone come out* [of the expert's] *pocket to finish the job...."* [2]

When the boys arrived at Frank's on Sunday, axes over their shoulders. Frank delegated Tawm the task of grinding. After a couple of hours of turning the handle, turn and turn about, the boys had tools that were razor sharp. Then Frank schooled Alfy and Euty in the art of swinging with a promise of further instructions with practical illustration when they went to get the logs out. The boys planned to go to the bush together with Frank Main to retrieve the logs for their houses and stables. After all the homesteaders had their logs out, they would hold a number of "bees" to raise the house walls for each of them in turn. Eventually Euty became expert with an ax and could build a corner with the best of them but that was yet to come.

After supper at Frank's, William Simms cut Alfy's hair that had been growing abundantly. Then leaving with many words of grateful appreciation, the boys trudged off across the prairie keeping to the high ridges to avoid the mosquitoes. After a few days, Alfy went to the land office to enter the land, leaving Euty on the site. When he returned, the brothers took up the business of ploughing. In keeping with the occasion the boys got up at dawn, had breakfast, and turned the oxen out early to get a good feed. Once they got some of the smallest poplar poles sharpened at the ends, they picked out a nice piece of sod. After they laid out pickets running east west with the aid of a compass, Euty went back for the oxen. After harnessing and then hitching them to the plough, they marched to the east end of the line of stakes.

Since Alfy had done some stubble ploughing at Frank Main's, *"I ... elected to guide the plow* [while] *Euty drove the oxen keeping them in line with the stakes we put up. As soon as the oxen started up I discovered that breaking the sod was much different than plowing old stubble land. The plow would not go in as I expected it to, but jumped from side to side making silly little scratches in the sod. We stopped operations to discuss possible causes for the unexpected behaviour of our implement, but could not fathom the mystery. Then we tried again with the same results. [Euty]… suggested that he try while I guided the oxen but the results were exactly the same.*

"*We were a despondent pair of embryo farmers, sitting on the vast unbroken prairie while the oxen chewed their cuds, flopped their heads from side to side, and swung their tails to keep off the flies…. [After a short time]… we heard "rattle, rattle" and a pony's head appeared over the ridge, followed by a buckboard in which Frank sat. He took the situation in at a glance. Having divested his mouth of a huge quid, and biting off a new one, he remarked' Well how's it goin' boys, I thought I would just run over and see how you were makin out.*'"[2]

[Climbing out of the buckboard, Frank] "*…walked over to the plow. First he took out the bridle belt that regulated the draft and raised it up. … Secondly he adjusted the rolling coulter that cuts the sod. [Because it was too low,] it kept the plough out of the sod. Then he turned the plough on its side to examine the share. The edge was as thick and dull as our axes were before getting them ground….*"[2]

Frank explained that ploughshares were not tempered. They had to be beaten cold on an anvil, with a blacksmith's hammer. He said a piece of rail was a good substitute and since he had a piece, the boys could bring their shares over the next Sunday. He would show them how to beat the shares. Meanwhile, Frank took a large flat file from his pocket, to make a temporary cutting edge.

Once that task was accomplished, Frank took the handles and with a "Gettap Jack, Tom," the plough sunk gently into the sod. Moving along the line of pickets, he turned a long, straight ribbon a foot wide and two inches thick, the grass turned downward. When he got to the last picket, the boys made a few adjustments, and then laid another ribbon close to the first. Alfy and Euty got Frank to strike two or three more lands before he returned to his farm. After his visit, the boys were full of confidence, and very thankful for both Frank's practical experience and expert instruction.

After Frank left, the boys made progress; the oxen walked the furrow sedately, drawing the properly rigged, sharpened plough. During the following weeks that they ploughed, they spent their Sundays at Frank's beating the share and maintaining the cutting edge because it would only last a week at a time.

Breaking would have been a pleasant task, except that occasional stones would throw the plough out. When this happened, the boys had to go back with all the equipment to pick up the missed piece. Euty got out the pick, axe and spade to remove all the stones that he could see on the lands Frank had struck. Later, they built a stone boat about five feet long and three feet wide. It had two good-sized poplar poles flattened on the sides with a draw bar notched and pegged at both ends, and small, flattened pieces pegged on the top.

The boat was a very useful piece of equipment for carrying much more than stones. They used it to hold clothing, implements, and their water jug and, when the Estlins finally had a stable, the boat transported the manure. It was not uncommon at winter dances, to see people wrapped in fur robes arrive sitting on boxes in stone boats, drawn by one or two steers, or oxen.

Alfy wrote to Point Edward indicating their location about ten to twelve miles from the Land Office. *"I think we have broken 5–6 acres.... The weather is good, except rather thundery. ... We might get on better with a shower or two to soften the ground...there are some very good hay spots... and a lake about ½ mile away with any amount of ducks...."* [12]

Again he stressed to the family not to buy cattle and not to purchase any major furniture. There were lots of poplar poles that would do just as well for bedsteads and lounges. They worried continually about spending money but much to Alfy's surprise, they had $244 dollars left rather than the $160, as Alfy had thought; somehow he had not remembered the original amount.

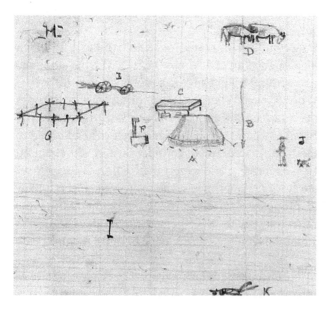

Alfred's sketch of camp enclosed in his letter to Point Edward.
Source:
Estlin family memorabilia, Sharon Hope

Slough on Emily Estlin's homestead 2011. *Source:* Sharon Hope

Alfy and Euty liked the life immensely. One of them got up at 4, turning the cattle out to graze until about six, when Alfy would hitch them up and plough until breakfast. That meal took place from 7–8 am roughly. Dinner was 12 noon until 2 and Supper 6–7 pm. Then Alfy ploughed until it got dark. Their meals settled into breakfasts of bacon, potatoes, hard tack or crackers, and dinners the same with the addition of pancakes. Teas were the same again with the addition of applesauce. Euty cooked fairly well. He was getting very fat, and Alfy was getting very thin, but he hoped to pick up once the breaking was over. Alfy was afraid that the women would find it tough on the land with the fearful mosquitoes that surrounded them and the fact there was no meat all summer. However, both the boys had been two months without meat and didn't miss it a bit.

There were a myriad of small details to attend to as Alfy and Euty settled in. They dug a small well, but thought the swamp or slough water best. They fetched milk and butter from Frank Main's, courtesy of his two cows. The mosquitoes plagued them to the point of smoking the cattle. The boys installed a kitchen garden on a gentle south-facing slope, where the soil was superb. In it, they planted a large patch of potatoes and turnips. When Euty went to the bush with Frank Main, he found that they could get at the timber easily. It was all poplar with nice straight boles. They could remove about 12 logs a day; it took about ten to build a side for the house.

Obtaining firewood was no trouble because if the boys started in the morning, they could get a load home by dinnertime. They just drove in, cut what they wanted (usually a large amount), with no one to stop them, and brought it home. They suffered for it though, with the blackflies and the mosquitoes that were so thick at times, they couldn't see through them. Besides their own fence logs and firewood, Alfy hoped that they would be able to get at least 500 logs out during the next winter which would sell like hot cakes at a dollar a piece.

Alfy decided on a story and one half house with a cellar, but he knew it would take some time to get the logs out. Once they got the roof on, Alfy thought they might be able to write for the family in Point Edward to come out.

The boys became a source of information for their friends in the east who considered coming to homestead. This amused them no end because they barely knew what to do but they dutifully wrote with costs and advice. A pony, for example, cost $50–$60 and a buckboard about $40. Alfy was still thinking that in the fall he and Euty could take the wagon and tent and spend a week looking over land west of Moose Mountain, and then once the crop was in next spring, the two of them could secure a section.

They longed for news from Ontario because the letters coming from Point Edward were so erratic. The letters came by train to Brandon, the furthest extent of the C. P. Railway at that time, and then by stage to Old Deloraine. There was also a post office at the Land Office, a mile or two further north. Letters reached the boys when someone going by the post office picked them up. When the boys finally got a letter, they tried to answer the family's questions as quickly as possible, and have their letter reposted again through the kindness of a neighbour. This method saved them taking a day off work to ride a pony (which they had to borrow) to the post office.

Prior's insurance situation was still not resolved, and Alfy became more or less convinced that they would not receive it. Others would take their money first. His father had gone through bankruptcy proceedings so the boys felt there would be demands on any money that came through. On July 16th Alfy wrote: *"...they won't care a pin about us.... Write lots of letters and send us some newspapers as we don't know what is going on in the world..."* [12]

The boys kept ploughing until the others were finished their work and then after a meeting at Frank's, they decided to get their house logs out together before haying. In this way all the homesteaders could work at their respective houses at odd times while they continued to hay. Meanwhile the boys had their own preparations to make to the house site. Alfy produced a detailed plan of the house, dividing the first floor into the kitchen 11x16, and a bedroom for his mother and the girls of 8x16, with the potential for three good bedrooms upstairs when he could afford the lumber to separate them. He felt there would be heaps of room for Euty, Charlie and himself upstairs and pile boxes there as well. The wall height was about 9 feet for the main floor and he had a combined wood and tool shed to one side. They pegged out the full size of the house, lining it by the compass, and then marked the cellar inside. They took the stone boat and collected the stones for the bottom logs to rest on, large flat ones for the corners.

Alfred's cross sectional sketch of the house.
Estlin family letters. *Source:* Sharon Hope

The boys finished ploughing about Tuesday July 18th, including the firebreaks around the house site, and then began digging the cellar. It was a tough job. The cellar was 16 feet long and 11 feet wide by 6 feet deep. They hit a stony bed of clay like concrete just as the weather became terribly hot. The bulldog flies, (named because of their large bodies), teased and bit them. One cannot imagine the enormous amount of dirt the cellar created. To top it off, the Muley ox nearly fell in the cellar and, as a result, wouldn't go within 100 yards of it. Euty told Alfy he was not going to dig a cellar when he set up housekeeping, or if he did, it was going to be a small one.

The boys found the tent very hot indeed now, so they camped out under the wagon box. Their attire during the day was a merim vest, thin pants, socks, shoes and a straw hat. They could barely keep that on. Sundays they visited, cut heads of hair, and wrote letters. The two took a walk over the farm one Sunday, and saw the turnips and potatoes thriving. Then they prepared to visit the Mains and Merlin and Latham, their usual routine. Alfy and Euty often stayed to tea or dinner with them.

Around July 23rd Alfy wrote that Euty, the cook, had gone to put on the potatoes for dinner; the boys had a bushel left which they hoped was enough to last until they could go to get more. *"…Please excuse the handwriting but lying on your tum tum with a pocketbook to write on is not productive of good penmanship. The dog is now assisting me to write.... You must provide yourselves with bags of muskit's bar with a slip string at the top and bottom over your straw hats...it keeps the brutes out.... "* [12]

Finally the boys were so pressed for provisions they had to make a trip for supplies; Euty maintained Alfy went to Brandon, which is likely. Hitching up the oxen, he set off while Euty guarded the site. As Euty watched the wagon slowly disappear over the rise, which seemed to take hours, he realized there was nothing as far as the eye could see. He was alone for the first time in his life, surrounded by complete and utter silence. There were a few distant neighbours but as far as he was concerned, they could have been in Ontario. Euty wondered what he would do with himself in the evenings when the chores were done.

Far away on the horizon there was a small cloud no larger than a man's hat. Later that evening, while listening to a plover call in the distance and a coyote yap eerily, Euty happened to look at the cloud again. It had spread up from the west and widened out. A pale light shot through the cloud and a warm wind sprang up, moaning through the grass. The wind increased accompanied by thunder. The collie crawled into the tent whining. One half hour later the storm burst. The wind came in stronger gusts, thunder crashed, and lightening seemed to pour out of the heavens. With a stronger gust of wind, the tent pins came loose leaving Euty and his bedding exposed to the elements as the tent blew away. Clutching at the flapping canvas, he rolled it around him as he lay on the ground. He managed to envelope the dog in one of the last folds. Once the thunder died down, he finally fell asleep still rolled in the tent. The next morning when Euty awoke to brilliant sunshine, he divested himself and the dog from the canvas, erected the tent again and set about drying their belongings.

The following morning Euty straightened up from cooking a final rasher of bacon to find a tall Indian looking wistfully at it. At a sign, his visitor joined in the repast. There was a keg of syrup that had fermented in the heat of the tent. While his guest waited, Euty made slapjacks with the remnants of his flour and poured liberal amounts of syrup over them. Apparently the meal met with the man's approval because after, he rose, picked up his rifle, poked Euty in the ribs, and strode off across the prairie. A few days later, Euty was very glad when he could see the wagon in the distance slowly making its way back through the rippling grass. [18]

Chapter 13
Logs and Hay

When the Mains were ready to extract logs from Turtle Mountain, the boys got up early in order to get into the bush before it got too hot. They took the box off the wagon, tying on their lunch, the axes and the chain. They were well along when they saw the others coming. There was Tawm with his horses, and Frank; Merlin and Latham with their oxen. When Tawm caught up with Alfy and Euty, he asked Alfy to take an axe and jump on his wagon, so they could go ahead to fall some logs. The others could "snake" them out, and load them when they arrived. Following his suggestion, Alfy went ahead. Not only was Alfy impressed at Tawm's dexterity with an axe, but also with his ability to lay a tree in a precise location. At first, he contented himself with chopping off the tops and trimming the limbs, but with a nice sharp axe felling looked so easy that Alfy finally plucked up his courage to take his place opposite Tawm. Then he struck blow for blow with him. Tawm showed Alfy how to make the tree fall where he wanted it, and how to make a proper scarf.

"When we got back to the others we found they had 'snaked' out a nice pile of logs that we had fallen. Frank took our oxen since they were well trained for the work, put a yoke on them, and with Euty helping, they pulled the logs quite efficiently. It was cruel work for both men and beasts—black flies, bulldog flies and mosquitoes by the millions." [2]

Then there was the heat—the sun pouring down without a breath of air into the valleys where the straightest timber grew. Finally the heavy green logs had to be lifted on to the wagons. After lunch, Tawm said they needed a few oak logs because each house required two rounds of oak logs laid on stones for the foundation. The side logs were 26 to 28 feet long and it was difficult to find oaks sufficiently straight that held their diameter but after a lot of searching they found the ones they wanted.

"Our next job was to make long reaches for the wagons so as to divide the weight of the logs evenly between the front and back wheels. We got some nice straight oak or ash poles about 16 feet long, flattened the butt ends, and bored a one and a quarter inch auger hole in them for the king bolt to go through. Then we smoothed the small ends down to go through the axle. By this time everyone was ready to load; soon we had six long logs and 8 short ones on each wagon." [2] The men wanted to get out of the heat and flies

as soon as possible so they started for home immediately after they were loaded. This was the first of many trips Alfy and Euty made for logs.

Between these journeys to the Mountain, Alfy made a number of shorter trips to fetch lime and sand, as well as taking care of a growing number of chores such as hoeing the spuds. Around this time, Alfy lost the dog at the store that was about 10 miles away from their land by trail. Alfy thought she must have followed some other wagon away by mistake; Euty and Alfy spent a miserable time because they were both so fond of her. She kept them alive and understood almost everything they said to her. The next night she made her appearance, hardly able to drag herself along. She evidently had been travelling all night with nothing to eat. She had a piece of rope around her neck that she had bitten through. Some "brute" had tried to steal her. Alfy couldn't fathom how the pup, at six months old, could find the tent on the vast prairie.

It was becoming a bit cooler now, so Alfy suggested to Euty that they might be warmer and more sheltered from the wind if they placed the tent in the hole that would be their cellar. He agreed and they were comfortable for quite some time. One night, though, there was a thunderstorm with a veritable hurricane accompanied by a deluge of rain. In a short time, there was six inches of water in the cellar. Although the tent itself stood up well being sheltered from the wind, everything they had was drenched. They consoled themselves with the fact that had the tent been above ground, it probably would have blown down, and then they would have lost their clothes and other light things. They moved the tent up the next day, digging a trench about it and pegging it down.

When the boys had about 35 logs at the house site, with the expectation of about 20 more, plus about six potential trips for joists and rafters, Charlie wrote Alfy asking questions about conveying goods from Point Edward to Manitoba. The Estlin letters continually overlapped, so no sooner did Alfy clarify a point then it arose again. Alfy stated over and over to bring as little as possible and no animals such as cattle, but communication was difficult with those living so far away in a different environment not to mention a lag of weeks in their letters. Since Charlie would be responsible for obtaining provisions, and transporting them from Point Edward, Alfy felt he should answer Charlie's inquiries with care. First, Alfy told him not to worry about the article that had appeared in the Globe stating that the government intended to reserve land. It would not affect them. Alfy believed that they could not be evicted. Then he responded to Charlie's question about obtaining a rail car.

"...You have no idea what expense, trouble and delay it would cause you. You would have to provide for the animals, ride with them, take them out and exercise them, and water them at least twice a day. The risk would be very great too, as many cattle if they survive the journey, die when they feed on the prairie grass because the change is so great. The idea of bringing up 2 or 3 yoke of oxen for other people... In the first place we cannot risk our money like that and in the second place we can buy oxen and cows cheaper here than you can bring them...Euty tells me a man was here today with a drove and offered him cows for $65 to $85...." [16]

Although several carloads of cattle had come to Brandon, there was no sale for them. Alfy hoped Charlie could bring a few fowls, but he also suggested a pig. What would it eat during the winter? Then there was Charlie's offer to bring up a milk cow. They didn't milk during the winter here like cows did in England, and the family would have no grain or roots to feed it during the first winter; the cow would want all the household refuse. The family would have very little income for two years, perhaps only 1–200 dollars the first year. Of course the boys might make some money from ploughing. The next year Alfy thought they might have income from 50–60 acres.

"...Don't bring any barrel pork..." Alfy suggested, *"...we have spiced roll of bacon and we don't get tired of that... You should get some hams, all sorts of groceries, and evaporated apples (lots)...."* Finally he said *" ...Now don't forget to tell me in your next letter the weight of the freight and the weight of the provisions, rate per 100 lbs to Brandon, bonding charges, and carriage of fowls...we will be going to Brandon to fetch the lumber, shingles and tar paper so we'll inquire about the furniture...we shall not need a box stove...."* [16]

Alfy wrote to Southwestern Railway about the land to make sure the officials told them directly it became their property. If the Syndicate got it, the boys would have to rush off to Winnipeg and secure it before anyone else did. If anyone else bought the land over their heads, they [that is, the Mains, Merlin, Latham, Alfy and Euty] agreed that they would not give it up but say: "we were improving it before it became your property".

On August 7th Alfy told the family he had heard nothing fresh about the land. The boys had nearly finished getting the logs out. They were amused when Charlie and Emily Estlin gravely told Alfy to inquire about Hudson Bay Company lands. The boys never saw anyone except on Sundays, and there were no other settlers near them familiar with the Hudson Bay lands that they could ask. However, in the next letter from Point Edward it was obvious that Charlie and Emily took the idea of purchasing Hudson Bay lands seriously. The price, Alfy told them was from $5 to $10 per acre, which meant that if they bought a ½ section with an average of $7 an acre, they would be paying $2240. Cash down would be $248. The family, were, of course, not in the position to pay these amounts. There was a risk that they might not get the railway land but Alfy was not afraid. It would be far better to pay for homesteads, and preempt a claim of 320 acres, than to take up Hudson's Bay land. Alfy would have about $100 left after the house, and with that, combined with the money Emily had, they would have to purchase provisions for a year, and make the first payment for the land.

Alfy commented that the family in Point Edward was spending money *"...on things we don't need for instance that furniture. I don't see that we need a box stove; surely the cook stove will warm the house enough. If you think it won't, I suppose you had better get a small one or a 2nd hand one as it will be little used...."* [12]

Alfy explained again that he would have to buy the windows, door, tarpaper, and shingles for the house. Everything in Brandon was fearfully dear. Alfy still hoped that the insurance money would come, but it was over 6 months since his father's death and nothing had arrived. The fare, Alfy informed the family, from Winnipeg to Brandon was $4 each. He let the family know that *"...We begin our hay making next Monday. We have all our logs out now and only have rafters and joists to get...I am going to ride 20 miles at noon in order to get this posted...."* [12]

Haying was like bush work. Tawm did the mowing and raking with his horses, while the rest of the party coiled, pitched, and stacked. The next time Alfy wrote to the family, he noted that he had not been able to fetch their letters for three weeks because they were so pressed with work. In fact, Alfy worked so hard that he could hardly write, spell, or express himself properly any more. The lack of letters was a great bother, but the pair had accomplished much more recently. At this point, the boys had between 15 and 20 tons of hay, and worked at odd times on the house when they could. Alfy had to do a compensatory day's work for Main in the bush. He left between 6 and 7am on a Friday morning, and did not get into bed until 3 on Saturday. He only had a snack. Then he was up again, and off to the bush for themselves at 6.30am, and back home again at half past eight at night. That amounted to 31 hours of work in 48 hours.

Every time the boys thought they were becoming experienced homesteaders, they stumbled. Euty dropped an axe in the bush but luckily a man brought it back a week later. On another trip to the Mountain, Euty took the wagon and broke it, which delayed them a bit. A man who lived about 2 miles away had 3 little boys and one not more than ten. The oldest boy took the horses and ploughed as a matter of course.

Soon the boys were going to fetch the materials that they needed from Brandon, or raise the house. After completing either of those two jobs, Alfy declared he would feel much better. Alfy spuded a stalk of potatoes, and found some the size of pigeon's eggs so the garden was progressing, but the gophers or ground squirrels troubled them. The animals swarmed and devoured everything in the way of flour, plants, and their other provisions. The boys killed six one week. The flies tortured them. The roof of the tent was black with insects. These flies bit nearly as badly as "moskiters", but Alfy and Euty could not get rid of them in spite of systematic killing with a net. At least they knew that most of these pests would be gone with the frost.

One Sunday, the boys put on their best clothes, and washed up thoroughly. After they tidied everything, Euty prepared to go over to bake as he always did. A man passed by their place. "'What's this?' he said, 'You boys goin to a wedding?' 'No' we answered 'only over to Frank's for a Sunday visit'." [2] He told them it was Saturday, so they changed immediately and got back to work.

The next week Alfy told the family that: "...*Euty has gone over to bake, we are to have a cake as an experiment...while I write the dog is lying next to the flour. Mr Gopher came to have a feed and did not see Kit. That gopher followed some 60–70 others.... We know everyone for several miles around, and they all take a great interest in us, and try to help us. We believe it is because we have sisters. Women are in great demand, there are only four around here, and they are worked to death baking etc., but there will be more now. Couldn't Captain bring up a carload?*" [12]

William Simms, who was a broad axeman, came over to hew the boys' foundation logs. Alfy and Euty helped Simms block his logs up firmly, take the bark off, run his line with a burnt stick, score it with the chopping axe, and then shear it down on both sides with the broad axe. The result was a thick oak plank. As soon as all eight logs were done, and the lower joists flattened on one side, Tawm came over to fit the lower logs to the stones. He made the notches for the joists to fit into, and then fitted the second tier of logs to the first, dovetailing the corners. The boys put the lower joists in later.

Because they had been working hard getting all the building materials ready for the "raisin", the boys were glad to get a call to go over to Frank's for the first "bee". They were anxious to learn, and besides, it was a welcome change from the continual work, from early morning til late; they didn't see anyone but each other from weekend to weekend.

When the day of the "bee" arrived, the boys went over in good time to look around so they could prepare for their own work when their turn came. They found Frank's cellar all finished, and the two rounds of oak logs neatly dovetailed together with the lower joists in their places two feet apart. The logs lay some distance from the foundation, the long ones at the sides, and the short ones at the ends. The largest logs rested nearest to the foundations followed by the next size, and so forth down to the smallest that would be placed at the top of the wall, and would end the row. The logs were all nicely peeled and hewn flat on one side; the side which would be turned "in". Rafters, plates, and jambs were all ready; when the other three corner men arrived, the men asked each other which corner they would like to take, and Tawm took the fourth. At the shout of "Timber" the others ran over, seized a log, and laid it on the building. Then they went to the other side, and did the same thing, while the corner men were busy fitting the dovetails.

William Simms and Frank made "toggles" that held the logs in their places, until the doorjamb was pegged in. The same thing occurred at the windows. After the men built a portion of the walls, they used poles hollowed out like a crutch placed at an angle against the ground to push the logs up. When the walls rose above the doors and windows, the upper joists had to be notched in between the logs then a few more logs were placed before the plates. The plates were hewn on both sides, so the walls would be level on them. Finally the two pairs of end rafters were set up, and well braced. After that, the "raisin" was over.

The boys wended their way home tired but extremely happy with what they had learned. They tackled their own work with renewed interest, and greater understanding. Merlin and Latham's "bee" was next but, before the boys had their own raising, they managed to get to Brandon.

Chapter 14
Together Again

It was the first week in September before Alfy and Euty were finally ready to purchase the shingles, tarpaper, windows, lumber, locks, hinges, nails, screws and so forth in Brandon. The trip took them a week. The boys were excited because they led such monotonous, isolated lives doing physical chores every day. It was a novelty to hitch up the faithful oxen, and set out for the new town some seventy–five miles to the northeast.

The weather, which was fine, made the trail dry and hard, so they crossed Plum Creek, as the Souris was called then, without trouble. In due course, they arrived at the busy town. Euty said that Brandon reminded him of a book he'd read about a dusty town where clouds of birds wheeled over the crops. He had never seen such flocks of birds as he saw there.

Once the boys found a stable for their oxen, they went with Frank to a small hotel that was called, Alfy thought, the Rosin House. They paid $1.00 for three substantial meals, a bed, and something for the dog. It took most of the next day to buy their stuff, and get the loads on. Alfy was obliged to hire an extra team when he discovered that they could only take half of what they wanted. This annoyed Alfy because it made the lumber that much more expensive. Although they couldn't do without the goods, the whole house wouldn't cost them as much as rent and firewood would for a winter spent in Ontario. Alfy just had time to go to the station to fetch the furniture because he wanted to take it with them but it wasn't there. The clerk said he expected it was detained at Chicago, St. Vincent or St Paul until the charges were paid. Alfy enclosed the weigh bill to Charlie, telling him to pay it, and that $5.00 was likely enough money to free it up.

For the return trip, the items had to be carefully packed and wedged to insure that they wouldn't slide during the continual jarring over the hard prairie trails. Frank supervised the packing and then they started shortly after dinner. Frank, Alfy and Euty made eight or nine miles that night, crossing the "Little Souris" to camp on the bluffs. The next day they got to the Souris proper where they forded the river successfully again, camping on the south bank.

After one more sleep, as the Indians say, the pair arrived safely at their site. The boys had left the tent and all their stuff out but the Indians never

Brandon in 1882. Permission given by Gordon Goldsborough Manitoba History Society. From S. J. McKee Archives at Brandon University, in the Lawrence Stuckey Collection, photo C1.

came. They really only had one regular visitor, and that was the Chief's son, [probably Sitting Eagle] but everything was exactly as they left it. The dreaded business was over.

The alkali water on the way to Brandon was so terrible that Alfy and Euty intended, in future, to sling a keg of water from the homestead under the wagon. They both had five days of acute diarrhea (Alfy couldn't wait to see how to spell it) that kept them back because they could not eat. *"We were so weak we couldn't work properly, however, a good square dose of painkiller put me straight, and Euty came all right without."* [12] Finally, they put a filter on their own water which also was somewhat alkali, and very muddy. The boys hoped when they dug a proper well, it would be different.

Merlin and Latham decided to return to Emerson for the winter having done all they could over the summer. They planned to open a store nearby the next spring. The brothers seemed to be accomplishing little now, and it felt as though they would never get the house up. They were still peeling logs and every little thing took time.

Euty and Alfy often longed for an hour in a good "confectioners". Half of their time was spent in preparing meals some of which they couldn't eat anyway. One week, all their biscuits were finished so they existed on slapjacks fried in bacon grease with treacle for pudding. On Sunday, Euty went to Franks to bake some "Choke dog" that they found very "lasting".

At another point, by the end of the week they ran out of food entirely. Euty had to go and bake, leaving Alfy with no breakfast until he came back. Alfy told Birdie that when she got installed in her new kitchen, she must prepare for appetites such as were never seen before.

"Our poor clothes—our socks suffer the worst. We should change them every day by rights, but we wear the same pair until we can't stop in the tent with them at night, then we put them on two or three times more. At this point, Euty washes them, and a nice healthy job it must be, but he [doesn't] seem to mind it."...He said he felt uncomfortable this morning as he missed his weekly wash last Sunday, and really must have one today. You should have seen his neck with a shirt he'd worn for 4 weeks in this weather... I am throwing on great style today with a white shirt. Euty says people will think I'm canvassing for M. P., as the only person we have seen with one on is Sutherland...." [12]

Now it was decidedly cooler at night. Alfy and Euty noticed the days getting shorter and the "miskiters" fewer. Yet the boys endured a fearful series of storms, when the wind blew like a hurricane. They hoped the rain would hold off until the hay was in. One of the oxen not only devoured an entire bag of eating potatoes, and a plate of bacon, but it broke the plate so now the boys had to improvise with the washbasin. The oxen were terribly thin because the brothers worked them too hard, however, the boys hoped that the animals would put up with it for a little longer. One ox went lame, but recovered. The ox they called Muley was very amusing, knowing everything they said to him. When Euty tried to work with him, he ran away, and kept dodging about. The ox ate potato peelings, slapjacks, dishwater, and bread. He walked about with a buffalo bone in his mouth smoking it like a pipe. The boys thought he was something like Charlie.

Alfy and Euty had an old rabbit too that insisted on living in the tent with them. Euty kept chasing it out with a towel. The pigeons were having a battle royal. Alfy and Euty had three roosters and one hen, so the birds fought constantly. The boys let the pigeons out because they were tame, but the large hawks came after them. The brothers only consolation was that all of this wasn't going to last long.

The turnips disappeared, the boys didn't know where; some stray cattle ate the potatoes down while they were in the bush, but the tops seemed to be picking up again. Alfy wrote to the family *"...I'll try to borrow a pony to post this in the evening but it is very bad getting back because you can't find your way over the prairie an hour after sundown. I am going to cut Euty's hair when he comes back. I don't think it has been cut since he left the Pt. He asked me to.... Did I tell you to bring us overalls and over shirts? I believe they are made of duck, and last well, in fact you can't wear anything else in the bush with comfort....*" [12]

Finally the monumental day arrived for Alfy and Euty's own house-raising. The "Commissariat Dept" caused them a good deal of concern but they managed to get the job done. Euty declared the raising a great success. " *...Thank goodness the old house is up and it is quite a size...I cooked 2 meals for 17 people, giving them bacon, potatoes, bread and butter, tea brewed in the kettle, and for dinner the same except for apple sauce cooked in the kettle....*" [19]

Everyone seemed to have enough to eat and drink. The only treat the boys had managed to get recently was some raspberries on the Mountain, and there weren't many of them.

Now Alfy and Euty returned to hay making. It did make the place look more inhabited to see a large mound of hay up on the prairie. The rick showed up and so did the house. Euty wished that the two of them had Charlie to give them a hand with the "blooming" hay, because it was very hard work, pitching it up on the wagon all day long. Euty had another project though: "*... We are going to make a commodious WC about 5 foot square, my special job, with a shingle roof, a thing that you won't see for more than 50 miles around....*" [19]

One important event occurred near the end of summer. A store started up only one and half miles from the boys that would be the Post office by and by. The Commission Trail passed right through the section. People would be bringing the mail up each week from Deloraine. This was going to be a great comfort to the family not only from the point of view of saving time in obtaining provisions but in communication with the world outside. It was going to be called Montifiore and the Estlin family adopted that name a few years later for their address.

Charlie took the initiative to write to the CPR Company about land. It did little good because the company's bureaucratic reply said nothing. "*... We do not know whether we will have any land in the locality specified. Nor do we recognize the claims of parties that squat on odd numbered sections; we entertain no applications for land not actually ours....*" [20]

The house was somewhat unfinished, having no doors or windows; the boys had to spend time putting up the remaining rafters, as well as the door and window jambs. Now the family could realistically come the first or second week in October. When Alfy and Euty began to give the family in Point Edward genuine arrival dates, they hoped the women wouldn't expect too much.

It didn't take long to get the roof boards on. After that, the boys put a coat of alkali mud in the cracks where the plate and roof boards joined. With the help of a couple of neighbours, they were ready to shingle. Fortunately their neighbours were experienced, so they did it correctly. They got the tarpaper on, well lapped, and, with a black stick and line, soon had a nice even course laid. The boys sawed off the ends of the roof boards straight, leaving a 12–inch projection over the ends, on which a 4-inch facer was nailed. After that it was easy work with two of them laying down the shingles, taking care to break the joints, and two others nailing them down. As soon as that task was finished, Alfy and Euty boarded up the gables, putting a small window in each, and made frames for the two doors and three windows. Next they laid the two floors, built a plank ladder called a "courtesy stair", and one ladder for the cellar.

After the boys had fitted the doors and windows, they were ready to do the "chinking". Chinking has to be done correctly otherwise it may fall out, leaving a hole when plastered with mud. As it turned out, they were only plastering on one side this first winter because Jack Frost stepped in unexpectedly, and froze the mud solid. They managed to get enough plaster on the inside of the house by keeping fires going, but the boys had to let it go at that. There were many other things they had to do including putting up the hay, and making some benches, and a table.

Meanwhile the members of the Point Edward baseball club invited Mr. Charles Estlin and ladies to a Social Party to be held at the Odd Fellows Hall on Friday the 29th of September 1882. Dancing began at eight o'clock. There were a number of people the boys knew on the arranging committees, so they understood how the invitation had arisen, but they could hardly imagine attending such a thing. Point Edward truly was another world.

Alfy and Euty had given detailed instructions to the family about bringing food, other provisions, minimal furniture and so forth. Now they prepared for the trip to Brandon to pick them up. The boys packed what was needed, and hoped that all the goods would arrive with the family. They left before sunup on the long trail to Brandon, which did not seem as long this time, having done it twice before.

"The change in the landscape was wonderful. What had been a wide expanse of unbroken prairie when we came there first, had now become a settlement...Now there were well-worn trails to the mountain, and from farm to farm, enabling us to visit each other more, as we could find our way after dark...." [2]

Alfy and Euty reached Brandon in good time to meet the train. Their poor mother nearly cried at the sight of them, sunburned black as Indians, unshaven and unshorn, with their clothes in rags from working in the bush. The pair wore their dilapidated straw hats with a dirty piece of mosquito netting on the crown; their boots were brown as a rusty iron with white toes due to the wearing effects of the prairie grass. It was not inspiring. Alfy didn't wonder that his mother, an English lady of the Victorian age, was shocked, but it never occurred to either of the boys that there was anything unusual in their appearance. The girls laughed, but the brothers didn't pay much attention to that.

The boys were delighted to see the rest of the family. After introducing them to Kit, Alfy and Euty took the family to a good hotel, kept by a Mr. Beaubier. It was a nice place where they stayed with the family again later on; Beaubier kept the Cecil Hotel in Brandon after that. The next thing was loading up. Alfy and Euty found they could not begin to take all the people, trunks, furniture, and handbags not to mention a number of other things they needed for the house. The boys loaded up two wagons with just what they needed most, and started off. These loads included the fowls, ducks, geese and pigs that Charlie had managed to bring. Emily had insisted on a small sanctum for herself in the new house partitioned off by a curtain. To decorate this space, she brought books, a bookcase, and a carpet so these things came as well.

Fortunately, the trail remained dry, and the mosquitoes had abated, so they all arrived home without any trouble. The next few days were very happy ones. Now a new and entirely different life opened up to Euty and Alfy. *"By and large, pioneers do realize what a woman means to a settlement. She is a missionary, doctor, and confidant whose advice is often sought. Her home is the meeting place where projects for the good of the community are initiated. Many women have earned a crown of glory for their self-sacrificing lives, and for the help they have given, often to total strangers, but they will never realize fully how great their influence is for good."* [2]

Apart from the joy of being reunited, there was so much to talk about and see. There was discussion about the crops, the house, pointing out the gophers, birds, and flowers; everything was new and fresh to the family. As soon as word got around that there were two girls at the homestead, freshly groomed gentlemen started to visit on a regular basis particularly on Sunday. This meant that the Estlin men had to stop work, and be polite, and that the Estlin girls and Emily had to feed the visitors. However, Alfy and Euty found that not having to cook their own meals as well as having an extra man to assist them, more than made up for the time they took off.

Euty and Alfy promptly gave May the job of bringing in the oxen, while the three brothers started to work on the stable. The trip to the Mountain was much easier, because the poles required for the stable were smaller, and the lack of insects made it enjoyable. They built four stalls eight feet wide, and an eight-foot wide passage with a good door made of boards in the middle. They gave it a slant roof covered in sod and then they plastered and chinked it. The next summer they laid a floor.

Charlie and Euty focused on the house, banking it up, making cupboards, and insuring that the big box stove had plenty of good dry oak and poplar, while Alfy started backsetting which was the name given to the second set of ploughing. Once the ground froze solid he had to stop. The house was barely adequate by modern standards, but Euty and Alfy thought it quite comfortable by the time winter came. May, on the other hand, disagreed and complained bitterly that it was extremely cold that first winter; the wind whistled through the cracks that had not been adequately filled. Alfy expected too, it was the fact that the women had not gone through a prairie winter before, and so were not acclimatized.

The three Estlin brothers were always on the look out for work and had several pieces of good luck that first year. An old timer had more grain than he anticipated which he wanted taken to Brandon to be sold. They took the grain, removing a fee for transport from the total proceeds from the trip. This experience started Charlie thinking about a future business. Secondly, a newcomer was willing to pay $60 for logs for his house, so the Estlin men were happy to accommodate him. The third job was that a man wanted a set of farm machinery transported to Deloraine, for which they would be paid $1 per 100 pounds or $40. This last windfall was ideal because the brothers wanted to buy another set of oxen and another plow now the family had an increased workforce.

As soon as they could, the boys made another trip back to Brandon to bring out all the remaining furniture. Alfy also wanted to get a set of sleighs, and provisions for the winter. That December when the boys went to the Brandon general store they patronized, they loaded up with a variety of items: a pair of mitts, 15 lengths of stovepipe, 15 lbs of nails, 1 pair of socks, 44 pounds of sugar, 50 pounds of oatmeal, one pr of oil skin moccasins, 1 pound chewing, 1 plug smoking, one small syrup jug, ½ lb lemon and orange peel, one snow shovel, and 4 pounds of manila paper. They managed to accomplish all of this before the snow got too deep.

In December as well, the three Estlins started to cut timber on Turtle Mountain for the granary, rails for a pasture, poles for the henhouse, the logs that their neighbour wanted and finally the firewood. Two of them made daily trips by sleigh to the Mountain as the sun rose, returning when it got dark. The third stayed at home to prepare the logs and cut up the firewood with the crosscut saw.

While homesteading that winter, the family had to keep the fowls, ducks, geese and the three piglets underground owing to the lack of proper outbuildings for them. In addition, the family had acquired a pig with no ears or tail called Anthony, and another large black pig called Ruth. The six ducks became May's. Birdie took the duck eggs to bed as a human incubator and they hatched out in the night, which was quite a surprise to her.

Chapter 15
Growing Pains

"One day we found the girls bursting with excitement. We received an invitation to a dance at one of our neighour's. Wishing to make a good impression, the girls hunted out suitable dresses while Charlie, Euty and I searched for collars and ties, polished up our shoes, and donned our Sunday clothes. We put the wagon box on the sleigh, put lots of hay in the bottom, and hitched up the oxen. Off we went leaving the Mater with the dog for company and a large pile of wood for the stove. When we arrived at the house, we discovered all the furniture piled outside. Seats made of planks, boards, nail kegs, and boxes lined the sides of the main room. All the settlers for miles around were there. After we had been 'made acquainted' with those we didn't know, the fun began." [2]

Two fiddles and a mouth organ supplied the music while a most important gentleman "called off". *"Most of the dances were square, which was something between a quadrille and a cotillion, lasting about ten to fifteen minutes. The movements directed by the 'caller off' were Greek to us, although the rest of the people understood them. The terms 'Shassy right' and 'alaman left' 'swing your honey', 'Dickey fly in and Birdie fly out,' came in a steady stream interspersed with other quaint sayings. These directions, delivered in a musical monotone constituted most of the dances, although there was the odd polka, waltz or schottische.*

"When the music stopped about midnight, we all sat against the walls. Everyone received a large plate that held two or three sandwiches, several slices of cake, and some cookies. We each got a cup, which we dipped into a boiler full of coffee with milk and sugar in it, as the boiler was carried around. If you were fastidious and did not like it this way, you could get a cup of water. The mound of food looked like far too great a ration but we discovered that one only ate part of it, then, putting your plate on the floor, you danced some more until about 3.00 am when you had another snack because the dance lasted until dawn so that people could see their way home." [2]

Since all the boys' friends were there, they felt quite at home, and enjoyed themselves. All ages attended and children simply found a spot to sleep on coats. The Estlins went home like the others in the early hours. Describing it to Emily, and listening to her comments was great fun for the

Estlin brothers and sisters, because she considered it very primitive and indecorous. No doubt it was from the Victorian point of view, but this was the only form of entertainment and social gathering they had. Alfy stated that young people required some form of company and diversion.

In the late fall, a Burnham friend asked after Harold Harker, Birdie's intended, suggesting that when he completed his time in Brazil he ought to try for trains in Canada. In the spring of 1883 Alfy heard from Harold, who was still working with the Railway in Rio de Janiero. In addition to his duties as superintendent, and balancing the books for the traffic department, he was looking forward to a long awaited cricket match between married and single men in his outfit; Harold had three men doing nothing but rolling the pitch for three days. He decided to put it about that he was married because *"this is a tropical clime and the young fellows here all keep ladies to mend their socks etc., and I don't care for such profligacy...it's duced hard trying sometimes especially when staying at a farm, and you are offered the pick of the farmyard to keep the mosquitoes away while you sleep...that is a regular custom in this country and all slaves aren't black you know, some are as white and good looking as you would wish, evidently the offspring of the farm owners...the working people never think of marrying, they simply live together...I have known some of my men change wives as often as three in a month.... You know, Alf, that when you can spare Birdie I am quite ready to relieve you of one of your responsibilities...I now have prospects of getting some good opportunities...I know that you all thought Birdie [was] wrong to get engaged to me when she might have had much better chances but I would never have bound her to an engagement had I not had great hopes of...earning good salaries.... "*[21]

April was a busy month at the farm. The water levels were high again, particularly with the Antler River but Alfy and Euty were used to that. The family lost the poultry over the winter and a portion of the cattle. William Underhill promised Charlie $7.00 for work and Charlie and Alfy entered into a financial arrangement with Frank Main for the sum of $125.00 for the use of his oxen to be repaid in September. The family also purchased an extra set of oxen as soon as they could. They harrowed their land several more times, then bought some wheat at $1.00 bushel that Frank Main sowed for them while they followed behind him with a harrow. There was a great shortage of seed potatoes that year so people tucked peelings into the newly broken sod. This resulted in a fair crop. After planting, the men turned their attention to breaking another 50 acres or so of prairie ready to backset. Just about the time the crop was up and growing well, the oxen broke into the field and ate some of it down but it recovered.

On the domestic front, Emily, who had jaundice again, was annoyed with the person currently doing the family washing. Using contacts she had, she started a long-term search for a suitable hired girl. It took several years to resolve the issue satisfactorily. In Bristol, Cousin Mary was the person who tried to find a woman for the Estlins. It had to be a person who didn't mind immigrating to a strange country and living in a basic, even primitive manner by Bristol standards. Meanwhile, Emily's friends expressed concern over May's activities. Putting the birds away at night was one thing but they did not like the idea of her helping with the ploughing because she would get coarse ideas. They wanted her to pay strict attention to her lessons.

May, like all the Estlins, contributed to the work, as it was needed. Birdie gave May her lessons, being well grounded herself. May had only 6 months of formal schooling in Point Edward, nothing else. She learned a great deal from a multi-volume set of books entitled the "Queens of England" and from the conversations on different topics that she took part in with her sister and brothers. The girls were always equally and fully engaged with their brothers in discussions on any topic and gave their opinions freely. Meal times were filled with conversation. Without the girls, the boys would not have progressed as they did.

The wheat grew well that year. Alfy, Euty and Charlie heard their neighbours talk about hail but the true meaning of its impact did not strike home, nor did they realize the danger of summer frost. When the crop ripened sufficiently and was ready to cut, Tawm came over with William Simms. They mowed it down with scythes that had wooden rails called cradles attached to them. Frank showed the Estlin brothers how to rake up a bundle of grain, make a band with about a dozen stems, and tie the band around the bundle, tucking the ends into the band. The men set the bundles on their butt ends, side by side, forming a stook or shock. These were the long stooks used in the old countries where rain was prevalent, so that the sheaves would dry out. The binding was hard, backbreaking work. The crop continued to be good so the sheaves were very heavy, but the family had the pleasure of knowing they were harvesting their own wheat for bread and seed for the next year. Charlie went to Frank Main's to learn stacking and to repay Frank for time that he had given to the three boys. Charlie, who took on this task as his responsibility, became very proficient and because no else wanted the job, he kept it during the family's early homesteading years.

About this time Tawm who became Tom, bought a pony from some passing Indians, which gave him the opportunity to visit more frequently.

When he began lending the pony to the girls, they became so fond of it that he eventually presented the pony to May. Nellie became her constant companion. May not only was able to bring the oxen in much more efficiently riding Nellie, but she could run errands for the family. May enjoyed riding over the prairies for long periods, and taking care of these small chores. She determined she would earn money like her brothers, by collecting buffalo bones for fertilizer. The bones were purchased for $20.00 a ton. However, no matter how many times she tried to collect enough, she never filled the required quota. Although this goal took her many miles away, wandering over the prairies on Nellie, the family never worried about her. May rode astride with a pair of her brother's cut down trousers under her skirt. The neighbours were absolutely scandalized but that didn't bother her one iota.

Unfortunately Nellie only lived until 1888; the brothers took her to Dr. Livingstone the vet, but on the way back, she crossed a creek dying on the far bank. May, who was inconsolable for a period, insisted in keeping a hoof from Nellie. Years later Emily, on a return trip to England, took the hoof and had a smith make it into a candlestick for her.

May Estlin's sketch of Nellie on her death. *Source:* Estlin family memorabilia, Sharon Hope

That spring, the Estlin family heard about a cattle sale east of old Deloraine so the brothers took the wagon and oxen, intending to purchase a cow, a three-year-old heifer and a calf. *"The cow was quiet and a good milker but the heifer was a nervous brute. When the heifer came in to be milked, she tried us sorely. She was agile as a cat, with a kick like a mule. Before you could milk her, you had to tie her legs. Even then, if you didn't get kicked putting the ties on, either you or she might kick over the milk pail."* [2]

After exhausting all the family's patience, they would let the heifer out so that her calf could do the milking. May, who received the calf as a present from her mother, having observed her brothers writing contracts with the neighbours, made up her own agreement: *"Given to May Estlin by Emily Estlin Sec 15 2 24 W Queene a heifer calf, all Queene's progeny, milk and butter to be the property of the said May Estlin henceforth and forever...."* [22]

In August, a neighbour supplied the family with lime from a kiln in order to finish the house off properly with mortar, a much better solution than mud. The brothers made improvements to the stable, put up a henhouse and built a granary with a sod roof; erecting the walls from the logs they retrieved the previous winter. They needed the granary because it was nearly time to thresh.

There were one or two threshing machines in the neighbourhood brought out from Ontario by their owners. Horses drew these machines. One was a tread type in which two horses walked up stairs in a box side by side; the other was an arm type, with six arms with a team of horses attached to each arm. The straw came out the back end; forking the straw was dirty, strenuous work. Sometimes it took up to four to six men to keep the carriers clear, especially on a large stack. It took a good man to stand at the end of the carriers, forking the straw in the blazing sun. However, no one thought of not helping if one was asked. It was generally expected that the farm owner would take the front perch but if he were busy someone else would assume that position.

During the summer of 1883, Alfy heard of a homestead near the Souris crossing where they had camped when they first came out. The boys were desperate for land so Alfy entered for it, although it was not a good quarter for two reasons. First, it was 25 miles away from the family's main focus of operations, and secondly, a ravine cut through it. After working on it, putting up a log house and stable, he abandoned the piece when a prairie fire destroyed the buildings. The crop was hailed out completely, but Alfy dragged wood and hay enough to last while he lived on it. He stayed the minimum amount of time that could be construed to be six months, thus fulfilling the homestead requirements.

As 1883 drew to a close, the family felt that they had made great improvements to their circumstances. They had comfortable buildings for themselves, and their stock. In addition, they had at their disposal, milk, cream, butter, wheat for flour, and seed for the next crop. Old Deloraine was only 12 miles away, with its store, post office and blacksmith. The family had quite a collection of animals by that time, the pigs and a new piglet born on Christmas Eve named Crispin, two calves, two cows and two heifers, and two yoke of oxen, Jack, Tom, Ted and Bob. In addition, they picked up another dog, Jim, a rough guard dog that survived being caught in a fox trap. The family thought he was too tough to die. He slept in a haystack because he certainly was not the pet that Kit was, who slept on May's bed.

Chapter 16
Rebellion

That winter passed quickly; the boys shot prairie chickens and rabbits to supplement their winter fare. With two yokes of oxen, when the brothers went to the bush for firewood, the loads were large enough that they could skip a few days if the weather was bad. When the spring came, they had all the poles they needed and got their crop planted in good time. They also had good news from Burnham: About six months before, the family had learned that the brickyard was unlet and the pond was full of water. Now they heard from their friends that the brickyard had been sold to a Mr. Hunt who had disposed of the machinery and planned to build there. The Estlins were relieved to hear there was activity in the old brickyard that had languished for so long.

In the spring of 1884, a friend of Birdie's in England sent 50 pounds to assist with her passage to Brazil. This action finally prompted a decision concerning her long engagement to Harold Harker. Harold's life in Brazil was very different from the family's farming struggles. They were living day to day by their own ingenuity and hard work. It appeared that Birdie and Harold were moving in two radically different directions. There was less comfort on the prairie, but more freedom from convention in some ways. One key factor in the decision about Harold, was that Emily felt that she couldn't spare Birdie who was running the household in the absence of domestic assistance and the Estlin brothers were all still at home.

Harold had never shown the least interest in coming to Canada; the bride followed the husband in those days. Birdie knew from Harold's letters what type of life she would lead in Brazil. When she finally broke off the engagement, the stress of the situation caused her to have a mental breakdown of sorts. It was a tragic dilemma. Birdie was really quite fond of Harold. Unfortunately, Harold was upset over the decision as well because he had expected her arrival. He protested, but he could do nothing from that distance. Birdie never married but remained with the family first as the main caregiver for May, and then, for many years, as caregiver for her mother.

In 1891, Harold died prematurely of a heart attack, having developed a heart condition after a bout of rheumatic fever that he contracted a few years before. He still was unmarried, and working for the same company in Brazil. As it turned out, Birdie, if she had married Harold, would have been stranded in Brazil without her family, a young widow likely with young children.

By July 1884, the cold wet weather made it very unfavourable for harvest. The brothers expected the wheat to be harvested around August 20th, the barley around September 30th, the oats around October 10th and peas around October 1st. The condition of the grain was only fair due to damage from wind and rain. The potato roots were poor and Alfy didn't feel it was worthwhile cultivating other crops such as currents or gooseberries. Hauling the grain to sell, or to the mill, when it was poor, was an effort without much reward. The nearest mill was at Deloraine twelve to fifteen miles away, run by William and Thomas Shepherd.

In order to sell their grain for the first two years, the Estlins hauled their wheat north to Brandon using their poor old oxen. They got up at 4 in the morning, and ate dinner on the prairie to insure that they made a stopping house by dark. After that there was a road they could follow, with a series of stopping houses every ten miles or so. In the fall of 1884, Alfy made the last trip to Brandon with 61.5 bushels of wheat in a train with three or four other wagons, which was their customary way of travel. There was a minimum of snow but the banks of the Souris were steep and bare. The party had difficulty getting their loads up, so they were late reaching Brandon. They did not arrive until the night of the fourth day, rather than at noon. When they came to sell the wheat, the buyers didn't want it, claiming it was smutty. Since none of the buyers would purchase it, Alfy sold his grain for 36 cents a bushel which, after paying his expenses for the trip coming and going, gave him nine dollars.

He obtained a box of groceries 16 inches long and a foot wide *"...in exchange for nearly two tons of the most valuable food product known to man"*[2] Alfy had just hauled the grain by ox cart seventy-five miles. He made a vow that he would never haul another load of wheat to Brandon, and thanks to the arrival of the train at Boissevain before the next harvest, the Fates decreed that Alfy kept that vow.

Hauling grain to Brandon.
Manitoba Archives

During that winter, an older gentleman appeared at the Estlin farm in his buggy with a nice team of drivers. It was cold and windy, with loose swirling snow, but not sufficient for a sleigh. The man's glasses had iced over and since the summer trails were covered with new snow, he lost his way. When he glimpsed a vague outline against the skyline, he drove toward it to get his bearings, encountering, rather to his surprise, the Estlin family home. They took him in and housed him until the weather quieted down. His name was J. P. Alexander, a genial Scot who was canvassing for votes at the time. He contested the Dominion Constituency of Souris two or three times, and was Registrar for the District when he moved up to the crossing. Although the Estlins had some misgivings about his safety, when the weather improved they sent J. P. on his way toward his home. The settlement was a considerable distance, but he managed to get there, much to the family's relief. The two families became firm friends particularly after the Alexander family moved to Deloraine.

In January 1885, the Estlin brothers went into the timber hauling business again, this time through a permit to take wood from a specific section for the sum of four dollars paid at Deloraine. The permit was for eight ends of wood and 1000 fence rails; they had until May to make use of the permit. It is impossible to know why they needed so many fence rails but it's likely they were planning for the additional homesteads Charlie and Alfy would obtain later in the year and they may have had a buyer for the rails as well. As spring progressed, however, all thoughts of farm work became secondary.

First there were rumours of Indians moving about in twos and threes going to and from the Reservation in the Turtle Mountain. Then horses were taken from farmers' fields and stables. Finally the family received authentic word of a rebellion of half-breeds and Indians in the Northwest Territories in what is now the province of Saskatchewan. The government sent soldiers from the East and Winnipeg mobilized their troops. The Government asked for men with wagons and teams for transport purposes so as many men as possible went off to get these jobs. It paid $5.00 a day all found which was extremely good money.

In April, the family heard that troop trains were passing through Brandon. Girls were serving coffee to the soldiers on these trains and getting kissed for their trouble. The girls started screaming and what happened became an issue in the town. The solders thought it just a lark but the men of Brandon were not amused. Encouraged by the Government to do so, the first volunteer Home Guards in southwestern Manitoba formed around and just north of Brandon but soon many other small communities followed suit.

Those with military experience left for a conference at Boissevain; Alfy went with four others. After they discussed the situation, they decided to comply with the Government's suggestion to form a company of Home Guards to patrol the boundary. The purpose was two fold: first, to prevent the American Indians from crossing the border to join the rebels and secondly, to protect the settlers. Each squad of 20 men, commissioned by the government, elected a Captain and a Lieutenant. The squads covered an allotted territory and the Government supplied rifles, bayonets and ammunition. Alfy was elected Captain and D. S. McLeod who served for many years as M. L. A. for the Constituency of Deloraine, became Lieutenant.

On the 18th of May the two collected a list of about 25 signatures that today reads like a pioneer roster. One of the signees was W. H. Stovin from the brothers' days on the Boundary Commission Trail; the first volunteer to sign was the Estlin's neighbour Frank W. Main. Alfy's brother Charlie Estlin signed as well. They all put their names to several oaths of allegiance and promises such as: "...*obligees have been furnished with a Snider Rifle, bayonet, scabbard, and twenty rounds of ammunition for the purpose of arming themselves to suppress any possible uprising of the Halfbreed or Indians...Upon the condition of the above written Bond ...obligees...shall upon demand deliver up to the obligor...the said Rifle, bayonet, scabbard and ammunition....*" [23] These items were to be handed over in sound condition.

An officer and a corporal's guard of four men left for Brandon with a light wagon to pick up the gear for transport to Deloraine. As it neared, Alfy and his men went to meet the wagon. Eventually it came into sight travelling very slowly. They watched the wagon's progress with curiosity. When it stopped, they went over to unload the gear. They found the officer in charge barely able to sit up to guide the horses while the guards were dead to the world. Brandon, in the spirit of patriotism, had been rewarding loyal militiamen with spirits of a more liquid variety. The citizens had bestowed a keg of liquor on these men and as a result the men had to carry the guards in and put them to bed before they could get to the rifles.

Alfy's company, the Medora Rifles No. 1, used to drill two or three times a week; after the rifles came they had regular target practice. Since most of the men were good shots and accustomed to rifles, it was an enjoyable exercise. The knowledge of the company's ability and preparedness did a great deal to reassure the settlers. It is possible that it also kept the American Indians in their own Territory since the company was not called upon to resist any invasion. Some years later, the government requested the return the rifles as promised, but a good number of them failed to appear, Alfy knew of at least one that was kept as a memento of the Rebellion.

The Dominion Day celebration that year featured the Home Guard in a rifle match but the pony and horse races were much more exciting since they were a close contest. The exception was Tom Main's "Duchess" which came in first with ease in the trotting event. Alfy participated in an instrumental performance with three others in the evening concert at the schoolhouse and A. P. Stewart and Alfy sang a duet "The Larboard Watch" which was said to delight the audience because their voices blended so well, Alfy having a deep bass.

Now that the Estlin family had a larger acreage, the oxen, although reliable, were too slow. The brothers bought a team of horses and a self-binder, the latter costing about $360.00. The material used for binding went through several changes but ended with manila cord

Sketch of a Metis.
Source: Estlin family memorabilia, Sharon Hope

that was very satisfactory. Although the family did not have a good crop that year because the wheat caught a frost when in blossom, the price was good so that by cutting the high ground, they gleaned enough to pay their expenses. The low lands were devoid of grain. The oats and barley, though, escaped the frost so they had plenty of coarse grain for the stock that was steadily increasing in numbers. The family supplies that summer from Bower Blackburn, Mundle, & Porter in Brandon, where they usually purchased their goods, included: 10 lbs blk tea, sugar, 2 jars mustard, 6 milk pans, 10 lbs 3 inch nails, 10 lbs shingles, rice, 1 lb saltpeter, 2 lamp shades, and 2 prs shoes.

On a very cold day in December 1885, a team of horses and sleigh drew up to the Estlin stable door. A man, dressed warmly in a fur coat, stepped down. The boys sent him to the house while they put away his team, and after he had warmed up he told the family why he was there. *"His name was J. L. Campbell and he was on his way to Old Deloraine to pick up a man called Williams who was working there and who had a homestead near the crossing. The purpose was to vote in the municipal election to be held in a few days. Since I had a vote from my homestead toward the Souris established the prior summer he wanted me to go too. He said he would pick up Williams and come back for me. Like a fool I said yes so I went. It was a terrible trip. We had to go off the Boundary Commission trail to pick up two other fools as weak minded as myself and like me did not want to refuse. The snow was deep and the horses could only walk. It was late afternoon when we arrived at a sod shack owned by a worthy couple Captain and Mrs. Higgins. We put up the horses, fed and watered them then the couple gave us supper before we made the rest of the journey to our driver's sod shack.*

"Campbell made us comfortable at his own place until the next day when we went down to the crossing to poll our votes. I think the polling station was either in the Gould's or Elliot's house. There was a dance to celebrate after the votes were counted since our side won by one vote. Of course, we four nonresidents all claimed that vote." [2]

The next day after the dance, the fellows started for home. The weather grew worse and worse so that by the time they got to the Estlin place and had dropped off the other two voters, it was a raging blizzard. Three days passed before the family's two new friends could leave. J. L. Campbell who

Ploughing on the homestead.
Source: Estlin family collection, Sharon Hope

had pressed Alfy into making the trip to vote, was elected reeve of Arthur Constituency and then became Registrar for the County of Souris River. John Williams, the other guest, became a member of Arthur Constituency for many years and Minister of Agriculture in the Norris Government.

The next year, 1886, was a memorable one for a variety of reasons. In April, Cousin Mary in Bristol announced that she finally found a suitable person to send to the Estlin family as a hired girl. Emily herself had not found anyone permanent either locally or abroad. There had been at least three disappointments the last being a C. Ellis from Bristol. Still Emily felt an Englishwoman would be best. The Secretary of Guardian House, Bristol recommended Elizabeth Williams to Cousin Mary. It was an institution that took in young girls of little means but good character to train as servants.

Both of Elizabeth's sisters currently were at this institution. Cousin Mary, who was quite well off, generously paid Elizabeth's passage as well as her food for the train. Elizabeth's relations were poor but respectable. When her father who was a sailor died, her mother remarried a worthy man labouring at the Bristol docks. There was a sick girl at home dying of an abscess that caused a craving for food.

Elizabeth unfortunately had married a smith who lived next door. This young man deserted her twice, pawning her clothes for drink. She had to go to her stepfather for seven months with her baby but she returned to her husband and struggled on until her baby died aged 13 months. Her stepfather pawned his best suit of clothes to bury the child. She was with her husband on the street when a woman with a ten-year-old boy greeted him familiarly and she discovered that the boy was her husband's. As a result of all this, she ardently wished to leave Bristol to avoid any future problems. Cousin Mary declared that *"…She is a capital worker in housecleaning, washing, plain cooking, and other things as well…."* [24]

Cousin Mary drew up a simple agreement in England maintaining that the language of Canadian agreements might be confusing to the girl. The agreement signed in early May between Elizabeth Ester Williams of Bristol domestic servant and Mrs Emily Estlin Turtle Mountain Manitoba Farmer, stated that she agreed to work for one year, at a sum of 14 pounds sterling and if she cared to stay a second year her wages would be raised to 16 pounds. Since she was not literate at the time, Elizabeth had the document read to her and signed it with an X. The girl arrived quite soon after Cousin Mary's letter. Thus began the family's very happy relationship with Lizzie as she became known, until she married and long afterward. The first thing the family did was to teach Lizzie to read and write.

Both Charlie and Alfy had to work their own respective homesteads as well as helping on the one in their mother's name. Alfy broke up 20 acres on his new land and built a stable, having relinquished the land 25 miles away. Charlie had a large field that he had prepared. They were ploughing and harrowing in early March, which was most unusual. The weather was splendid up until the end of April. However the weather during June was dry with several thunderstorms, and one light frost. It continued to be dry thereafter. The prospects for grain were reasonably good initially in some places but it was very bad for root crops from the start. *"As the drought continued, the gophers began destroying the crops wholesale coming off the prairies, with its dead grass, into the green fields; twenty-acre fields were being completely cleaned out. The gophers mowed down the wheat and sucked out the sap.*" [2] Alfy mentioned the issue of gophers on several prior occasions to the government but received no response.

It was Alfy's opinion that unless some measures were taken to curb the destruction that the gophers were causing, farmers in future would not be able to raise wheat. The gophers needed to be stopped on the wildland before they reached the farmers' fields. The only means the homesteaders had of fighting them was either trapping, or shooting them with a .22 rifle. Though the Estlin brothers killed hundreds of them, they kept coming. The family had no barley, no potatoes, no other roots, and a very poor showing for wheat with just enough for seed. Hay was fairly plentiful because the sloughs dried up so the brothers mowed them. The grass was coarse and weedy but sufficient to see the livestock through the winter.

The Department of Agriculture circulated questionnaires each year trying to judge the potential for poor and good crops. The government asked about labour, for example. During poor harvests, there was little demand for labourers as far as the family was concerned; the men earned $25 a month with board so none of the farmers could afford them. The method the farmers used for big tasks was to arrange work exchanges among neighbours.

In the midst of dealing with gophers and drought, a letter arrived from the Dominion Land Office signed by Mr. Ruttan Assistant Secretary. It concerned the Estlin homestead. Emily received the right to homestead their South East ¼ section and to purchase the SW section for $2.50/acre from the Railway. The family could pay ¼ of the total purchase price in cash and the balance with interest in three equal payments. Alfy drafted a gracious reply on behalf of his mother only asking if Ruttan wished the family to prove residency; they were willing to do that either by affidavit or physically going to the Deloraine Land Office. Luckily the family got a small windfall from England that helped to make the land payments and keep them going.

The District had a fire that year in which Charlie lost everything that he had invested in his homestead and many of the Estlins' neighbours lost much more. Mr. Gerry, the man that the boys had met at the Souris crossing, lost his sod house.

Mrs. J. P. Alexander, living at Sourisford at that time, took part in a survey called "What women say of the Canadian Northwest" sponsored by the railway. She advised newcomers to bring plenty of blankets and warm clothes but not furnishings. She regretted the lack of schools and churches nearby, but extolled the climate that she declared caused children to grow like mushrooms. As for Indians, most settlers were not afraid of them and even hired them from time to time. She and many other women like her considered themselves quite content with their lot. Emily Estlin also responded to the questionnaire on prairie pioneer life. When she was asked if she was content she replied that the Estlins were too far from markets.

Chapter 17
Struggles

It was hard for the Estlin family that winter. Like many settlers, the money they had brought out was gone. They had no grain to sell or to feed the cattle, and no pigs or poultry for market or to eat themselves. They ground roasted wheat for coffee, used unroasted for porridge, had some very lean pork and beef, a few eggs, and a little milk. They managed to get through the winter by selling mink and fox pelts. In the early days there were plenty of mink around the Souris; the brothers heard mention of 20 being taken there before the place was settled. As you might imagine, the family was very glad to see the green grass the following spring and the appearance of ducks and geese.

G. R. Renfrew and Co.furrier, business card, 1886.
Source: Estlin family memorabilia collection, Sharon Hope

In the spring of 1887, the Estlin brothers did most of the work with the oxen because they had no oats for the horses. It was much slower but by working longer hours they managed to get through in good time. When they put the garden in, they had noticed a few bugs the previous year but nothing substantial. This year, the insects were much more numerous. The brothers recognized them as the Colorado beetle. When the beetles came from North Dakota on warm south winds, they spread over the country.

John Brondgeet at Waubeesh near the Turtle Mountain heard Alfy was considering sheep so he offered him ewe yearlings for ten dollars and a ram lamb for five. Alfy bought the ram lamb for four dollars. Money was always a problem; the family was constantly juggling funds. Alfy had corresponded with a Robert Gifford in Toronto who had written many letters of inquiry before coming out to homestead around 1885. He called in a note Alfy had with him in March saying he was very hard up and even offered a discount if he paid it in full. Subsequently Gifford was sentenced to 18 months for forging checks in Winnipeg although many of his friends asked for leniency in sentencing. After that news got around, he went off to another part of Manitoba to prospect for land and the next the Estlin family heard of him, he had moved to Vancouver where he fell in with a bunco steerer [confidence man] who relieved him of $300.00.

In April, another debt caught up with Alfy from the previous year. F. T. Stewart, a Deloraine attorney, wrote him a letter concerning collection from N. J. M. Nems [sp?] for herding six head of cattle in 1886 at $1.80 a head for a total of $10.80. The attourney stated it would be served at the next Court unless paid.

Fortunately that summer, the family had a good growing season. Alfy had his new homestead only one mile from his mother's home and Charlie's was only six miles south of the family. They put their hay up on their own lands then prepared to cut the grain for all the holdings. The family now had about 300 acres of grain to cut with only one binder and only one team of horses. The brothers solved the problem for a while by tying on a smart steer on the outside and the horses on the pole, changing one ox for another every three hours. When they began to have trouble with the binder, their progress slowed and then they found the wheat was ripening faster than they could cut it. The brothers began to run double shifts, day and night to make up the time. They put one coal-oil lantern on the end of the pole and one on the binder so the driver could see whether the sheaves were tied or not. Since this arrangement worked well, they were quite optimistic of getting the wheat cut before it shelled too much, until one night the big wheel of the binder went into a badger hole. It went in with such a bang that the big arm snapped off at the elbow. Alfy was off duty having a sleep when Charlie called him to see what they could do about it.

It was a short clean break in cast iron, but time was precious and the nearest arm was in Brandon so Alfy sent Charlie off with the pony and buckboard. He drove day and night stopping only long enough to feed and rest the pony. He was back on the morning of the second day. Meanwhile the boys had patched the break with pieces of wrought iron, wire and binder twine so it would work. They didn't lose much time until they came to put in the replacement. Working on it was compounded by the fact they didn't have the proper tools. However the brothers made up time by continuing to work double shifts until they were finished at last.[2]

Although the brothers had a large amount to thresh that year, (some fields yielded 30 bushels an acre), the job was much faster because the steam thresher had made its debut. Since there was an abundance of straw, farmers only stacked oat straw. Most of the wheat straw was bucked; a long pole with a horse hitched to each end drew the straw away from the separator. After the machine pulled the straw away, it could be burnt so that the field was ready for ploughing. This lightened the workload considerably.

Charlie, trained as a clerk in England, kept detailed accounts in a notebook about each trip to the elevator. The trips were usually every other day starting just before Christmas, and then carrying well on into the next spring. He listed amounts, prices, those involved and expenses such as pills, meat, insurance, and merchants like Cavers

Harvest.
Source: Estlin family collection, Sharon Hope

and Stewart in Deloraine as well as the Estlin promissory notes. Charlie's grain records sometimes included other farmers for whom he took grain to the elevator, such as Tom Main and J. L. Campbell. He was gradually transforming into a grain merchant.

Initially, bills were in Emily's name. She kept the family money sewn into one of her three petticoats, "the eiderdown" one. The only financial loss the Estlins sustained in the early years was when a young hired hand stated he had a sprained ankle that necessitated leaving him alone in the house. Although Emily's diamond ring that she kept in a drawer disappeared, all of the family money remained intact. Needless to say, they never saw or heard of the hired hand again.

The homestead, which was close to the United States border, did receive some visitors. One morning a handsome black bearded man arrived at the door, driving a herd of 45 horses. In the most cultivated accent, he asked to purchase some of the potatoes he saw growing in the garden. Now these plants had been grown from $1.00 a pound seed and all had to be saved to make more seed for the next year. The family was reluctant to part with any. Again, the man asked in a most genteel manner if he could receive some potatoes. Whatever the family gave him, it was not the potatoes.

It was only when the Northwest Mounted Police arrived in the afternoon the family discovered the well-spoken man was a horse thief.

Since the homestead was so close to the Turtle Mountain, and the Indian Reserve there, the Indians came by fairly regularly asking for food. The Estlin family never had any trouble from Indians; after the family gave them what food they could, the Indians left peacefully. Usually adults were at home but on one occasion May was by herself, when an Indian suddenly appeared at the kitchen window and startled her. She wouldn't open the door. He left after lurking about for a long time hoping for the return of the older family members and the usual gift of food.

The family home always lacked sufficient space; the original size was only meant to be a temporary measure. The following year the brothers built a kitchen with an upstairs, and more stable room. These additions were built of logs except the roof and floor. They also had to build shacks on both Alfy's property and Charlie's homestead. The men needed more horses because they had steadily increased the acreage so they exchanged one yoke of oxen for an extra team of horses. Now the family had 4 horses and four oxen that provided plenty of power for their needs.

Letters were still the main method of keeping in touch. Here in the District, May became friends with the younger Alexander girl, Margaret. Margaret was nicknamed Dot, after she sent notes to May punctuated with

Bringing in the hay. *Source:* Estlin family collection, Sharon Hope

a dot after each letter. The girls passed these letters when one of boys, often Euty, went to the Alexander farm. In January 1889 Margaret wrote from Sourisford to May thanking her for a Christmas present sent via Birdie: *"... My foot is getting better nicely. I think I will be out next week. I think Flora is a darling pony. I am going to have a ride on her with you down to the well with the cattle...."* [25]

With the money from a good crop in 1887 the family bought some things they needed, supplemented their monotonous diet, and the boys bought special presents for their mother and the girls. The brothers were full of hope that in the spring of 1888, they would at last see an end to the family's financial struggles. That hope was blighted immediately because there was another frost when the blossoms came. The farmers had tall handsome wheat stalks but no grain. The family had to thresh the wheat crop just to obtain enough seed. The Estlin family had plenty of oats and barley since these crops were not caught by the frost but there was no market for them. That winter the family had beef and pork to sell, as well as eggs and butter to trade for groceries. The brothers shot prairie chickens and rabbits as usual and Alfy got some work auditing the municipal books that was very congenial to him. It widened his circle of acquaintances and friends considerably.

A year or so later, the family had the worst drought they had experienced to date combined with a vicious fire that swept down from the west, jumped the Souris River and swept into the Turtle Mountain leaving a black ruin behind instead of grass. It began with a very mild winter with so little snow that the family hardly used their sleighs. By the beginning of March the land was bare; because the weather was very warm, the farmers were all on the land disking and harrowing. The Estlins did not plough because they were afraid of drying out the soil further nor did they wish to sow early in case of a hard freeze. However it did not matter how they planned or worked their land because there was no rain all summer. Consequently the gophers swarmed in from the dry open prairie again literally devouring the crops. The brothers shot and trapped them by the hundreds; in one den alone by their granary they counted around 175.

The brothers' next worry was hay. The slough and meadows were baked dry so they mowed the dry prairie grass that had a little green tuft growing through it. The Estlin's neighbours shook their heads, saying: *"you're wasting your time, the damn stuff is no good."* [2] They kept at it putting together all they could, then sprinkling some salt on it as they stacked it. As a result, the family stock pulled through the winter while many of their neighbours' animals did not.

Harvesting what grain they could was a terrible task. Although the brothers tried all sorts of tactics, the grain was so short that the binder would not cut it. Finally they had to use the mower and risk losing half of it as it fell out of the rake. After the harvest was all done they had 300 bushels of wheat, no barley, and 80 bushels of oats. This amount was from 300 acres of land. As one of their neighbours put it: *"One seed has been blessed and multiplied two fold."* [2] After their tiny harvest, the brothers tried to plough the land but it was so hard and dry, ploughing was almost impossible. Someone suggested they take one of the ploughs off the old gang plough and use the oxen. This worked quite well although they had to plough deeper than they wanted in order to keep the plough in the ground at all.

One of the first things the brothers did was to plough the firebreaks around the house, the outbuildings, around the straw and the haystacks. They made these breaks wide, burning any grass between them. Everything was tinder dry. The Estlin family could see small prairie fires in the west each evening. It was fortunate that the brothers completed the firebreaks as thoroughly as they did because not many days after they finished, Alfy went to the Mountain for a load of wood. By the time he had his load cut, the acrid smell of smoke filled the air but Alfy didn't pay much attention to it.

Alfy was busy loading his wood into the wagon when he heard galloping hooves on the hard beaten track. In a few minutes, he saw Charlie on the pony, riding lickity-split through the scrub and brush piles. Charlie was white as a sheet and said he didn't expect they could get out alive, because the fire was coming in, forming a great wall from the west. He had ridden ahead to warn his brother of the danger. When Alfy asked about their buildings and hay, Charlie said the breaks were good. Euty and the girls were watching in case any stray weeds blew across them. The two brothers needed to get out of the fire's path if they could. They threw the chains across the bolsters and tightened them to keep the small number of poles in place that Alfy had already loaded. Alfy hitched on the horses while Charlie went ahead on the pony to find a way out.

The smoke grew thicker and thicker which made the horses very uneasy and hard to manage but the brothers knew the locality well. They made their way to a valley that had a spring running through it. This valley flattened out as it came out of the Mountain and the grass remained green there. They stayed in that spot until the fire had passed, then they drove home over the blackened waste, very thankful for their escape. [2]

This was the family's worst fire in memory. It came down, jumping both Antler Creek and the Souris River which were low, and did a great deal of damage to buildings and hay stacks in the District that were not properly protected. It also burned up the prairie grass badly needed as pasture.

The winter following was one of great difficulty. The Estlin family had two consecutive failed crops and no one else in the District had any money. Few settlers had any straw or hay. Practically no one had any coarse grain to fatten pigs or cattle. Many cattle and horses died because the fire burned up the grassland. How people survived Alfy didn't know.

The family barely managed to get along. They had meat even if it was lean, and wheat enough for flour and porridge. There was always some butter and milk. Many people had absolutely no crop or stock. Water was an added worry that winter. The lack of rain and the great heat dried up the family's slough, which had never failed them before. Although the brothers dug several holes in it, the holes froze solid because the reeds and rushes were not there to hold the snow and mitigate the temperatures. The first move to solve this latest problem was to melt snow. Now melting a boiler full of snow for washing is one thing, but when one owns six horses, pigs, twenty head of cattle of which four are working oxen, it is quite a different matter. The family had a big iron box as large as the cook stove top with a tap in the bottom. It was all one man could do to keep this filled with snow, the firebox full of wood and animals at least partially watered. The following year was dry as well but by the autumn the rains arrived.

In addition to the Estlin brothers and sisters who were still at home, a cousin, Ernie Goodland had come out from England to join the family around this time in a training capacity. Alfy received a stipend from his father, Charlie Goodland, to teach him farming; Alfy's uncle wrote from England that he considered three years should be sufficient for Ernie to take up on his own. Charlie Goodland wondered about the weather on the prairies compared to British Columbia saying: "...*What do you think Alfy? Do you know anything about the Pacific Side? Vancouver? I mean is the climate more suitable for farming...?*" [26]

In 1891 there was an excellent crop with 40–50 bushels of wheat per acre so the Estlin brothers hoped again that their financial difficulties would be over. Alfy wrote in a light hearted way to his aunt Kate that he and Ernie were going to pick out a ¼ section so Ernie could start making his fortune. Ernie's mother Kate replied snappishly that she thought Ernie should be receiving some remuneration because he was an experienced hand now and she had no doubt he would receive it because it was promised.

No sooner did Alfy have Ernie settled than his uncle sent another proposition concerning his younger cousin Bert. Alfy was irritated and said so. His uncle was very amused by the consternation his letter caused. Charlie Goodland maintained it wasn't his intention to burden Alfy with an unprofitable addition to the family but it was much better for Bert to be with Alfy than going elsewhere on his own.

"...I thought an able bodied fellow willing to work was always worth his keep in Manitoba. Well I gather you are willing to take him if we can agree on terms." [27] He proposed that Alfy take Bert for one year board, wash and lodging and teach him the rudiments of Manitoba farming. Goodland would give Alfy 20 pounds cash down and at the end of the year further arrangements would be made. "...I presume that this will not interfere with your own arrangement with Ern. He is getting on very well. You all appear to be saturated with the idea that this year's crop is to be a failure. I don't see why you should anticipate disaster. The chances are, I think the other way, you had several bad years and now may fairly expect to have several good ones...." [27]

Alfy's uncle went on to describe Bert's physical strength. Alfy reluctantly agreed to take him. Bert Goodland came out, worked with Alfy and then ran the post office at Goodlands. He later moved to Chilliwack. Although a good businessman, he had a much more distinguished career in the military during and after WWI than he ever did farming. The final cousin Charlie Goodland sent out was the youngest, Roger, who was not suited to farming at all. Thankfully Alfy had little to do with Roger's training.

The Estlin family was always contending with some difficulty. Some years before, May had a parasite or tapeworm and had to be "dewormed". They never discovered where she got it. In 1891 Mater had a neck affliction that they hoped was only goiter that could be treated with iodine or something. Euty was taken seriously ill while away from home. He had begun framing a house with the McLean brothers in a nearby municipality. He moved about looking for work of this type where there was a need. Charlie went up to take care of him and managed to get him to John Crawford's, a fellow carpenter, where Mrs. Crawford tended to him. Charlie's aunt remarked to him in a letter: "...You seem to have managed splendidly under most trying circumstances and I really think you must feel that Euty owes you his life to your sustained care...Poor fellow what an awful place to fall ill in! ...This is an unlucky illness just when it seemed that Euty had grown strong and well. He has an unfortunate knack of being ill in other people's houses...." [28]

In 1892 Elizabeth Williams, the family's hired help, left to marry Fred Wickham. Cousin Mary worried that Birdie would be left alone to cook for the threshing crew. She had always looked out for Birdie and renewed a debenture that she had put in Stuckey's Bank on her behalf. It was with a very safe company according to Cousin Mary. She went on to discuss future plans for both Euty and Alfy with their sister: *"...Your domestic advice is quite exciting...but I do not know how you will get on without either of your brothers...I hope that Alfred will not leave his present home for another year at least.... Euty must be doing well if he contemplates marriage.... I hope the young lady in Melita is worthy of Euty...he ought to have a refined, intelligent, practical wife and I trust he has not been precipitate in his choice...."* [29]

Euty continued constructing houses locally over the next few years while Charlie moved toward the political arena. Charlie was returning officer for Polling Station 71 for Selkirk in 1891 where J. Daly had 35 votes and his opponent 34. He also had coordinated the polling in 1888 where he paid the bills for the constable, schoolhouse, and returning officer. Charlie was a staunch member of the Conservatives and attended the Souris District meetings to the point that he was elected officer and a delegate for the Winnipeg convention.

Chapter 18
From Farm to Town

With the advent of the railway at Deloraine, which caused the old town to move closer to the line, an expanded community sprang up almost overnight. There was a store, implement warehouse, blacksmith, and, of course, the Post Office. Now the Estlins received more or less regular mail and newspapers. They even could send telegrams and, most important of all, they were able to buy necessities without a long trip to Brandon. With the opening of the post office at Montifore in 1885, the Estlins had an address much closer to their homestead.

In 1890, Dodds Hardware and General Store moved to the then unnamed cluster of businesses on the Souris. The next year, J. L. Campbell, the Registrar of the Electoral District, started a lumber and hardware business in the small community. The grade for the railway was laid out in the same year in front of a ramshackle collection of ten or so stores that formed Front Street and what would become Main Street. A photograph taken at the time clearly shows the immense prairie stretching away behind these structures making them look rather temporary and vulnerable. Once the decision about the railway route was known, a Northern grain elevator and a grist and flourmill located there. In one of the first community decisions ever recorded, the village council bought a cemetery on the small promontory that was to be the original site of a town called Manchester. The railway bypassed it and it never grew. The new town was Melita.

The municipalities increased in number with corresponding changes to the boundaries as settlers flocked to southwestern Manitoba. Before the major settlements evolved, the trails followed the path of least resistance, detouring around difficult low or steep spots or major watercourses. As the region became more populated, roads crossed the country, marked out in road allowances.

As roads were built, residents worked on them, giving what was called "Statute Labour". One gave a certain number of days work according to one's land holdings, reporting to the master or foreman of the ward when and where it was required. The work consisted primarily of fixing low spots, building temporary bridges with poles from the Mountain and road grading.

The improved transportation widened the Estlins' circle of friends as well as providing them with access to a variety of entertainments, fraternal societies, and church services. There was even a traveling circus that came to Melita when the village was only a few years old. All of these possibilities gave them a richer and better quality of life.

Deloraine proudly sponsored a number of formal entertainments. One of the first that the Estlin family knew about was a concert that took place in Cavers Hall on October 8th 1890 to raise money for the English church building fund. "*...A brand new upright grand piano was used thanks to the kindliness of Mr. A. M. Herron the American Consul at this port....*" [30]

Mabel and Alfred B. Estlin in 1893 at their first house. *Source:* Estlin family collection, Sharon Hope

Tickets were sold at Cowan's drugstore. Both A. P. Stewart and a man with a ferocious beard called "Flesher" sang. This was John Flesher, now the land agent; his son was the telegraph operator in town. John had thirteen children in all. Mabel Flesher, John's daughter, was 17 or 18 at the time. In March 1893, Alfy married Mabel Flesher.

Charlie, quite a man about town by this time, became Honorary Secretary for the First Annual Bachelors Ball held in the spring of 1893 at Melita. Joseph Campbell, who worked with Charlie, was on the committee.

View of Melita circa 1893. C. P. Estlin's implement outlet tall sign on left. *Source:* Estlin family collection, Sharon Hope

Mrs Graham, wife of the town's local grocer, sent a written reply that she would attend; the local paper deemed it as a great success. No sooner was Melita's Ball over than Deloraine promptly had their 2nd Annual Calico Bachelors Ball in April at Cavers Hall. That summer the Deloraine cricket team was organized and photographed. Charlie was in the photo but he was not named to the team that played in Winnipeg at the First Annual Tournament.

While Emily and the girls remained on the original homestead 15-2-24 and Alfy worked his homestead 2-2-24, Charlie began negotiations for the sale of his land: 4-1-24. During 1893, Charlie had started an implement business in Melita combining it with his grain merchant position so he did the logical thing and moved to town. After his sale, Charlie established a large house on Maple St. During 1894, Euty started the same type of implement business in Deloraine.

Aunt Agnes wrote to Charlie: *"...I was grieved to hear of the bad crops and the general state of depression in your part of the world. I was much gratified to hear how much you had been helping all thru the time of trouble caused by May's illness* [probably scarlet fever]. *Some day it will come back to you, those sorts of acts always bring their own rewards...I hope your position is tolerably certain with regular pay... I suppose Alfy and his wife will struggle along on the farm and you three live on as little as possible in Melita. Your mother is a wonder; she seems to grow stronger as she grows older. It is vigorous of Euty to think of a machine warehouse and with his great practical knowledge...provided he gets paid...."* [31]

Unlike his brothers, Alfy was indeed, as Aunt Agnes put it, still struggling along on his farm. He had further problems with the weather and his crop. This time it was hail. The insurance agency maintained that the climate was not suited to growing crops, while indicating that they would not be paying full premium for losses that year.

In 1895 southwestern Manitoba had yet another dry year and hail. This totally destroyed Alfy's crop and garden. As a result of the unrelenting physical labour and worry, Alfy fell ill. This state caused his pregnant wife much anxiety because she was inexperienced in knowing how to care for him. Alfy was hot and listless. Mab poured cold water on his head that eased the discomfort for a time. Mab appealed to Emily her mother-in-law: *"...Alfy thinks there is something distinctly wrong with his head and the medicine is only irritating it. Tomorrow I will send for Dr. Tomulin... have you a pair of clean sheets you could lend me?"* [32] Cousin Mary astutely suggested that: *"these blightings ... point to a different occupation for Alfred,*

Family home in Melita established by Charlie Estlin. Emily Estlin in the foreground.
Source: Estlin family collection, Sharon Hope

J. L. Campbell (left) and A. B. Estlin in the doorframe of J. L. Campbell's lumberyard, Melita, Manitoba.
Source: Estlin family collection, Sharon Hope

and perhaps coming at this moment, he can take up something less arduous and anxious...." [33]

Charlie had continued working with J. L. Campbell, and his local lumber company. J. L. was diversifying, moving more into the insurance and real estate fields by that time. When Charlie heard of the devastation, he wrote to Alfy in early August saying Campbell was anxious to get someone in the office and he was negotiating. J. L. thought Alfy would suit and he wanted him to come up to Melita to see about the job as soon as he could. He encouraged Alfy to get rid of the farming burden. Charlie assured Alfy that they could get Euty to come to Melita, since he was only at Pierson, and they could all talk the matter over. Alfy came up, talked to J. L. and then accepted his offer. He had a small son only a month old by this time and no doubt he was anxious for a secure wage.

Charlie promptly wrote to see what his mother wanted to do if Alfy left since the women couldn't remain alone without one of the brothers to keep an eye on them. Emily said of Alfy's leaving: "It must be done". As Aunt Agnes predicted, Emily and the girls moved to town with Charlie. The house even had a furnace that delighted the female members of the family to no end!

As it turned out, Alfy had been considering the lumber trade for quite some time. Mr. Patrick, T. A. Burrows, G. B. Hauser and Alfy had formed an association of sawmill owners called the Western Lumberman's Association. Now they wanted to form a retail group. The main purpose of the new group [the Western Retail Lumberman's Association] was to improve business practices and keep the retail lumber trade out of shopkeepers' hands. Alfy eventually became vice-president and then president of the retail association.

In an ironic twist of fate, Ernie Goodland, Alfy's former protégé, wistfully expressed an interest in marriage in a letter to England having seen Alfy enter that blissful state recently, but his formidable mother Kate was not amused. *"...I consider it would be the greatest mistake, just consider the position of your affairs, you are barely started yet. Your farm is not half finished, you have had no crop, you have no spare cash...."* [34] Ernie never married.

Programme card for the Deloraine Concert 1895.
Source: Estlin family memorabilia collection, Sharon Hope.

In the spring of 1895, Euty sang in the Brass Band Concert held in Chapin's Hall at Deloraine. The tune was "Ise goin back to Dixie"; he also acted in a farce as Skipes, "A little deranged in the upper story." In November, Mr and Mrs Henry Smith requested the Estlin family's attendance at the marriage of Margaret to Euty, at Chesterfield Farm.

Birdie benefitted financially from her English investments through the kindness of Cousin Mary as well as from her domestic enterprises starting in 1895; she received 50 pounds on the "Bristol and West of England Canadian Land Mortgage," drawn on Messrs. Robarts & Company, followed by other sums over the next several years. In 1896 she had a small business of her own raising chickens and selling the eggs along with some butter from time to time. Her notebooks were filled with days that chickens were placed in the granary to "sit". Maggie and Euty, Mabel and Alfy were frequent visitors to Birdie and May, at Charlie's house, averaging once a week. Euty was now building houses on his own around the Districts, this time in Killarney.

Charlie's dance card was full for the 1899 Seventh Annual Bachelors Ball; he was the only unmarried male Estlin left. Even after several children, Alfy's wife still danced and enjoyed a polka and schottische with Charlie. Emily helped to organize the Merry Maidens dance a few months later. She may have thought it was high time May found a husband since she was 25, considered well past the usual age for marriage. May was not in any rush, however, and the choice of men was not really to her liking. She became engaged to a man she considered "dull". Perhaps the engagement was meant to stave off other unwanted suitors until she could find the right person. Emily had received a joyful note from J. P. Alexander declaring that his daughter Margaret had made him a granddad ("Funny isn't it?" he said). Comparisons may have been made while describing Margaret's new role as a mother.

C. P Estlin's dance card from the Melita Bachelor's Ball, 1899.
Source: Estlin family memorabilia collection, Sharon Hope

In the summer of 1898 the family took a holiday together, perhaps the first since arriving in Canada. Near the Turtle Mountain, creeks connected Lake Max, Lake Lulu, Lake Oscar and Lake William. The Mountain was still heavily timbered with oak, elm, ash, Manitoba maple and birch. Then there was scrub growth consisting of chokecherries, pin cherries, high bush cranberries, Saskatoons, alder and poplar. It had such natural beauty that the lakes made an ideal spot for a holiday. Max Lake, as the family always called it, was quite big by English standards and the biggest of the Turtle Mountain lakes. A family called Hurt lived nearby with a little girl known as Girlie. Robert Hurt ran a sawmill at one end of the lake.

Although Emily did not go, the rest of Estlin family did, including Birdie's little dog Toto. Starting in June, once they got there, they just stayed on. The family put up striped holiday tents for the men supplied by Robert Hurt who also had a free gas motor launch available for visitors and vacationers. The brothers and sisters explored by boat, walked and fished. Altogether they averaged a party of 10, because in addition to all of the Estlins, there was Frank Aitkens, an accountant, who kept the books for J. L. Campbell and Ferguson and his brother Arthur, a machinist in Boissevain. Charlie brought a camera and took a lot of photographs.

The girls, who were in a house, [likely the Hurt's], declared they couldn't bear to leave they were having such a heavenly time. Birdie commented that Mrs. Hurt didn't want them to go and leave her alone

At Max Lake, the men, according to Birdie, were very kind and waited upon the women. The gas launch was delightful. Birdie and May were in it every moment except for meals. In fact, May got quite expert at steering. They developed rapacious appetites and Birdie declared they all were getting quite fat. The family cooked outside the house on a small box stove and since the provisions came up from town there was not much to do in the way of preparation. May and Mrs Hurt drove with Marvel, [May's horse after Nellie] into Boissevain for provisions where the girls had to get new blouses because the ones they brought got so dirty. Birdie wrote: "...*I think we shall be here until the middle of August anyhow .... Toto is devoted to the launch. It is so lively here among the trees and this is a large lake* [so] *we can go for miles around the different islands in the launch. May and Frank Aitkens are great chums. I don't think we shall stay at Deloraine more than one night* [to] *go to see Ernie as our clothes are getting pretty used up with the bush and the boating. The little squirrels run about quite close to us and steal bread....*" [35]

Mr. Hurt wouldn't dream of letting May drive all the way to town alone which she found frustrating. She claimed that she could be there in a matter of one hour and 15 minutes as it was only 14 miles and Marvel was well rested. However, she was having such a good time nothing could dampen her enthusiasm. "... *Frank is my special chum and favorite but Mr Arthur is fine too so jolly. I can row quite competently and scull a bit under my chum's tuition...Frank is the most patient good-natured creature on earth.... We have such a fine time, no restraint or stiffness at all....*" [36]

Frank Aitkens fishing outside Melita.
Source: Estlin family collection, Sharon Hope

Chapter 19
Ascending Stars

As the Estlin family entered the 20th century their focus moved from rural farming to town entertainments and business. They still had financial worries, but the day-to-day struggle for existence was behind them. Their stories became linked to enterprises and travels.

Alfy became involved with many civic activities, joining the Order of Foresters in Deloraine, and tree planting around Melita. He ordered 100 Russian poplars and through the Souris River Agricultural Society, got a speaker to explain to farmers how to plant and care for the trees. The next year Alfy helped organize the Melita bicycle races, complete with a cup. He served on a jury in Brandon for an attempted murder trial of a Birtle man accused of poisoning his father. They found him not guilty.

Euty was working in Winnipeg as head of his own construction business but left in 1900 for Marble, North Carolina to run a placer mine for a New York firm. Winnipeg was not the boomtown it had been when the family first arrived in the province. In fact, it was extremely difficult for a self-employed man to make a living there in small business by 1900. There had been a steady decline in employment for some time.

Euty first settled in Valley Town County in Andrews, NC, which was near Marble. Andrews was a relatively small town then, about 10 years old when his family arrived. Resting at the foot of the Great Smokey Mountains, the Valley River meandered through the green farms which made a beautiful setting for the communities along its length. The county had a long history related to the removal of the Cherokee Indians and to mountain life. A tannery opened in Andrews in 1898 that provided some employment for the tiny place. The town of Marble was named for the high quality white, blue, gray and pink marble which was quarried there. It was located on the western edge of the township. After a short time, Euty's family moved to Murphy, the county seat, on the southwestern side of Marble, which was a much older town.

Euty's daughter Emily, his eldest child, wrote to her grandmother Emily at Christmas 1900: "*Santa Clause brought me a mouth organ, hammer, pinchers, pliers and a little saw just like Daddy's, a box of candy and some mitts...When Mummie and I go out driving she lets me hold the reins... Mummie's chickens go to bed in the trees...the kitty cat sleeps under the stove....*" [37] After the birth of his first son in North Carolina, Euty asked various family members for potential names. Cousin Mary, after due consideration, suggested Edward to him after her uncle Edward who had died of consumption at 24. She said he was much beloved particularly by her father but now no one remembered him. Edward Archibald was duly christened.

One story related to Euty's stay in North Carolina concerned attending a picture show in one of the larger towns. Euty was accustomed to blacks since he had hired a black general labourer to cook and help in his household. During the show, a black man was thrown from the balcony of the theatre to the lower floor. Since the man was obviously hurt, Euty turned to see who would help him. Much to Euty's horror, the people around him simply ignored his circumstances saying, "He's just a negro his own people can help him". It is likely that this was Euty's first encounter with racial prejudice. By 1902 Euty and his family were back in Winnipeg. Everyone hoped his construction business would be a successful venture in the near future. He began to build grain elevators and bridges that did prove quite profitable.

The same year that Euty had a son, Alfy had one as well, Campbell, but he only lived 14 months. He got a fever that he wasn't strong enough to overcome. While Euty was away in the United States, Alfy telegrammed to Cousin Mary to help find a hired girl for his wife since Lizzie had been such a help to the Mater. She found Emily Brooks and agreed to pay her way out. Emily had an unpleasant stepfather that forced her brother to immigrate as a farm laborer. She wanted to come as well. As usual, Cousin Mary was delighted to have found just the right person for the Estlin family.

By 1901–1902, Charlie was fully involved with grain transport. He recorded grain intake not only for his village but for places such as Lyleton; documenting the series of insurance policies on the wheat, the rail car numbers, the wheat's owners for each car, his hours with J.L. Campbell (309.5 to be exact) and finally the numerous and complex loans and other financial transactions that the Estlin family engaged in. These financial agreements now began to involve Frank Aitkens. Charlie seemed to have days working for the CPR, days unloading lumber, and calculating freight on cordwood, which was likely related to his work with J. L. Campbell. He was the consummate entrepreneur, juggling as many jobs as he could.

The year 1903 was an extraordinary one for all kinds of events: Sadly Cousin Mary, the Estlin family loyal supporter and kind guardian for so many years, died in November of 1902. She had a tumor diagnosed about eight months before and the doctors could do nothing. Birdie and her mother went to England the following spring since there was some contention over Cousin Mary's will and all the Estlin siblings were significant beneficiaries, particularly the girls. Cousin Mary's first thought was to leave the money to open a home for retired governesses but her executors deemed it too hard to administer. The will was settled eventually with Birdie and May getting 1000 pounds each and the "boys" 100 pounds each. Cousin Mary was forever generous. Emily and Birdie had a wonderful time visiting all the relatives. Emily even opened the Taunton flower show that year, and visited Burnham. Over the summer in Melita, May went to Boissevain, where the Aitkens lived.

May made the wise decision to break off her engagement with her "dull suitor" and marry Frank Aitkens. The Estlin brothers were all delighted since they had known Frank for years as well as his Aitkens brothers. Both families got along extremely well. In the fall, Emily and Birdie were intent on getting London outfits both for May and themselves that would be appropriate for the December 10th wedding. They ordered a wreath of orange blossoms, a veil and May's dress.

The local Melita paper wrote the wedding up in style, describing May as "...One of Melita's brightest and most popular young ladies...The groom supported by Mr. A.B. Estlin as best man having taken his proper position, the bride soon entered leaning on the arm of her brother Mr. C. P. Estlin... the bride's wedding gown a London creation imported for the occasion was white silk with chiffon wedding veil...the bride carrying a bouquet of white carnations and margarites looked unusually charming. The happy couple withdrew to the home of Mrs. Estlin ...the lucky groom has spent several years in Manitoba and now being identified with the firm of Campbell and Ferguson Ltd, has decided to take up his permanent abode in Melita where he has erected a neat residence in an attractive part of town...." [38] The newlyweds settled into a house that Frank had built near Charlie, Emily and Birdie.

Left to right: Emily Maude (Birdie), Frank Aitkens, and May Estlin (Aitkens).
Source: Estlin family collection, Sharon Hope

Meanwhile, in Winnipeg, a man called White working for Euty's company, was injured while building a grain elevator in Starbuck the previous summer, and brought a suit against him. In lowering some planking the rope slipped and the planks fell on White breaking his arm and inflicting other injuries. Euty claimed he told the man to be careful and not to lower more than one plank at a time. Euty contended that the accident was caused by White's own negligence. The jury found Euty not guilty and White had to pay court expenses.

Charlie, whose life had become extremely hectic, took a boat cruise to Rat Portage, then on to Fort Frances and Mine Centre, thoroughly enjoying his trip and the break from his many enterprises. Shortly after, he became acting mayor for Melita and then won the mayoral election against John Crerar by just two votes the next year. One of his first mayoral duties in April was to issue a warrant for apprehension of Peter Davis who allegedly committed an assault on Dora Boorman a resident of the town.

Dora heard someone running behind her. As she opened the door to the house where she resided and stepped inside, the door was pushed from her hand and *"...I felt someone clasp me around the head and shoulders. I screamed... I struggled to get away...."* [39] The man was taken into custody. Charlie also served on the town cemetery committee with Alfy.

Charlie, as mayor, went to Winnipeg to discuss the reduction in grain rates. He told a reporter that the farmer got the benefit of 2 cents a bushel the next day after the reduction came in. Furthermore the price of wheat went up in sympathy with the outside markets due to Roblin's deal with the CPR. The benefit to farmers was four times what it was the previous year.

In the following year, there was a severe snowstorm beginning in February that caused a coal famine in Melita. Charlie acknowledged the help and cooperation of the CPR that managed to open up the line coming from Estevan to where two cars of coal had been stuck some 10 miles from Melita. However in March, when the tracks were clogged again by a blizzard on March 20th, no trains ran for five days.

When May had a son in September 1904, Euty's remark was to give him a decent name. The comment had some merit considering the old fashioned names held by the current Estlins. She named him Charles. Her daughter received the family names in 1907, Alice Maude. Maude, who never used her first name, hated both names.

Over the summer of 1906, Charlie took another much-needed vacation, this time to England. As he crossed by train to Montreal, he commented that the country around North Bay was farmed indifferently and that the land was poor for crops. On the other hand, he thought Ottawa was a beautifully situated city. Ted Jaques, who had married Margaret Alexander, met him at the Montreal station and they toured the city before getting tickets on the boat. After choppy seas caused Charlie to go back to his cabin without breakfast one morning, he joked in his diary: *"It is now church time in Melita and if the choir are as I expect, they will be singing 'For those in Peril on the Sea'. If they could see us they would sing it with their whole souls. 2.20 pm. Not enjoying myself... Ted has just remarked: 'Paying a hundred dollars for this.'"* [40] Charlie visited Brentford, saw his old offices and found the place where he used to lodge. He found the town much improved. Moreover, there was a fine new bridge at Kew over the Thames. After conducting a little family research, Charlie went off on a stag hunt with a distant relative, Charles Ware. The hunt took place outside Cloutsham. *"The first stag they found would not run so was killed and the second one went over the hill toward Porlock and was killed."* [40] Charlie's vacation was short. By Aug 24th he was sailing home on the Empress of Ireland and arrived in Canada on the 30th. It was his third trip out.

Following his holiday, Charlie became an unofficial Provincial Municipal Inspector overseeing Municipal expenditure. He was wrestling with problems in Victoria Municipality where *"the amount of work is enormous and enough to drive one crazy, such innumerable errors, all the columns in the rolls have to be cross checked and so many corrections makes the additions very hard. My kingdom for an adding machine. Poor old Joe has petered out a little and gone to Winnipeg for a rest and I am trying to get the rolls finished by the time he returns. I have been at them all the week and part of last...."* [41]

In Winnipeg, Euty, in a stroke of marketing genius, started a paper for builders and contractors called the "Northwest Contractor". It included a list of tenders called for and plans prepared for new buildings. The editorial matter was also considered excellent reading. It caught on like wildfire and Euty sold it within a year to a Toronto publisher who made it into a standard trade journal. On the home front, he was becoming quite domestic, getting the dinner, helping to do the dishes, and getting breakfast. However there was much more excitement in store for Euty than this settled life.

In 1907, Ferdinand Aitkens, Frank's brother, wrote from Winnipeg about a scheme which he proclaimed would be good for them all. Ferd was going to form a syndicate and get good reliable men of position involved in order to provide financial backing. He was impressed, he stated, with the inventor, Mr. Everson [sic].

The mysterious invention was a street sweeper prototype and Euty, assisted by Ferd, threw himself whole heartedly into the project to get it produced and on the market.

Euty calmly suggested that Charlie, Frank [Aitkens] and Alfy might raise the capital the others needed for the venture. The family disagreed.

Ferd stated in November to Frank: *"Your cable and C.P.'s give me your strong opinion. Our machine will do the work…to the extent of 200 pounds per mile; the City of Westminster pays 500 pounds/mile but whether they will go with contracts is another matter."* [42]

Euty, undeterred by any opposition, or lack of investors, pressed on. Failing to find anywhere suitable to build and market the machine properly in Canada, he looked to England. With the assistance of Ferd, who was returning to England anyway, and accompanied by the inventor Everson, he shipped the machine to Britain. Once he arrived, Euty declared that both Liverpool and Manchester were fine for sweeping but they had very little asphalt. They took the machine to London.

"This is the finest place on earth for sweeping," Euty commented, *"you travel all day in any direction over asphalt and black paving perfectly smooth and dirty.…I don't anticipate any trouble getting started once our Syndicate is formed."* [43] Euty indicated that in addition to the larger machine, they would need four or so smaller machines or dodgers to go in smaller spaces and curved areas where the larger sweeper couldn't go. He didn't see anything in the traffic to interfere but suggested that nights and Sundays might be best for the sweeper's use.

Euty (left) and Alfy at Niagara Falls, June 1908.
Source: Estlin photo collection, Sharon Hope

In 1908, Ferd remarked: *"Everson is definitely peculiar. He expects everyone to fall down and worship his invention and find the cash."* [44] The problem was Ferd had to find 750 pounds to build the big machine with no security of any kind, no information and nothing in writing. Euty, working with Everson, said they thought Ferd would approach some friends who would take sufficient interest to put up the money out of friendship but anyone Ferd approached wanted to see something definite in the way of return.

Streetsweeper. Source: Estlin memorabilia, Fran Aitkens

Ferd wanted to get a contract based on the satisfactory performance of the machine that would convince investors it was sound. Everson objected to any strings. Ferd intended to get ready to leave for BC where he had land in the Okanagan that he was going to farm. This plan had been in place long before the sweeper materialized and he left shortly after.

In June 1908 Alfy and Euty passed through Toronto and talked to J. Campbell who, by this time, had a wholesale lumber business based in that city and branches in places like Melita. Indications were Campbell wanted Alfy to take a more responsible job related to his company. Charlie alluded to Alfy being in Winnipeg in subsequent letters but Alfy eventually returned to Melita.

In 1909 an article appeared in a Winnipeg paper describing the testing of a New York sweeper. *"...The machine was tried in West street near Vesey to let "Big" Bill Edwards, cleaning Commissioner, see what it could do. The monster came ...under the guidance of W.R. Emerson [sic] the inventor, a chauffeur and another man who sat in the rear and raised and lowered that part of the machine which gobbled up the dirt."* [45]

Soon other sweepers earned newspaper attention locally and abroad while articles announced the need to obtain international patents. Euty applied for a Canadian patent first in 1910 and for another later. Aunt Agnes wrote that year they were sorry for Euty's disappointment about his machine. When he wrote to her, he apparently had hopes of starting another company. Unfortunately, the final outcome for Euty and his machine is not known.

During this time Alfy had been continuing his civic commitments in Melita and became President of the Board of Trade in the town. Compared to his brothers' accomplishments, this might not have seemed much of a prize but Alfy enjoyed Melita.

Both Euty and Charlie had banner years in 1910 on a provincial level. Euty sent a telegram to Emily stating that Charlie had finally been officially appointed Chief Registrar Government Relations for Manitoba. The newspaper declared that the appointment was a popular one and that the department was to be congratulated on securing the services of so competent a person to fill the position. He assumed an even greater workload.

While Charlie was in Regina, he complained that he was blown hither and thither and didn't know where he was going next. *"I finished that 'course' down at Wolseley and got a message to report here. I have been taking stock of lumberyards and probably this will be some more of it. Things are booming here a long way more than Manitoba. The hotels are all jammed up with 'Fair' and I have not got a room yet...."* [46]

On March 23rd Euty went to see the Manitoba Attn Gen. Mr. Campbell. When he arrived, Campbell indicated he knew all about Euty's elevator construction business and asked if Euty would call at the Gov't office in the morning when he would introduce him to the Minister of Public Works. When Euty got back to his office, the phone rang and the President of the Grain Growers indicated that he was their unanimous choice for the job. Euty began building elevators under the newly formed state-owned elevator line that was administered by the Department of Public Works.

Emily wrote to Charlie: *"We are pleased and delighted...the good news of Euty's appointment.... ...it is a good thing that it is all right at last...We drank Euty's health and sent a box of strawberries on the strength of it ... it snowed a little this morning and we had to make a little fire in the furnace which was very comforting...you left a little bundle of papers do you want them?"* [47]

In June, the Estlin women went off to Appleton Wisconsin for an extended visit to Emily's cousin, Judge John Goodland. John treated them like royalty with drives in the Goodland car, parties, picnics, moving pictures and in particular, baseball games. Emily wrote to Charlie, *"The Melita people would be horrified to see the baseball games going on, on Sunday. The country... is very beautiful. ...They do not grow much wheat around here mostly rye. I am writing this while the children are making a great noise strumming on the piano. I see Euty is very busy with the Elevator. Cousin John has a beautiful car....*"[47] The women snatched every opportunity to take drives in John's car.

There was an underlying reason for this US visit; the family contemplated a major move. In July 1910, Charlie remarked cryptically that when he came out, they would all be old timers and able to take him around. By January 1911, Charlie and Frank found themselves booked into the Dominion Hotel in Victoria, B.C. as part of a reconnaissance trip to the city and the country surrounding it. May had wished to leave Melita since the children were born because she felt people were too interested in her affairs. She wanted to get her children to a place that was not so narrow-minded as she described it. Frank's brothers had been in B.C. for a while and maintained it was an excellent place for farming. A family friend, A. E. Cameron, was also planning to move to Victoria and others they knew from the prairies already lived there.

Charlie reported that Victoria, even in January, was almost like summer when he looked out his window. He was absolutely determined to live there as well. He thought it much more bracing than Vancouver or Chilliwack but added as a cautionary note, that they would discuss it upon their return to the prairies. He remarked that it didn't seem to rain much and they had looked at the city thoroughly by walking around.

Based on this trip, Frank, May, the two children, Emily, and Birdie determined to leave for B.C. as soon as possible. By accident or design, A. E. Cameron, their friend, was coming to Victoria from Melita at exactly the same time. He offered to take their household effects to Vancouver Island since he was taking a load of horses of his own. The family was gone by May 1911; they bought a farm in Gordon Head on Tyndall Avenue north of A. E. Cameron.

Charlie was happy to hear good accounts of Gordon Head once the family arrived, and in replying to Birdie's letter he reassured the family: "*I suppose you are expecting all the time that something will happen to spoil it which has been the inevitable experience here...I hope you will have a new lease of life and enjoy it all thoroughly, the climate is not so nerve racking...I hope the strawberries will be a success...I will feel more like coming out in the fall.*"[48]

He wrote again to May: "*My star appears to be in the ascendant at the present time, I suppose I should feel complimented at being selected as this is special work but it's the salary I appreciate most. This rather clinches the thing for Alf... now he will go back to Melita and Mab will stay here for a month...I am not really sorry that events have changed as I really did not hanker for work in Melita ... but this really suits me better...People all over are talking about boom for Manitoba I don't intend to boom myself but will take advantage if the opportunity offers...."* [49]

With a major portion of the Estlin family in BC and no longer sharing the same prairie dreams, or the same conditions, relationships subtly changed. However, the siblings never stopped being a family and looking out for each other.

The year 1911 seems the appropriate place to end the Estlin family's immigration "saga". This year (2011) represents the one hundredth anniversary since the first Estlins came to live in British Columbia. Charlie Estlin died unmarried in 1913 of cancer. He came to live with the family in Victoria B.C. after an unsuccessful operation in Manitoba and died less than a year later. No doubt Victoria was where he wanted to be.

Neither Alfy nor his children settled in B.C. Alfy died in Melita of renal failure in 1938. Euty came to British Columbia with his children, eventually settling in Vancouver as a consulting engineer, where he died in 1951. The Estlin women, who all remained in Greater Victoria, lived past the age of 90. Birdie, the oldest sibling, died in 1951, Emily, their mother died in 1927, and May, the youngest, died in 1968.

Chapter 20
Final Perspective

No observation can be truly unbiased and the Estlins are no exception. Susannah Estlin is critical of Catholic services because she was a Unitarian Minister's wife but she also gave balanced descriptions of the French people and their condition. She praised them for their fortitude but criticized their housekeeping. In some cases she believed the English people could learn from the French with respect to particular modes of conduct or customs. During July 1789, she hoped that political change might better the condition for French citizens but she admitted later that it had not. Susannah appreciated the beauty of Paris when she arrived, and continued to appreciate it while she was held in the city. She joined a party of individuals for protection and then waited, not dissolving into panic or cowering in her hotel, but going out each day to see the sights and learn as much as she could. At the same time that she displayed courage, she did not tempt fate by drawing too much attention to their party.

John Prior, like any 20-year-old, wanted to enjoy himself in London. He showed typical impatience with older generations and was somewhat sensitive to criticism. However, despite his perpetual sightseeing, he was prepared to take up arms against the Chartists to protect his bank. Although he took a great interest in the life of Bacchus, and spent innumerable hours attending soirees of various types, when his brother Alfred was ill, he stepped in to give his brother personal care. Whereas Susannah rode an ass, frequented coffee houses, and tasted new food, John Prior, her grandson, swam in the river, ate at the Poplars, and learned new dances. He frequently walked or rode about darkened London streets at night, which in the Victorian age could not have been safe. Thievery was rampant in London, as he described in his diary, yet he expressed no real concern, patiently tracking down and retrieving his umbrella. He passed off cholera with a sentence as if it were a cold.

The Estlins' immigration to Canada tested their Somerset metal to the utmost. While suffering a personal loss, they contended with having no money and having no knowledge of the Canadian prairies, yet they persevered, finding land and taking advantage of every possible opportunity to succeed. When at last they left farming, their struggles were not over.

They continued to try to achieve some degree of success in business, which took, more or less, 14 years to be realized. The robustness of their spirit is truly admirable considering the circumstances.

These three snapshots of life show changes in language and expression, changes in perceiving class, new patterns of church attendance and religious duty, and modifications in accepted or appropriate social custom. Although Susannah talks of class, John Prior barely alludes to it, except to subtly express a respect for those in eminent positions. As for those below John Prior in the work world, he barely mentions the sweeps, and never comments on the hundreds of street vendors and shopkeepers that he must have seen daily or the servants he encountered. Like Susannah, John Prior associates with his fellow clerks, his school friends, and his relatives, in other words those of similar social status. For John, entering mid shipman Woolgrove's world for a short period was conducted in the same manner as sampling a new fruit.

Strict religious and moral adherence was once part of daily English life in Susannah's time, but religious influence diminished to a weekly custom in John Prior's youth and finally disappeared altogether in the 1880s Canadian prairies where virtually no churches existed. However, even Alfy and Euty did not work on Sunday but went visiting once a week in their best clothes. Social niceties and good breeding did not matter much in the Canadian west, where the ability to build a log house and harvest grain was paramount. In Emerson, Alfy commented that he hadn't had a collar on for weeks but did not miss it.

Written expression has evolved considerably from Susannah's time to the 21st century where shorter sentences, standardized spelling and fewer commas are the accepted trend. Contemporary language requires more direct expression and perhaps we have lost some elegance in English usage as a result. Foreshadowing the use of photos, John Prior Estlin's sketches are priceless. Whether the Illustrated London News provided him with inspiration or not, they make his diary special. He would be surprised at our current reliance on imagery.

Writing reveals as much about the writer as it does about the subject matter. In Susannah we see a woman with a sense of humor and a zest for life. In John Prior at 21 we see the beginning of a renaissance man, interested in architecture, performance and entertainment, drawing, public health and ships. In the final narrative we see the mature John Prior, where his interests have expanded and deepened. The last piece introduces us to Prior's children where Victorian filial duty plays an important role. This work documents son Alfy's dedication to his family, his sister Birdie's role as caregiver and his brother Charlie's concern for his sisters and mother as they moved to Melita.

The final record shows above all, that persistence, patience and having a goal can overcome the most daunting obstacles. It also demonstrates the surprising but infinite ability of people to adapt to circumstance.

Notes

1) May Aitkens recollections to her daughter Lorna Aitkens: nd-likely the late 1950s or early 1960s.

2) Estlin, A. B. nd. The Old Commission Trail, Unpublished Memoire. Compiled by Lynda Villeneuve.

3) Estlin, E. S. nd. Unpublished memoire.

4) Series of letters: John Prior Estlin to Charles Estlin 1880.

5) Series of letters: Emily Estlin to Charles Estlin1880.

6) Letter: Alfred Estlin to Edward Bagehot 1881.

7) Telegram: Anonymous to Edward Bagehot 1881 quoted in Charles Estlin's letter.

8) Series of letters: Charles Estlin to Emily Estlin 1881.

9) Letter: Charles Estlin to Birdie Estlin1881.

10) Letter: May Estlin to Charles Estlin 1881.

11) Series of letters: Alfred Estlin to Charles Estlin 1881.

12) Series of letters/postcards: Alfred Estlin to Emily Estlin 1882.

13) Series of letters: Charles Estlin to Alfred Estlin 1882.

14) Series of letters: Eustace Estlin to Emily Estlin 1882.

15) Letter: Edward Small to Emily Maude Estlin 1882.

16) Series of letters: Alfred Estlin to Charles Estlin 1882.

17) Telegram: Emily Estlin to Alfred Estlin 1882.

18) Estlin, E. S. 1933. Looking Back in Manitoba. For Publication in the New Era, Melita newspaper.

19) Letter: Eustace Estlin to Birdie Estlin 1882.

20) Letter: CPR to Charles Estlin1882.

21) Letter: Harold Hayes Harker to Alfred Estlin1883.

22) Note: May Estlin to Emily Estlin 1883.

23) Document: Anonymous copy of the signees'oath for the Medora Rifles 1885.

24) Letter: Mary Ann Estlin to Emily Estlin 1886.

25) Letter: Margaret Alexander to May Estlin 1889.

26) Letter: Charles Goodland to Alfred Estlin 1890.

27) Letter: Charles Goodland to Alfred Estlin 1892.

28) Letter: Mary Ann Estlin to Charles Estlin 1891.

29) Letter: Mary Ann Estlin to Birdie Estlin 1892.

30) Flyer: Details given for entertainment 1890.

31) Letter: Agnes Senior to Charles Estlin1894.

32) Note: Mabel Estlin to Emily Estlin 1895.

33) Letter: Mary Ann Estlin to Emily Estlin 1895.

34) Letter: Kate Goodland to Ernest Goodland 1894.

35) Letter: Birdie Estlin to Emily Estlin 1898.

36) Letter: May Estlin to Emily Estlin 1898.

37) Letter: Emily Estlin granddaughter to Emily Estlin–grandmother 1900.

38) Newspaper clipping: Anonymous from the Melita paper Dec. 1903.

39) Warrant for arrest: For Peter Davis signed by Charles Estlin mayor 1903.

40) Trip Diary: Charles Estlin1906.

41) Letter: Charles Estlin to Frank Aitkens 1907.

42) Letter: Ferdinand Aitkens to Frank Aitkens 1907.

43) Letter: Eustace Estlin to Charles Estlin 1907.

44) Letter: Ferdinand Aitkens to Frank Aitkens 1908.

45) Winnipeg newspaper clipping; Street Sweeper Testing. 1909.

46) Letter: Charles Estlin to May Aitkens 1910.

47) Two Letters: Emily Estlin to Charles Estlin 1910.

48) Letter: Charles Estlin to Birdie Estlin1911.

49) Letter: Charles Estlin to May Aitkens 1911.

Selected References

Boissevain History Book Committee. 1981. Beckoning Hills Revisited – Pioneer Settlement Turtle Mountain Souris – Basin Areas.

Brenda History Committee. 1990. Bridging Brenda (Vol 1 & 2), Brenda Municipality.

Campbell, Charles F. Municipality of Arthur and its History. Melita–Arthur Historical Committee.

Deloraine History Book Committee. 1980. Deloraine Scans a Century, 1880–1980.

Estlin, A. B. The First Settlers. Melita–Arthur Historical Committee.

Estlin, A. B. Land Titles Excerpts. Melita–Arthur Historical Committee.

Estlin, E. nd. Unpublished Memoire.

Hurt, Alice Selina 1970. Turtle Mountain Corduroy.

Melita–Arthur Historical Committee. 1983. Our First Century Melita and Arthur. Altona: Friesen Printers.

Malciw, Johnny. 2009. Settling and 'Selling' Canada's West: The Role of Immigration. Ryerson University. Thesis.

Melita–Arthur Historical Committee. "Pioneer Picnic".

McClelland, James and Dan Lewis. 1975. Emerson. A Centennial History. Town of Emerson. Altona Friesen Printers.

Ritchie, James. 2001. Turtle Mountain Tales, Deloraine, Man. Moncur Gallery of Native History, Co-published by: Boissevain & Morton Regional Library and Boissevain Community Archive.

The Sourisford History Committee. Sourisford and Area from 1879.

Villeneuve, Lynda nd. The Old Commission Trail. Unpublished Memoire of Alfred Bagehot Estlin.

Women's Institute. Melita's Tales and Trails. 1879–1967.

Wright, Norman Ernest. 1951. In View of Turtle Hill – A Survey of the History of Southwestern Manitoba to 1900. Deloraine Times Publishing.

Index

About the Author

Sharon Hope was born and raised in BC's Greater Victoria area and is the great-granddaughter of John Prior Estlin. She has worked on various family materials most of her life.

Sharon pursued degrees at Oregon State University and UBC as part of a career that spanned 40 years in forest ecology and silvicultural forestry; she has recently returned to nonscientific writing, a passion she had as a young woman.

She is the co-author of Celebrating Our Past (2006) with Valerie Green, which is the history of the Gordon Head School, in Victoria. She has written numerous unpublished poems and fictional short stories as well as published articles of general and academic interest.

Sharon is currently compiling information for a book on the history of Mount Douglas High School in Victoria.

CPSIA information can be obtained
at www.ICGtesting.com
Printed in the USA
LVHW08s0502190818
587344LV00001B/4/P

9 780987 745910